EMOTIONAL ADDICTIONS

A Reference Book for Addictions and Mental Health Counseling

Wylie, Texas 75098

Peter D. Ladd

WITHDRAWN

University Press of America,® Inc.
Lanham · Boulder · New York · Toronto · Plymouth, UK

Copyright © 2009 by
University Press of America,® Inc.
4501 Forbes Boulevard
Suite 200
Lanham, Maryland 20706
UPA Acquisitions Department (301) 459-3366

Estover Road
Plymouth PL6 7PY
United Kingdom

Library of Congress Control Number: 2009926587
ISBN: 978-0-7618-4623-9 (paperback : alk. paper)
eISBN: 978-0-7618-4624-6

This book is dedicated to students and practitioners of addictions and mental health counseling, and for those who are interested in a new approach to understanding addictions and mental health disorders

Contents

Preface

The impetus behind this book came from a number of directions that eventually converged, and writing it seemed an important step in the areas of addictions and mental health.

The idea of emotional addictions, according to my definition of them, began in 1993 after writing a chapter in a book about emotional addictions with at-risk students (Miller, 1993), and successfully fulfilling the mandates of a grant from the New York State Department of Education in association with the New York State Office of Mental Health. At that time, public school students in New York were receiving information on the dangers of drugs and alcohol abuse through curricula that gave them the latest facts pertaining to the subject. However, a needs assessment in the age group between 13 through 18 revealed that 83% of these students stated that drug and alcohol prevention education did not comprehensively cover the nature of their addictive patterns, especially about how they were feeling (Miller, 1993).

During this same period of time, my work in the area of emotions had reached a point where working with at-risk students on addictions seemed the logical next step. On a one year sabbatical from St. Lawrence University, I piloted a program on emotional addictions at the Pinewood Alternative School, and was struck by the importance of giving these students a map or a pattern of their feelings that they could understand and use. It seemed to make the drug and alcohol curriculum come to life, and gave them the belief that addiction was not completely their fault.

For the past 30 years, I have been working on the Akwesasne Mohawk Reservation, as a teacher for St. Lawrence University's Graduate Program in Counseling, and also as the Clinical Supervisor for Akwesasne's Holistic Health and Wellness Program, which combines mental health and addictions counseling, but also includes a traditional medicine program staffed by healers from the Mohawk Tribe. The program at Akwesasne is directed more toward a community model of counseling rather than a medical model, and has allowed me to observe the basic needs of Native people suffering from addictions and emotional distress. Over the years, I have come to the conclusion that mental health and addictions counseling treat many of the same clients, and the closer these two professions understand each other, the larger benefit will be given to clients who seek help in either program.

Of course, such a belief does have its drawbacks. Having been trained as a clinical psychologist, I realize how many institutions have adopted the fine work found in such guidelines as the DSMIV manual for diagnosing mental health issues (Psychiatric Association, 1994), and I am aware of the numerous tests that make up diagnosis for certain types of addictions (Marlatt, 2005), and I am also aware that such work will continue in both fields. However, my experiences have encouraged me to put forward a new approach to addictions and mental health counseling that maps out the emotional experiences of everyday people, and describes how these emotions can become addictions, much like physical addictions.

Most of my encouragement has come from colleagues and their clients who have stated that, on occasions, emotions do appear as addictions with many of their characteristics such as, denial, addictive thinking, dependency, compulsive behavior, tolerance, and withdrawal. Furthermore, counseling emotions as addictions has implications as to how these emotions should be treated. Counseling for emotional addictions seems to offer alternatives to counselors who practice traditional diagnosis and treatment for mental health disorders and physical addictions. It also may offer new alternatives for clients in understanding emotions that seem to have taken over their lives. Personally, I believe it offers an alternative for helping people going through difficult human experiences who are looking for any remedy to ease their pain.

I have taken a phenomenological (experiential) approach in this book, and have included more than feelings in making up my definition of emotional addictions. I make the assumption that beliefs, thoughts, behaviors, physical conditions, the emotional climate, and feelings all go into an emotional experience and somewhere in one or more of these, clients and counselors can find ways to alter emotions that are causing dysfunction. Within this book, I attempt to define and describe what I am calling emotional addictions. My experience tells me that such phenomena exist. I am hopeful that others will agree with me, and will continue describing and refining this idea.

Peter D. Ladd
St. Lawrence University
January 6, 2009

Acknowledgements

I would like to thank the clients and counselors who allowed me to use their human experiences as the foundation of this book. A book based on human experience can only be enhanced by "real life" stories, and I want those who allowed me to use their stories to know how greatly I appreciate their generosity.

I would like to thank Jennifer Gaudreau and Clare Kilpatrick Benz for reading this book and being so generous in their comments about it.

I would like to thank the following colleagues on the Akwesasne Mohawk Reservation for their contributions to this book namely, Ann Marie Churchill, Sabrina Jacobs (Toweson), April White (Kanahwii), Donna Benedict (Ioterakeha Otsista), and Carol Thompson, Tammy Mitchell, Louise Tewakierakwa, Tina Mitchell, Leona Barnes, Andria Cook, Kanietahawi Sharrow. .

I also would like to thank Joanna Munger who proof read the manuscript and made timely suggestions for clarity and understanding. Also, at St. Lawrence University, I would like to thank Jim Shuman for his support and guidance, and to the graduate students who encouraged me to write a book that described human experience.

I would like to thank Donna Allen, Linda Zerbe, Tish Jepsen, Lisa Blanchfield, and Dorian Ladd for their the encouragement and the time sacrificed in support of this project.

Finally, I would like to thank my wife, Kyle Blanchfield for her constant support, and for her expertise, as a colleague in St. Lawrence University's Graduate School. Ideas are meant to be shared, and sometimes sharing creates new ideas. I would like to thank Kyle for sharing ideas with me for the last 30 years on a personal and professional basis.

PDL

Introduction

The concept of addiction plagues many aspects of contemporary life. For example, the United States government spends over 250 billion dollars each year on problems relating to drugs and drug addiction (NIDA, 2005). Combine the cost of addiction with the indirect pain and suffering for adults and children, and what emerges are dangerous implications for our society.

Research has responded to the addiction crisis by conducting physical and psychological studies of alcoholism, cocaine use, and any number of other forms of substance abuse. This research can be combined with process oriented addictions such as, a gambling addiction. Until recently however, studies clarifying the addictive characteristics of everyday emotions have not entered mainstream research on addiction. This is understandable because research on the addictive characteristics of emotions can fall into many categories. Some emotions such as anger or anxiety may lean toward a physiological understanding while others such as apathy or guilt may be best understood from a psychological perspective. Beyond this, may be some skepticism whether there are such phenomena as emotional addictions.

Without scientific research to support such a claim, we turn to the area of human experience for answers. For example, can the experience of jealousy in everyday living be studied for its addictive characteristics? Or, can someone experiencing resentment become emotionally addicted to a lifestyle filled with frustration and victimization? These are the type of questions posed in this book, and from such questions it is hoped a dialogue will emerge for more in-depth studies of emotional addictions.

Counseling as a Human Experience

Relying on human experience to validate the possibility of emotional addictions has its benefits and its disadvantages. Instead of investing in the clear, rational procedures involved in natural scientific method, we are investing in a more phenomenological method of research (Ralkowski, 2007). In this book, stories of people actually experiencing what is being defined as emotional addictions have been accumulated and studied for their experiential value. Since this work is primarily a reference book for addictions and mental health counseling, the use of human experience to understand emotional phenomena seems appropriate. More effective counselors rely on the human experience of their clients for guidance and direction.

Definitions of ten emotional addictions based on the human experience of those who have lived with these emotions will be explored, beginning with anger and continuing through anxiety, apathy, egotism, envy, guilt, jealousy, resentment, revenge and self-hatred.

In order to accomplish this task, case studies supplied by many different counselors and their clients were reviewed. This required a clear definition of how counselors and clients would be perceived in the research. In the field of counseling, there appears to be two distinct perspectives on the role of clients and counselors. One perspective depicts counseling as being controlled by experts, who diagnose the problems of their clients, and help them make changes in their lives. There are numerous books describing important counseling skills where counselors use their expertise to help clients make these changes. The other perspective relies on the human experience of *clients as experts* with counselors providing clarity and direction at appropriate times during the counseling process (Ashenberg, 2004). In this research, we are relying on clients to guide us to a better understanding of what is being called, emotional addictions. Therefore, the following chapters are not about important counseling skills, but about developing a reference book based on human experience.

A Phenomenology of Emotions

Before describing each emotional addiction, an infrastructure or "emotional pattern" is needed to give us a better understanding for what comprises an emotional experience (Figure IA). The following elements are included in a phenomenology of emotions, and we will see that more than feelings are involved when people become emotional. In other words, specific variables are present when someone experiences anger, guilt or jealousy, or any other emotion. Let us look at variables to consider when having an emotional experience.

Physical—People may find that physical concerns play a part when being emotional but the role may be different for each emotion. The importance of physical concerns may have something to do with the type of emotion being experienced as much as the type of person becoming emotional (Wyer & Scrull, 1993). For example, physical elements probably play a larger role in a person's emotional experience with anger than with guilt. Some people are more physically prone to be sensitive, aggressive and demonstrative than others, and the experience of anger may rely more on human biology to effectively express itself. In comparison, the subtle nature of guilt most likely would rely less on a person's physical makeup. In understanding a phenomenology of emotions, it would be in our best interest to understand how physical concerns affect different emotional experiences.

For example, Tommy a twelve year old boy, was considered "high strung" and had been diagnosed with attention deficit disorder. His parents had many different opinions as to why he was this way, different than the diagnosis, and they expressed them when Tommy was brought to a counselor for his anger problems. John, his counselor, was noted for his thoroughness, and welcomed Tommy and his parents to his office. During the counseling session, he informed Tommy's parents that he would be checking numerous possibilities as to why Tommy seemed so agitated. After a few weeks of trying to help Tommy, John observed that Tommy seemed bothered by the fluorescent lights in the waiting room. He asked his parents about Tommy's vision, and it was disclosed that Tommy's father had the same problem. They both had an oversensitive physical reaction to artificial lighting.

In this example, the emotional experience of being agitated was resolved through understanding a physical concern that affected Tommy. Even though Tommy's situation was not a classic counseling experience, we still need to consider the physical side of our client's emotions. For example, some peoples' emotional states are directly affected by physical concerns such as, autism or anxiety associated with a malfunctioning thyroid condition (Zager, 2005; Leaman, 1992). In understanding a phenomenology of emotions, physical concerns are a part of the equation, but not all of it.

Beliefs—Our beliefs can have a major impact on a phenomenology of emotions. Research shows that our beliefs can lead to certain behaviors, (Zager, 2005) and that can be said for emotions. For example, believing that "The only good people are white people." may make a bigot angry most of the time, especially in a multi-cultural society. In a phenomenology of emotions, our belief systems may set the stage for what emotions we express. Combine a consideration of our physical characteristics, with our beliefs and our emotions can be dramatically influenced. For example, a male who believes he needs to possess a female in a relationship, may be more prone to the emotion of jealousy. Or, a learning disabled person who believes that others have more opportunities, may experience the emotion of resentment. In both of these examples, it was specific beliefs that influenced a certain emotional reaction.

In counseling, we have observed our client's emotional states, and have looked for answers to these emotions by surveying our client's beliefs. For example, if you show severe bouts of the emotion envy, it may be important to seek out the belief behind being envious. It may be the belief that, "In

Phenomenology of Emotions

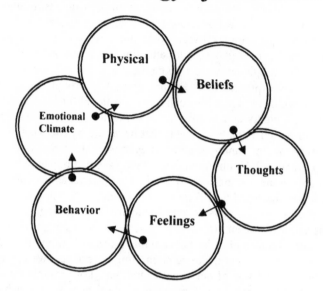

Figure IA

Phenomenology of Addictions

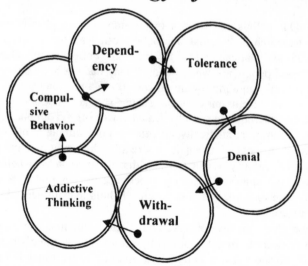

Figure IB

order to be acceptable, you must be tall and thin." If you are not, you may have an envious, emotional experience. A phenomenology of emotions requires more than feelings to be understood. Sometimes feelings are the symbolic expression of a far deeper emotional belief. An emotional experience includes more than just a physical reaction. It includes specific beliefs about one's emotions

Thoughts—Included in a phenomenology of emotions are the thoughts that accompany an emotional experience. Thoughts can hold a major role in how we express our emotions. If our thoughts are based on reliable and valid information, then our emotional response will be different then if our thoughts were gathered at random (Longabaugh & Morganstern, 1999). For example, a person who has reliable and valid thoughts about why another person is mounting a verbal attack may have a different emotional response than a person who randomly thinks about the verbal attack. The calculated thoughts made in the first example may elicit an emotional response of compassion or empathy while the random thoughts of the second example may elicit anger or resentment.

When counseling highly emotional people, it may be important to consider their physical concerns and their beliefs, but leaving out how someone is thinking about an emotional experience will limit information needed to accurately help clients. At times, our clients may demonstrate highly irrational thinking that has a direct impact on emotions. For example, if a client's thoughts are scattered, random, over-generalized or incomplete regarding their feelings, it may be our responsibility as counselors to help organize their thoughts. Many clients are severely impacted when negative thoughts dominate their thinking during an emotional experience (Leaman, 1992). For example, the negative thinking taking place when someone is criticized may elicit the emotion of guilt, while positive thoughts may bring out the emotion of concern. In a phenomenology of emotions, the thought process used when going through an emotional experience should be considered along with one's physical concerns and beliefs.

Feelings—Physical characteristics, personal beliefs and patterns of thinking can directly influence our feelings, and it is feelings that we most associate with an emotional experience (Norman & Ganser, 2004). For nonprofessionals, getting in touch with feelings may be enough in understanding emotional experiences. Yet, feelings may only be a part of what is needed to counsel clients. In a phenomenology of emotions, feelings become the most tangible part of our experience. For example, if someone acts unreasonable towards us, we may get angry, if someone violates us in some way, we may seek revenge. However, to understand what anger or revenge means in a counseling setting, more than an expression of feelings may be necessary.

We may need to find out if there are physical reasons for these feelings, or what beliefs are triggering such feelings, or what are our thoughts on these feelings?

However, let us not ignore pure expressions of feelings as valuable in their own right. In counseling, expressing one's feelings is one of the higher forms of communication. Beyond our facts and opinions are our feelings. Sometimes counselors may not want to focus on physical concerns or beliefs or someone's thoughts. Sometimes an open and unencumbered expression of feelings may be the best therapeutic stance (Lemoire & Chen, 2005). For example, a client in counseling may break into a rage and needs simply to vent feelings. For the counselor, this may not be the time to pursue one's thoughts and beliefs. It may be important to express feelings without including any other emotional characteristics. In a phenomenology of emotions, expression of feelings can be a major consideration, but it must be said that feelings are only a part of understanding emotional phenomena. In counseling, to understand emotions, a combination of physical concerns, beliefs, thoughts and feelings must be taken into consideration.

Behaviors—The combination of people's physical make up, beliefs, thoughts and feelings directly influence their behavior. In a phenomenology of emotions, behavior seems to be what counselors commonly consider during treatment. For example, in anger management, it may be a combination of cognitive and behavioral techniques used to treat an angry client. Or, it may be behavioral techniques that treat a client who has anxiety over being in public. Or, it may be a combination of feelings and behavior that a counselor uses when treating a client for loss. In a phenomenology of emotions, behavior, along with feelings, become the two visible and sometimes dramatic expressions of an emotional experience. It would be difficult to counsel a client's emotional experience without looking at behavior. It is what we remember when understanding the emotions of others.

For example, when bullies create fear in the hearts and minds of their victims, it becomes the act of bullying where we focus attention. Counselors want to change the behavior of bullies, and want the emotional experience around them to be more stable and reasonable. Furthermore, behavior is the most researched portion of an emotional experience. It lends itself to quantification and replication, and has received the most attention when studying emotions (Ashkansas, Hartell & Zerbe, 2000). For example, if we are going to study someone who displays a chronic need to be jealous, we most likely will start with studying his or her behavior. The connection between the emotions of clients and their predictable behavior still dominates research concerning emotions (Mano, 1991). However, in a phenomenology of emotions, understanding emotions through people's behavior is not enough. In order to capture the entire emotional experience, researchers also need to consider the characteristics of what was previously discussed in this Introduction.

Emotional Climate—Ironically, the characteristic that has considerable influence on people's emotional experience, turns out to be the characteristic least discussed. People who have emotional experiences are having them within a climate of emotion that surrounds these experiences (Ladd, 2005). For example, if you wake up and feel happy about starting your day, and go down to the breakfast table where your relatives are sitting around with bitterness on their faces, "How long do you think it will take before you also are feeling pangs of bitterness?" In a phenomenology of emotions, the emotional climate in which people's emotions take place can have a direct influence on personal emotions. Sometimes the emotional climate can become bigger than the people in it, as found in an angry mob or mourning the loss of a loved one. In such cases, we may have a personal emotional experience that is directly influenced by the emotional climate.

The problem for researchers who study emotions is that each emotional climate is different, and its effect on people's emotions is different. However, in a phenomenology of emotions studying emotions without considering the climate in which people experience these emotions is like evaluating the sea worthiness of a boat without considering the type of water where it will be used. The bias of this book is that counseling and psychology, in general, should include studies based on a more human science not only natural science, where human experience is elevated to the realm of understandable possibilities. In a natural scientific study of emotions, the emotional climate seems secondary because it is difficult to control its validity and reliability. Therefore, the purpose of natural scientific method is to develop facts that are valid and reliable. Studying emotions from a human science perspective assumes you cannot completely control for reliability and validity. In a more phenomenological method of research, facts are not as important as human possibilities. Under this form of research the emotional climate becomes one more possibility to consider in the overall understanding of an emotional experience.

A Phenomenology of Addictions

In the last section we considered what elements need consideration in a phenomenology of emotions. We will find in the next ten chapters that each emotion creates a different phenomenological experience. However, our interest is in how these emotions can develop addictive characteristics, and how these characteristics affect addictions and mental health counseling. To meet this challenge, it became important to create an infrastructure for what is an addiction, (Figure IB) and combine it with the infrastructure of each emotion. This combination was the basis for forming ten unique emotional addictions. In this section, we will consider what might be considered in a phenomenology of addiction. There are certain characteristics that prevail no matter what type of addiction is being studied. The following describes these characteristics.

Dependency—Professionals are familiar with the concept of dependency in addictions and mental health counseling. Simply put, it is when people go beyond *wanting* something, to *needing* something. Dependency is different than desire. It becomes a need, and we can see this taking place in emotional addictions (Ray, 1990). For example, we have our moments when we get angry at some unreasonable circumstance, and express ourselves through anger. However, our anger is specific to that situation. It relates directly to what we are experiencing. This is different than getting angry in almost every situation. In our first example, the situation caused our anger. In the second, our anger is applied to many different situations. In a sense, we depend on anger to get us through these experiences. In other words, we have formed a dependency on getting angry.

Much like an alcoholic who depends on alcohol to face difficult situations, a person with an emotional addiction may depend on a specific emotion for a comparable result. For example, a person addicted to resentment may feel frustrated and stuck regardless of the situations he or she faces. The resentment becomes a crutch to depend on when experiencing conflict. The resentful person faces emotional experiences using a dependency on resentment to face these situations. In this example, we may ask, "Why would someone gossip and indirectly attack others for no reason?" It may be they depend on an emotional addiction of resentment to solve their problems.

Denial—In addictions, denial is practiced as an excuse so people can continue using something; even though, it may be having negative effects on relationships, job performance and other social activities (Siossat, 1998). For example, the alcoholic who makes excuses, and defends their drinking may be in denial regarding the impact their drinking is having on the family. In this example, denial is used to cover up a problem that may be obvious to others, or may be hurting others. Denial becomes a dangerous facet of addiction because it denies addicted people an opportunity to face their problems.

In an emotional addiction, denial may be used in a similar manner. For example, people may make excuses for their jealous behavior and call it possessive love, when underneath they are using force to express their jealousy. In this example, these people are in denial of their jealousy, allowing them to continue using abusive behavior. Just as observed in a physical addiction, denial allows people with emotional addictions to continue using their emotions at the expense of themselves and others. In counseling, we have clients who express denial in many ways. For example, we may have clients who deny hating themselves, yet practice self-destructive behavior. Or, we may have clients who deny they are vengeful, yet spend days planning to get back at a person they believe has violated them.

Withdrawal—In physical addiction, withdrawal is a physical and psychological rebellion against the loss of gratification that comes from a drug's addictive characteristics (NIHM, 2004). It is a period where the body and mind go through a painful re-organization in order to function without the use of the drug. However, the body and the mind do not completely forget the gratification they have encountered. Thus, the saying, "I am a recovering alcoholic." Or, "I am a recovering heroin addict." Groups such as, Alcoholics Anonymous, Synanon and others, are organizations developed to deal with the incomplete withdrawal symptoms of drug and alcohol addiction.

In an emotional addiction, withdrawal from emotional gratification can be as powerful as withdrawal from physical or psychological gratification. For example, a counselor may try to help a client with their shame. They may work on their self-esteem and a positive attitude. However, the counselor may have to consider their client may have felt ashamed for many years, and has practiced shame during these years. The reality may be that the client has an emotional addiction to feeling ashamed. The counselor may need to understand when removing shame from their client's emotional experiences, there may be withdrawal symptoms. Because of this, they also may have to counsel for such emotions as, anxiety, fear of failure and possibly fear of intimacy. Clients with emotional addictions may suffer symptoms of withdrawal if not counseled correctly. Furthermore, clients having bouts with emotional addictions may have recurring incidents of withdrawal even after recovery has taken place. For example, a client having recovered from a personal identity based on shame, may have recurring withdrawal symptoms when another judges their behavior as shameful.

Tolerance—In drug and alcohol addiction, tolerance is described as needing to take increasing quantities of a substance to obtain the same effect (Chung, Martin, Winters & Langenbucker, 2001). For example, some alcoholics can function at blood levels of alcohol that would be intoxicating, coma-inducing, or lethal to the average drinker. People acquiring a tolerance of this caliber, need to chronically continue to drink over a certain period of time. However, in later stages of some addictions, tolerance reverses itself, and what was tolerable begins to break down, usually causing serious physical problems for the people who once were able to tolerate their addiction.

In emotional addictions, tolerance may play a comparable role in people's emotional experiences. For example, people suffering from an emotional addiction of anger, may not notice their constant explosions towards others as a problem. What may shock others as far as explosive behavior may be perceived as normal to someone with an anger tolerance. Furthermore, tolerance in emotional addictions seems to follow a similar path as physical addictions. For example, that same person with an emotional addiction to anger may go beyond developing a tolerance for anger and need bigger and more profound explosions to satisfy the addiction. Counselors who have worked with clients suffering from an emotional addiction may be surprised by how much dysfunctional behavior these clients can tolerate. Combine tolerance, denial, dependency and fear of withdrawal symptoms, and some clients may have an equally hard time recovering from an emotional addiction as with a physical addiction.

Compulsive Behavior—Addicts, at some point during their addictive behavior, cross a line between voluntary and compulsive behavior. For example, alcoholics can reach a stage in their drinking where memory, perception and neuro-motor functioning becomes more compulsory than voluntary. A physiological chain of events develops where the alcoholic perceives drinking as a necessity, and the neuro-motor impulses in the brain follow with a compulsive act of drinking to excess (Esterly & Neely, 1997).

In emotional addictions, a similar pathway may be in use where a line is crossed in our emotions, and we act more compulsively than with forethought or meaningful intentions. For example, people suffering from an emotional addiction to anxiety may have every intention to stop being anxious. They may understand that; other methods are available when becoming anxious, that one's anxiety is more myth than reality, and that by creating a sense of security and safety their anxiety may be reduced. Even when knowing how to create coping techniques against further anxiety, people still may compulsively have anxiety attacks. They may have crossed the line between voluntary and compulsive behavior, where they cannot stop their unwanted anxiety. Combine this type of compulsive behavior with; denial of controlling anxiety, a dependency on using it, tolerance for living with it, and withdrawal symptoms when it begins to lessen, and you have some of the characteristics of an anxiety addiction.

Addictive Thinking—The addictive thinking that takes place with people having physical addictions can also be found in emotional addictions (Twerski, 1990). But, before we compare the two, a comparison of addictive thinking and critical thinking may be in order. There are specific characteristics that are used in critical thinking. First, critical thinkers usually check out their assumptions about experiences in life. For example, if you are from the Sahara Desert and you move to the northeast United States, you may assume you know about snow. This assumption may hold true until you have an accident while driving in it. Many addictive thinkers do not examine their assumptions much like the driver from the Sahara Desert. They work from unchecked assumptions such as, for example, assuming that heroin will be a way to solve all problems.

In addictive thinking, our unchecked assumptions lead to narrow perceptions of our world. In critical thinking, our checked assumptions lead to broadened perceptions. For example, the heroin addict that was going to solve all problems by taking heroin now has narrowed heroin as *the* solution to solving problems.

In critical thinking, our broadened perceptions lead to more calculated decision making. In addictive thinking our decisions are more random. For example, a heroin addict with unchecked assumptions and a narrow perception of how to solve problems is more inclined to make random decisions rather than calculated ones. For example, the heroin addict may decide to randomly use larger amounts of heroin to solve future life problems.

Critical thinkers who; check out assumptions, broaden their perceptions and calculate their decisions are more inclined to act rather than react. Addictive thinkers with unchecked assumptions, narrow perceptions, and random thinking are more inclined to react. In emotional addictions, this pattern of addictive thinking mimics thinking in physical addictions, and both can lead to reactionary behavior.

Emotional Addictions and Counseling

There seems to be a different approach taken with mental health counselors and addictions counselors when treating clients. Mental health counselors focus more on disorders where the emotions and behaviors of clients are understood through such works as the Diagnostic and Statistical Manual IV (First, 2000). Addictions counselors treat addictive patterns of behavior found in physical and process oriented addictions (Rose, Chassin, Presson & Sherman, 2000). Furthermore, if a client has both a mental health disorder and an addiction, the addiction may be treated first or if treated simultaneously, it may be treated as a dual-diagnosis (Ortman, 2001) in consultation with both mental health and addictions counselors.

Without getting into an extended history of both professions, let it be said that mental health counseling and addictions counseling were established as two different schools of thought that collaborate with each other, but are perceived as different forms of counseling with different philosophies and different methods of certification. However, what will be presented in this book does not come from either school of thought, but originates in the human experience of people with emotional addiction problems.

In everyday experience, emotions and addictions are not necessarily separated by schools of thought, and the phenomenon of experiencing an emotional addiction may need an understanding from both points of view. This book is an attempt at giving both mental health counselors and addictions counselors a new perspective on human experience, and an opportunity to cross over the political lines drawn between these exciting professions. From a human experience perspective, people in pain are not as concerned with professional dividing lines between different approaches to counseling. They are concerned with reducing their pain. Sometimes the most effective professionals to help these people are mental health counselors. Other times, people who are in pain are better served by seeing addiction's counselors, or are best served by having a professional who understands both. This book is intended to give mental health counselors a new approach to working with addictions and addiction counselors a new approach to handling emotions and mental health.

Summary

In the field of counseling, the actual counseling experience seems to rely on possibilities more than facts. We have demonstrated this in our descriptions of a phenomenology of emotions and addictions. For example, when counseling for emotions, we may help our clients by discussing the possibility that physical health is affecting their emotions. At other times, we may discuss what our clients believe about their emotions, or how they are thinking about them. We may have discussions only on feelings, or on how emotions affect behavior. Counseling for emotions may also create discussions about the emotional climate that is affecting our clients' emotions. As counselors, we must be open to all of these possibilities.

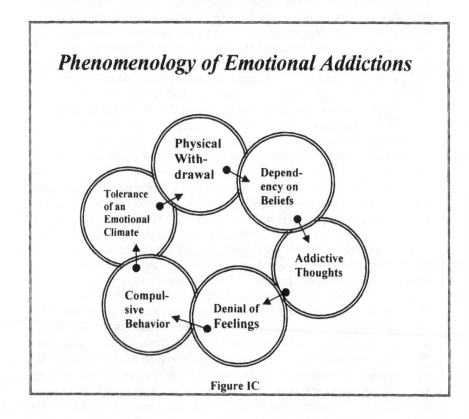

Phenomenology of Emotional Addictions

Figure IC

The same holds true for addictions counseling. For example, we may be counseling for how our clients demonstrate denial of certain addictions, or how they depend on them. We could engage our clients in discussions regarding their addictive thinking, or how they are able to tolerate certain addictions. We may point out compulsions that are created by addictions, or how our clients are facing withdrawal symptoms when trying to recover from them. In all of these discussions, we are looking for possibilities to engage our clients with the hope of creating change.

In counseling for an emotional addiction, again we benefit more from possibilities than facts. For example in counseling, we may talk about the possibility that physical withdrawal may be a part of experiencing an emotional addiction, or how depending on certain beliefs may create a foundation for an emotional addiction. We may discuss the possibility that emotional addictions can be affected by addictive thoughts, or how clients may be in denial of certain feelings. We may discuss the possibility that an emotional addiction may emerge from compulsive behavior, or how clients may learn to tolerate an emotional climate found in society that surrounds an emotional addiction (Figure IC).

In all of these examples, accurate facts can be helpful in providing information for recovery; however, creating possibilities that directly address our clients' problems seems to be the main reason people seek counseling. For example, giving clients facts without exploring possibilities in counseling is like giving someone a car without teaching them how to drive.

The foundation of scientific inquiry is based on the formation of facts. Much like any field in science, facts comprise the bulk of the research in these fields. In psychology, this approach also prevails. However, as researchers, we must be prudent not to let our facts limit our possibilities. Psychology is a field of inquiry where understanding only facts may limit meaningful information found in human experience. Studying human feelings and behaviors has offered psychology an opportunity to gather facts that pass the test for reliability and validity. Such facts can be found in research such as in, the DSMIV or the latest research on the physiological impact of drugs on our bodies. These factual resources and others are the foundation of our understanding in the fields of mental health and addictions. Yet, we should not assume that only facts are important. In other words, facts should not limit us from what is meaningful.

This book will focus more on possibilities than on facts. A phenomenological approach to research was used for this reason. In psychology, sometimes a combination of facts and possibilities brings us closer to what it means to be human. The following is an attempt to humanize the perspectives found in mental health and addictions counseling. It may be possible that human beings can become addicted to their emotions. At the present time, this is a hypothesis, not a fact. It still remains in the realm of possibilities. However, our human experience has directed this research to the possibility of emotional addictions being an everyday phenomenon. This book explores that possibility.

Chapter 1: Anger Addiction

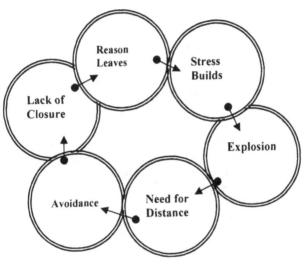

Figure 1

Background

Anger can be found in many different contexts and expressed in numerous ways. From a physiological perspective, anger is what happens when tension builds in our bodies from an outside threat, and ultimately results in adrenaline shooting through us, setting the stage for some form of fight or flight phenomenon to take place (Siegman & Smith, 1994). From a sociological perspective, anger is what happens to us when the boundaries of everyday living are threatened by some outside force, and we are compelled to defend ourselves against these threats (Allcom, 1994). From a psychological perspective, anger is what we experience when feeling that life has become unreasonable and we feel threatened, and we need to attack in some way, in order for reason to return (Feindler, 2006). In all of these different perspectives, it may be noted that, what was accepted as physically, socially or psychologically normal has been dramatically disrupted. Anger is our safety valve when our normal lives are threatened and some response is mandatory.

In the fields of addictions and mental health counseling, counselors may experience anger from their clients at all three of the above described levels. Anger is a phenomenon that has followed us through pre-historic times and seems to be a basic part of our makeup, no matter what level we perceive it. However, over thousands of years of expressing ourselves through anger, we have made attempts to control its irrational nature (Reiser, 1999). This became obvious with the growth of civilization where anger began its downward spiral as an acceptable behavior. In our present day society, anger has taken a second seat to resentment which has been designated as civilized anger.

One of the few areas that anger seems to hold a certain level of acceptance is with different forms of counseling and therapy. Sometimes in counseling, we encourage our clients when they get angry, especially if directed at the dysfunction inhibiting their growth. We also may see anger more therapeutically than anxiety, depression or denial of problems. Counselors like to direct anger into productive forms so that society does not feel threatened by irrational intentions or by unreasonable behavior (Chalk, 1998).

Many forms of anger management have been created to make anger civilized and controllable, and schools, families and workplaces have counselors available for anger's unpredictable nature. If we were to be candid about anger, civilization has a sketchy report card when it comes to controlling it. We still have disagreements among ourselves, and war and insurrection do not seem to be diminishing any time soon. Unfortunately for most of us, we live with violent expressions of anger, and it appears that the world has become semi-numb to such events (Deluca, 1995).

On an individual basis, our complacency seems less intact regarding anger. We do not seem to tolerate people exploding with rage when the rest of us are coping as best we can with life's problems. Our concern has become so great that anger management can be found in all walks of life, and with all types of professionals trying to control anger (Blum, 2001). In most of these attempts at anger reduction, we seem to define it either as some form of disorder or as aberrant behavior. Oppositional defiant disorder, conduct disorder and juvenile delinquency are a few of the names we give to angry people, and we vigilantly try to keep these people within the boundaries of our society.

In this chapter we are attempting to define anger in a different manner, and not concede that it is only found in forms of aberrant behavior or as a disorder. We will define anger through the perspective of an emotional addiction. Treating anger as an addiction has implications for how we perceive it, and how it is treated in counseling and therapy. Hopefully, we can expand our understanding of this ancient phenomenon with the realization that life may create addictive tendencies in certain people who eventually use anger as a filter for all of their behavior, not only in unreasonable circumstances.

Case Study

Fred was a conflicted person. He had recently married into a family that was open to many different religions, races and gender identities. Yet, Fred was trying to make his way through these, so called, liberal values. His own background reflected a very different set of values. Even though his mother was a compassionate woman, she struggled with drug and alcohol problems which left her an unlikely mentor for Fred's personal value system. Fred's father was another story. He was an avowed racist who even started a dispute when African American music was played at Fred's wedding.

Fred was like a bomb that needed the slightest ignition in order to go off. For example, he was gathered with his wife's family, and they started talking about common themes such as politics, religion and life style. Fred's in-laws were shocked at the level of anger and rage he held for people different from himself. Actually, it was so obvious that everyone except Fred were frozen with shock at the epithets he projected across the room. As he looked into the eyes of his newly found in-laws, Fred did not know the trouble he was in. Whatever comments he had made when in the company of his racist father, had little positive effect on his newly acquired relatives. He truly loved his wife, Nicole, but some habits die hard, and his anger about others was one of them. The irony of his behavior was that he avoided any hints from his wife that he should be careful around her parents. For the most part, Fred had spent little time with others different from himself. His anger was prefabricated from the depths of his racism, and his brand of reasonable behavior was limited to his narrow point of view.

Finally, Fred went too far and his brother-in-law called him a racist. However, this only made Fred angrier. He told his wife that he was not going to speak to his brother-in-law ever again. It was only after his wife threatened to leave him that he decided to get help. Confused and conflicted, Fred sought help from a mental health counselor named, Randy. After telling him his story, Randy knew that Fred had anger management issues. Subsequently, he used behavioral techniques in anger management training to help Fred reduce his anger, and join his partner in a productive and healthy life. However, all of Randy's anger management training did not work. Fred would try these skills over the next few months, only to have violent outbursts at issues that did not seem to bother other family members. Finally, Randy proposed that he and Fred look at his anger from a different perspective. Instead of looking at it as a behavioral problem or possibly as a disorder, Randy suggested they view Fred's anger as an emotional addiction; one that had such symptoms as, denial, dependency, compulsive behavior, tolerance, addictive thinking and withdrawal. Randy told Fred that in physical

addiction people who wanted to stop have to first accept that an addiction may be inhibiting them from stopping. What they wanted to do and what they needed to do were different. For example, an alcoholic who realizes that alcohol is wrecking his or her life wants to stop but needs alcohol regardless of their intentions. He told Fred, that his situation was similar. He wanted to stop being angry but he compulsively would explode, in spite of his wishes. He told Fred that he wanted to look at his anger as an addiction that probably had been practiced for any number of years. Instead of questioning Fred's desire to fit into the family of his wife, Nicole, Fred should visualize an addictive pattern of feelings and behavior that caused him to express uncontrollable anger whenever some incident went against his value system.

As Fred's counseling progressed, he began to realize the depth of his addiction. It was so powerful that it stopped him from love, companionship and intimacy. It was the one theme that clouded all others. It was an emotional addiction to anger, and he had learned it at an early age. Unlike others who embraced racism and bigotry, Fred unconsciously became addicted to it. He used a pattern of behavior that stopped him from meeting the goals and desires of his marriage. Similar to a drug or alcohol addict, Fred became addicted to anger, and it was now controlling those areas of his life that he believed were important.

The Experience of Anger

The experience of anger begins with a person's perception of what seems like a reasonable situation, suddenly becoming unreasonable. We all have a sense of what we feel is reasonable behavior either emanating from others or from circumstances within our worlds, and we all seem to know when a change has occurred that makes our worlds unreasonable. Sometimes, we accept life as unreasonable and do little in response to it. Other times, we irrationally act, as an expression to a world that has been disrupted. Anger seems to be one response that we use to counteract these disruptions. For example, someone hits you with a rock for no apparent reason. Under these circumstances, it may not be the time for making a reasonable response. You may find yourself reacting out of anger for a provocation that does not seem to make sense. Physically, you may have an angry stimulus/response reaction. Socially, you may have an angry response to someone

breaking some social boundary such as, angry over someone using rocks as weapons. Psychologically, you may respond to someone or some thing crossing over a line in your belief system such as, becoming angry when someone embarrasses you in front of others by hitting you with a rock. In all of these examples, reason leaves, and you may find yourself embarking into the experience of anger (Figure 1).

Fred, in the case study, was one of these people. He found individuals from different races, colors and creeds to be unreasonable choices in his belief system, and he responded angrily by using racial, sexist or religious slurs. Reason seemed to leave anytime these themes entered his consciousness. For Fred, there were certain areas of his life that were automatically a threat. Unlike Fred, many of us have particular issues that may cause reason to leave, but there may be any number of extenuating circumstances for our behavior, and we might classify them as situational, or not being present all of the time.

Stress
Builds

When we experience anger, reason has left our consciousness by sending a signal to the amygdale of our brains, to prepare for some imminent threat about to take place (Nelson, 2006). Physically, the amygdale sends a message to the pituitary gland to begin pumping adrenaline through our bodies to either fight the threat, or to make flight from it. Our muscles tense and we become hyper-vigilant towards the world around us. Socially, we may focus on those actions from others that are disrupting our social order such as, being in the middle of a mob, and becoming stressed for no apparent reason. Psychologically, we may become angry when our belief systems become disrupted, and we find ourselves unable to accept the words of others because they seem unreasonable. In all of these, we are preparing ourselves for some emotional exchange that is not based on logical behavior (Figure 1). In fact, our behavior becomes irrational, not in the sense that it is now dysfunctional, but in respect to rational behavior no longer being able to rectify the problem.

Many of us find ourselves in the position of reason leaving and having stress build. In an imperfect world, not all situations will appear reasonable. For many of us, the opportunity or the will to get angry is not present, and we bury our anger, causing other accumulated problems to take over. Developmentally, most of us have our anger controlled as we become older, and wiser. For example, a temper tantrum at five years old is quite different than one happening as an adult. Yet, there are those moments in all of us where stress builds in response to some form of unreasonable actions in our lives, and this prepares us for some form of outward explosion.

The explosion stage in anger is the one we are most commonly used to observing, and the one that causes us the most personal change. Up until this point, we could define our feelings as some form of anxiety or resentment, but with an explosion, anger becomes clearly defined for ourselves and those who observe it (Figure 1). Our stress is released in some form of dramatic behavior. Sometimes, we attack a problem such as, getting angry at a car that will not start. Other times, we attack people such as, when punishing a child for their unreasonable behavior, and other times we attack both, as found in our going to war against a country and its people. The important point to remember is that the explosion needs to take place. Even when we say, "You look angry!" we are commenting on the possibility that someone could explode if something does not change.

In the case study, as long as Fred kept his racial biases to himself, most of his relatives probably would not respond to his behavior. It is only after he exploded with anger that shock was visibly noticeable. Many times, it is the explosion stage in anger that is most judged, and it is the stage that may create the label of, "angry person" in the minds of others. In the case study, this certainly held true. Fred was caught between his anger and his love for Nicole. He initially sought out counseling to control his explosions, and like others, was seeking some form of anger management to alter his behavior.

Probably one of the most ignored aspects of anger is what to do with it after the explosion has taken place. For example, an explosion of anger is not the most opportune time to resolve a problem. We may have heard of examples where two people are exploding and a third person approaches them and says, "What is wrong here?" If you think about it, such a statement seems a bit absurd. Reason has left both parties. They have become highly stressed and are now exploding at each other. Not exactly the best time to ask a logical question and expect a reasonable answer. Yet, how many people try to settle their anger while they are exploding? Instead, there seems to be a more reasonable approach that can be taken. After the explosion has taken place, it may be advisable to get distance so reason can return (Figure 1). How many people have had angry explosions in a car or an elevator and continue to fight because they could not get away from each other. In family counseling, a couple fighting with each other where one party says, "I'm leaving!" and the other party says, "You get back here!" makes little sense in resolving an angry dispute (Vogel, Epting & Webster, 2003).

For these reasons, needing to get distance from an explosion may be one of the most important steps in resolving any angry dispute. Distance gives angry people an opportunity for reason to return. It allows people to calm down and try to reasonably perceive the problem. And, there are two major types of distance that can be obtained when explosions take place. There is physical distance where leaving the scene of the explosion helps in re-establishing reasonable behavior, and there is temporal distance where having enough time pass may accomplish the same goal of having reason return. Most of us who have become angry, unconsciously understand the need for distance when engaged in angry disputes, and most of us calm down and let reason return. As we will see later in the Chapter, that is not always the case with people practicing an emotional addiction to anger.

For those of you who have exploded with anger, have gotten distance and have let reason return, the next stage of anger may be crucial. Some of us will decide that being angry was not worth it, and will get on with our lives with the hope that all will be forgotten, and in any number of cases, that is exactly what happens. We explode, get distance, and eventually let anger go. Most of our angry explosions seem to be handled in this manner, especially if we were angry at another person and they in turn, have let it go. However, what happens when either we cannot let it go, or others are having a similar problem? For example, a fourth grade teacher had a fight with her husband and the next day exploded at her class. In subsequent days, she began to notice a difference in the students. They became more reserved and cautious. Finally, she went to a friend and asked what she should do. The friend asked if there was any incident that caused the problem. The teacher finally admitted that she had become angry with them but was avoiding saying anything. She believed it would eventually go away. Incredibly, she avoided them for over a month. Her friend told her to tell the class that her angry explosion was over. The next day, she announced to the class that the explosion that took place a month earlier was now officially over. At that moment, the whole class breathed a sigh of relief. The experience of anger is not over when we want it to be over, or even when we think it should be over. Simply put, "Anger is over when we make sure it is over." Methods for avoiding this reality only seem to extend it.

What is needed for anger to end is some form of closure. As stated before, sometimes this happens with the passage of time. However, there are circumstances when an intervention needs to take place (Figure 1). In the above example regarding the angry teacher, she needed to tell her class that she was no longer angry before they could let it go. They had not achieved proper distance from the explosion on their own. They needed her to announce that her angry outburst had ended, and she was not angry any longer. Without giving her class closure, she extended the life of the angry experience. For example, in the case study, one of Fred's problems was that he realized his angry outbursts cast a negative impression on his acceptance into his wife's family. It is highly possible that he sought out counseling for this reason. Without closure, he ran the risk of being perceived as an unreasonable person, or a volatile person, and who is to say whether that was not the case?

As we will see in the next section, there are people who do not find closure when expressing their anger, and with a lack of closure, they create a climate for experiencing more unreasonable behavior. Constantly cycling through angry explosions without closure may create more angry explosions, and a tendency to avoid closure, in general. For those who fall into this vicious cycle, levels of anger may increase and what was found reasonable may decrease. They may be initiating a cycle of behavior that repeats itself. Without proper understanding of this phenomenon, they may fall into an emotional addiction based on anger where people adopt anger as a life style.

How an Anger Addiction Works

As described in the last section, all of us have moments of anger, and all of us find justifications for life becoming unreasonable. We are not perfect, and neither are moments in our everyday living where we become stressed and explode with anger. Yet, angry explosions seem to be only half the story. Getting distance and facing our unreasonable behavior, helps us obtain closure on these events, and it may be the avoidance of fallout from angry explosions, that makes such experiences linger much longer than we would like.

However, there are people who do avoid the fallout from their angry explosions, and do not obtain closure from these experiences, and for these and other reasons, seem to be angry most of the time. These are people who have created a pattern of behavior that feeds on itself. In other words, they do not need someone or something to be unreasonable in their presence. They have a predisposition for unreasonable behavior, and have developed a pattern of behavior that reinforces this predisposition. Such people may be viewed as having an anger addiction, where they find it difficult not to be angry or difficult not to get angry. The following addresses some of the characteristics of an emotional addiction to anger:

Reason Leaves and Addictive Thinking—In an angry experience, there are many reasons for us to abandon our logical behavior and begin to prepare ourselves for a reaction to an unreasonable outside event. However, when we think about someone with an anger addiction, it may be important to understand the type of thinking that dictates one's behavior. Fundamentally, it comes down to how much in this life are we willing to accept as reasonable? For example, in the case study, Fred used addictive thinking when he thought about others in areas of race, greed and color. His parameters for reason were extremely narrow. Basically, if you were not like Fred, than he may be angry with you. The problem with this type of thinking is that it tends to appear safe and easy within the minds of those using it. Unlike any type of critical thinking where we check out our assumptions, broaden your perceptions and evaluate our conclusions, addictive thinking avoids all of these steps (Halpern, 2003). By working from unchecked assumptions, narrow perceptions and random conclusions, people do not have to work at being reasonable. Many of them do the opposite. They work at being unreasonable. They find viewing their world as unreasonable, allows them to keep their lives simple, in declaring, "Here is what I can accept, and here is what I find unacceptable."

In the case study, Fred adopted the addictive thinking of his father, and it was only when confronted with more critical thinking found in counseling did Fred begin to change. Counselors have seen this type of thinking before. Numerous drug and alcohol abusers also practice addictive thinking (Terwski, 1990). They may take drugs to avoid critical decision making, and they may find themselves making habitual decisions in their place. For ex-

ample, if you are having trouble with your family, you can use critical thinking to solve these problems, or you can make a habitual decision and take
drugs. In the case study, Fred was using addictive thinking when perceiving
people different than himself. However, instead of taking drugs, Fred got angry.

Stress Builds and Dependency—Unfortunately for Fred, his addictive thinking created an enormous amount of stress within his life. His addictive thinking lowered his need to critically think through problems; however,
it trapped Fred into predictable responses that showed little change. If he met
someone from an unacceptable race, he treated them with anger regardless of
the circumstances, thus earning him the label of either bigot or racist. For
Fred, judging people became uncomplicated, you were either with him or
you were against him. In an emotional addiction to anger, the fallout of addictive thinking seems severe. With the same addictive thought process, any
person can develop a similar response. Fred became similar to a rat hitting a
feeder bar, where a certain stimulus resulted in a similar response each time
his racism got the better of him (Honig & Fetterman, 1992).

In the experience of anger, the similar response that seems to take place
is for someone to become, stressed. In other words, addictive thinking seems
to make people more unreasonable, and unreasonable people seem to become stressed more easily. And, in an anger addiction, not only can a person
become stressed more easily, but they may, over time, develop a dependency
on becoming stressed. In the case study, Fred may have developed a problem
with stress. He may have used it any time unreasonable circumstances entered his life, and if circumstances were unreasonable, Fred could depend on
stress to be ever present in his life.

Treating stress as a dependency may help counselors with clients who
show signs of anger. Stress management and anger management can be helpful skills to use during counseling; however, there are people who seem to
depend on anger and stress as a way of fulfilling their values and beliefs.
Behavioral skills to reduce anger and stress may be competing with a client's
dependency on both of these, in order to define his or her identity (Powers,
Cramer & Grubka, 2007). In the case study, Fred relied on anger and stress
as a part of his personality. In the same manner as his father, Fred found
much of life unreasonable. In counseling, it may be important to go beyond
skill training and look deeper into a client's dependency on anger, or a dependency on stress to fully help someone get over both of them.

Explosions and Compulsive Behavior—Some may say that exploding with anger is a compulsive act, based on a build up of stress, and
some unreasonable experience happening in one's life (Ladd, 2005). However, in an emotional addiction to anger, it may be the type of compulsive act
that takes place that separates it from everyday angry explosions. When
someone who is not addicted to anger explodes, it tends to be for certain

circumstances that present themselves. For example, if someone is talking to you and slaps you in the face, you might compulsively act by slapping them back. However, it does not mean that everyone who you talk to will slap you in the face. Your critical thinking skills may consider a similar situation to be quite different, and if slapped in the face again, who can determine how you will react? An emotional addiction to anger does not make such specific distinctions. Someone addicted to anger, may compulsively react as if all similar situations are identical. For example, in the case study, Fred even in hearing mention of a race other than his race compulsively exploded without even considering the circumstances taking place. Much like an alcoholic compulsively takes a drink when under stress those with an anger addiction may compulsively explode when under the same type of stress.

As counselors, this type of explosion becomes more complicated than someone exploding for some unreasonable event. It is a pattern of explosion where someone reacts to pre-determined categories in life that are unacceptable. Exploding through anger is a compulsive act, but in an anger addiction, the explosion may be based on pre-determined factors that caused it to become compulsive.

Needing Distance and Denial—After an explosion of anger, distance is needed for reason to return. In most angry explosions, people get distance after they have stopped venting over their unreasonable experiences. They may decide that the problem got out of hand, and they need some time for themselves, in order to calm down and re-gather their composure. In an anger addiction, people's need for distance seems to be in denial. For example, take terrorists who explode with violence against people they despise. In many respects, they are in denial of the concept of distance after angry explosions. In this example, there seems to be an ongoing sense of anger where distance does not completely negate chances for future explosions (Haddad, 2004).

In counseling, we may experience angry people who compulsively explode but do not seem to ever get distance from such angry feelings. In some respects, they are in denial of a need for distance. Their goal seems to be in keeping the anger alive, albeit at a reduced level. Their sense of denial almost guarantees that distance will not work. For example, in the case study, Fred does not ever achieve complete distance from his racism. There seemed to be no sense of giving up the underlying reasons for his anger. His explosions seemed to be an ongoing statement of his prejudice toward others. This can be reinforced by what happens physically. Without getting distance a person's adrenaline levels may stay elevated in preparation for future explosions (Johnson, 1990). Randy, his counselor, must establish some form of distance between Fred and his beliefs. Fred's acceptance of, a need for distance, may help him prepare for confronting his anger addiction. Denying a need for distance may only keep Fred addicted to his anger.

Avoidance and Tolerance—Most of us look for distance after an angry explosion so that we can calm down and have reason return. However, people with an anger addiction may not achieve distance. They may dismiss their explosions in order to avoid thinking about them. In effect, avoiding angry explosions does not create proper distance. In the case study, Fred avoided the people around his angry outbursts until his brother-in-law called him a racist. Even then, he avoided the possibility of having a problem. Instead, he told his wife that he did not want to ever see her brother, again. His tolerance for avoiding his anger was greater than facing it. We could see Fred spending many months or years avoiding resolution of his anger because he had already developed a tolerance for how it affected others.

The cycle that Fred was practicing was filled with addictive thinking, dependency on stress, compulsive explosions, disregarding a need to get distance and finally, tolerance for a problem that he avoided. Much as an alcoholic develops a tolerance for overusing alcohol, Fred had developed a tolerance for overusing his anger. He accomplished this by avoiding feeling and thinking about his behavior. Originally, he avoided his angry outbursts in front of his wife's parents. Later, he avoided the intervention made by his brother-in-law. His avoidance of facing his angry outbursts can be attributed to his tolerance of them. Fortunately, his wife forced him to seek help by threatening divorce. This was an action he could not tolerate.

Lack of Closure and Withdrawal—People with physical addictions may experience withdrawal symptoms when they stop using drugs (Faupel, 1991). An emotional addiction to anger may also create withdrawal symptoms but for a different reason. When angry people deny their need for distance, and avoid their behavior after an angry explosion, they may be missing an opportunity to get closure. Without facing the problem or getting closure, people with an anger addiction can become more unreasonable about people and their surroundings. In effect, their anger has come full circle. Beginning with addictive thinking, leading to more stress, and ending in angry explosions, an anger addiction begins to move on its own momentum.

By understanding the dynamics of this addictive cycle of anger, counselors can be better equipped to use anger management or stress reduction techniques in treating their angry clients. In the case study, Fred could be treated through anger management techniques. However, Fred's practice of anger management techniques could change his behavior, but may not be enough to influence the beliefs behind his addiction. However, if Fred can realize that over the years he has become addicted to a pattern of beliefs, feelings and behavior, as the basis of his anger, then he may begin to disrupt this pattern. Without changing his thinking, feelings and behavior, he may continue to experience symptoms of withdrawal to an emotion that could have serious consequences in his marriage and his life.

Emotional Connections

What separates our everyday anger from people who are addicted to it, can be complicated. First of all, there are circumstances in the world where anger seems justifiable, and would not be considered addictive such as, being angry at invaders attacking your country. However, how about anger that comes from a life of abuse where unreasonable behavior flourishes and people have continuously gotten hurt? How deep does this type of anger reside in any given person that he or she may spend the rest of their lives angry at the world, or angry at relationships with others?

In this section, we will explore the possibility of an anger addiction with specific circumstances. The two themes we will focus on are alcoholism and inter-generational child abuse. Both of these have had impacts on peoples' lives where anger is observed, and on occasions must be treated. Yet, let us look at treatment beyond anger management skills that have become popular in recent years. In treatment for anger, let us perceive it as an addiction, while looking for patterns that can help angry clients.

An Anger Addiction and Alcoholism—For those who have worked with alcoholic clients, how many clients also are suffering from some form of anger problem? In some respects, anger and alcoholism can become intertwined (Chafetz & Demone, 1962). Some alcoholics drink because of their anger, and some angry people use alcohol to nullify their angry feelings. Furthermore, in the treatment of alcoholism, getting in touch with angry feelings may be vital for recovery. Yet, treating anger as an addiction may not be the approach followed by many drug and alcohol counselors. In spite of this, there are alcoholics who stop using alcohol and still have garnered the label of "dry drunk". It is in this area where understanding anger from an addictions perspective may be useful. Sometimes when a person is referred to as a dry drunk, we are implying that some other addiction is still present, or at least, some similar pattern of addictive behavior is now being displayed in spite of the absence of alcohol.

One of these addictive patterns that may be present is the addictive pattern of anger. Some alcoholics can let go of alcohol but cannot let go of their anger. In fact, some of these people treat anger as a drug, and will explode anytime the stresses of life become overwhelming. Much like an alcoholic takes a drink to relieve stress, someone with an anger addiction explodes with anger for the same reasons.

Example—John was a Vietnam Veteran who had been through more than most people could endure. He had earned the Silver Star for bravery and survived being held in captivity for over a year. At the age of sixty, he had spent many years drinking and drugging, and most of this time he complained about his country and its wars. However, in spite of all the violence and disillusionment, he had found Jesus ten years ago and made a remarkable recovery from his alcohol addiction. His faith kept him from further drinking, and it set the ground work for how he tried to conduct himself around others.

John's faith helped him from continued drinking, and he was proud of this. However, his angry outbursts were another matter. John used to be a mean drunk in his alcohol using days, but now he was simply mean. People did not have to say much to him before he would go into a tirade, about almost anything. It appeared John left his drinking behind but still was fully involved in his anger. John's anger became so noticeable that his family and friends were becoming frightened around him. In desperation, they asked if he would see a counselor for his problem.

Jake was a drug and alcohol counselor who also had experience in the field of mental health. He met John for the first time, and was told that he was coming to rectify anger management problems. Jake was well versed in the skills needed to help John, so he spent the first six weeks helping him with these skills. Even though John was a fast learner, it became apparent to Jake that just learning skills would not be enough. What he proposed to John took him aback. He told him that, he believed, that John was suffering from two addictions, and he had only gotten one of them under control. He also said these two addictions were so intertwined that controlling one without the other would create certain problems, eventually. The two addictions he was referring to were alcohol and anger. Jake understood that both had a long history with each other; and even though, John's anger was discussed in his alcohol recovery, no one had actually declared it an addiction, or treated it as an addiction. For the next several months, both of them discussed John's anger as an addiction. Here was a connection that seemed to work for John and was the impetus for his recovery.

Summary—Treating anger as an addiction may have certain advantages, especially when an intractable pattern of behavior seems to be blocking a client's recovery from feelings of anger. In the example of John, this certainly seemed the case. Sometimes an overwhelming trauma such as the Vietnam War can cause post traumatic stress disorder, and John more than likely suffered from it. Without treatment for this disorder, John began looking for other solutions for how he felt. One of his solutions was to drink alcohol and wash away moments that were personally traumatic. His other solution was to explode with anger at whatever demons he had inherited from the traumatic events that followed him through his life.

There is no question that John is a prime candidate for post traumatic stress disorder counseling. Yet, the road he pursued was in the drug and alcohol arena. From this approach, he became rehabilitated from alcohol and found religion as his guide. However, his underlying anger became as addictive as his alcohol consumption. Actually, before he stopped drinking, he would practice both simultaneously by being a mean drunk. After, he stopped drinking he still possessed the same pattern of feelings and behavior that caused his alcoholism. Instead of becoming completely rehabilitated, John pushed all of his energies into an emotional addiction to anger. Jake, his counselor, may have realized that sometimes it is important to use the most understood approach to a problem. Instead of treating his PTSD, he treated him for an anger addiction. It seemed to be an addictive pattern of behavior that John understood.

Here is a case where the more possibilities offered to John, the more comprehensive the treatment for his anger. Instead of the counselor being the expert, and treating John's anger with anger management skills or treating his anger through some form of post traumatic stress counseling, his counselor let human experience dictate the problem. When we look at how John was using anger, it may become clear that it was being used in a similar fashion to, for example, an alcoholic using alcohol. It was John's human experience with anger that signaled to Jake, his counselor, that it would be better treated by seeing it as an emotional addiction. Sometimes the most accurate experts in treating clients for their problems are clients, themselves.

An Anger Addiction and Inter-Generational Child Abuse—

Counselors are familiar with the term inter-generational child abuse (Corby, 2006). For those who are not, it is the process of being abused as a child and then having one's own children, and abusing them in the same manner. In effect, you could end up with three or four generations of abuse in one family. Therefore, child abuse becomes inherited from one generation to another. The saying, "You go with what you know." holds true with these families, and we find abuse being learned as a pattern of behavior that is passed down from one generation to the next. For counselors, the question that may arise from inter-generational abuse is, "What exactly is the pattern being passed down?" In this section, we will consider an emotional addiction to anger as a significant part of that pattern. Addictive thinking, a dependency on stressful feelings, compulsive explosions and an avoidance of closure, may be elements of anger that abused individuals learn from their abusers, and they may be the elements of anger that are used to continue abuse with one's own children.

Unfortunately for clients who have been abused and are now abusing their children, the specter of guilt, shame and anxiety may loom heavily within their consciousness, and in most cases, counseling for such feelings can be effective. However, it may be a factor for a complete understanding of one's inter-generational abuse, to become knowledgeable of the pattern of behavior that was passed down from one generation to the next. Furthermore, it may be important that child abusers have an understanding of anger as an emotional addiction, and that abusive behavior is not necessarily a part of their overall personalities. Much of the guilt and shame emanating from abuse seems to accept the assumption that, complete fault lies in the abuser. Looking at abuse from the perspective of an emotional addiction may change such an assumption.

Example—Paul lived in abuse for most of his life. Living with alcoholic parents was only the tip of the iceberg when he considered the abuse he was now inflicting on his own children. As a child, he was constantly beaten and abused both physically and psychologically. It seemed that his parents were rejecting him and tormenting him, no matter what circumstances awaited him at home. And, then there were the nights of drunken brawls between his parents that seemed to end with him being beaten by the loser of these brawls. In many respects, he would secretly hope for his father to be victorious, because his beatings were far more intense and physically more severe when his father lost. This was Paul's life for as long as he could remember. The only time he felt safe is when he visited his father's parents. It was only then he could rely on there being people meaner and more out of control than both his parents. Yet, such safety was short lived because eventually his guilt would engulf him for having such thoughts.

As a married adult, Paul vowed that he would never be like his parents. He despised what happened to him during his childhood, and wanted his children to have a better life than he did. Yet, times were difficult for Paul. The economy cost him his job and constant demands from his wife and children uncovered feelings from the past. His family's demands and judgments of Paul made him angry, and old patterns of behavior were beginning to surface. The first time he hit one of his children was a breaking point in his life. After that incident, the floodgates of abuse opened and threatened his entire family. The person he vowed to never emulate had been reborn and was terrorizing his family.

However, this time, the abuse was in competition with Paul's guilt and shame. He could hardly look at his family after an abusive event took place, and it was something that weighed on his mind, most of the time. Finally, Paul sought help by making an appointment to see a mental health counselor, Frank, who was recommended to him by a friend. During their first session, Frank heard Paul's story of abuse dating back to his grandfather, and all of the anger and guilt that seemed to accompany this abuse. Frank listened to Paul's condemnation of himself as an evil person, who was ashamed that he turned out exactly like his father and his grandfather. He heard how Paul had decided that he would never forgive himself for what he had done to his wife and children, and that he was in counseling not for himself, but for ideas on how to keep his family safe.

Frank listened intently to Paul's words, and finally responded to what he heard. Sometimes the client understands their problems better than their counselors, but finds ways of avoiding them. What becomes problematic is facing these problems in a clear and accurate manner. This is what Frank had to eventually tell Paul when Paul made attempts to rationalize and practice avoidance, regarding his anger. Here is what he said:

Look, I have been listening to you condemn yourself for hours each week and how you see yourself as an abuser. You were born an abuser, and you had parents and grandparents who were abusers. In many respects, you look at yourself as, "damaged goods." Yet, in talking with you, it seems to me that you are a nice guy who loves his family but feels out of control. How about if my description is accurate? How about if you are a pretty nice guy but you cannot control yourself? How about if I told you what was passed down from one generation to the next was not some kind of "evil genes" but an emotional addiction to being angry, and we should treat this problem as one would treat any addiction.

Over several months, Frank and Paul did not focus on Paul's bad behavior but came to an understanding of how an anger addiction works, and what Paul needed to do to get through such an addiction. In the end, Paul did not focus on his shame; however, his shame diminished with his getting control over his anger addiction. Paul left counseling with a plan to control his anger and a perception of himself that was not haunted by abusive experiences from his past.

Summary—During the counseling session with Paul, it became clear to his counselor, Frank, that Paul carried a perception of himself that was self-defeating, where he not only blamed himself for his behavior but he believed that he was from a blood line of abusers. Instead of focusing on Paul's so called abusive personality, Frank decided to help Paul understand how he had become addicted to a pattern of anger that was learned long ago. His addiction to anger made him feel similar to anyone with a physical addiction. He described that addiction was immersed in his experience of being out of control. He also explained that getting addicted and staying addicted were two different phenomena. As a young boy he harbored anger toward his parents, yet at the same time, he was learning to be like them. His addiction to anger followed him into his adult life and resurfaced in his own family. Frank posed the following questions to Paul. Having learned a pattern of anger when young is not the problem. The question is, "Do you still want to practice this pattern?" Also, believing that you are bad person when you were young is not the problem. The question is, "Do you still want to believe you are a bad person?" Or, are you a victim of an anger addiction that has not been successfully controlled?

For counselors, it may be more productive to treat a client's addiction rather than treating a change in their personality. This especially makes sense when we do not know what kind of personality someone might demonstrate when addictive behavior is removed. Counselors will tell you that treating an alcoholic for mental health counseling, when he or she is still using alcohol, makes treatment more difficult (Hensely, 2001). The same may apply for an emotional addiction. The connection between inter-generational child abuse and an anger addiction may lead to treating some abuse cases, differently.

Again, human experience may need to dictate the type of counseling used. Common practices for mental health and addictions counseling may need to consider new ways to look at problems. In the example of inter-generational child abuse and anger, this could be the case.

Potential Counseling Solutions

- It may be important to map out how someone is becoming angry and when they are demonstrating their anger. Behavioral techniques (Thompson, 2003) for demonstrating their pattern of anger on a daily basis may create clues as what is generating this anger. Sometimes clients are not aware of those cues that make them angry, and they compulsively explode without knowledge where the explosions are coming from.

- It may be important to point out how perceiving unreasonable circumstances in life may be controlled by how one thinks about them. Sometimes, people may use addictive thinking to understand life's problems. Some form of cognitive behavioral therapy may be needed to help creates some form of critical thinking about unreasonable events (Fall, Holder, & Marquis, 2003).

- Active Listening (Ihde, 1976) can be an effective technique especially when angry people need to vent their feelings. This technique works well during the explosion stage when people need to get out their anger and not have it judged. It seems that making judgments too soon with angry people does not allow them to fully vent their feelings. Furthermore, active listening may not be a technique that others will seek out during an explosion.

- The skill of "pacing" may be important when talking to an angry person (Schwartz & Andrasik, 2003). Here is a skill where you want your client to slow down their; talking, breathing and thinking to match the pace that you as a counselor are talking, breathing and thinking. This skill also works well with more than one angry person.

- One of the most important skills for clients to use in an anger addiction is getting distance after the explosion has taken place. This becomes an important step in treating an anger addiction because many angry people who get distance do not use it for calming down, and letting reason return. Without distance, adrenaline may be still pumping through one's body causing even a physical response that does not allow the angry incident to be over.

- Avoidance of facing an angry explosion after an angry outburst has happened can create problems for the next time someone becomes angry. Facing one's angry explosions and thinking about how to do things differently is a rational and reasonable way to be prepared for getting closure to an angry outburst.

Anger Addiction Short List

- Seeing life as unreasonable most of the time can be the beginning stage in an anger addiction.

- Angry people can control their stress by pacing themselves. By breathing and speaking more slowly when feeling stress begin to rise.

- When exploding with anger, attack problems not people.

- Get distance after an angry explosion so reason can return and you can obtain closure.

- Do not avoid the fallout from an angry explosion. Face the fallout and seek closure.

- Without closure from constantly being angry, may cause someone to stay angry at a lower level, all of the time.

- Help clients learn how to get physical distance after an angry explosion, and also distance pertaining to time.

- Watch out for angry people who demonstrate addictive thinking. For example, "If you are not for me than you are against me."

- Angry clients may develop a tolerance for avoiding their behavior. Show how a tolerance for avoiding angry behavior can produce increased levels of anger.

- Understand that getting distance from an angry explosion is a productive way to allow reason to return. It becomes more difficult to get addicted to anger when you use distance to calm down.

- Remember when people are charged with abuse, they may be harboring an anger addiction.

Format for Other Emotional Connections

This is an opportunity to develop a connection between an anger addiction and some other real life experience. This could mean making a connection between an anger addiction and some form of physical addiction, or a connection with another process oriented addiction. Also, this could be a connection between an anger addiction and a mental health disorder. Finally, this could be a connection between an anger addiction and an everyday life experience where an anger addiction makes an impact on this experience:

Briefly describe the connection between an anger addiction and your chosen phenomenon:

Write an example of how an anger addiction is connected to your chosen phenomenon:

Summarize your thinking on this connection:

Chapter 2: Anxiety Addiction

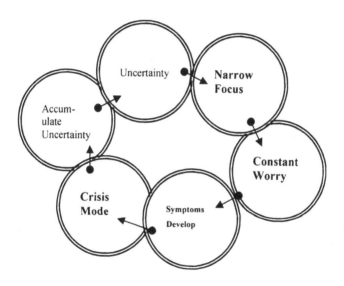

Figure 2

Background

In considering the emotion of anxiety and viewing it as an emotional addiction, first requires an understanding of the depth in which this emotion has been addressed in the field of mental health. We can see this by looking inside the, *Diagnostic and Statistical Manual of Mental Disorders, Fourth Edition*, commonly known as the DSMIV (First, 2000). In it, you will find a myriad of ways the emotion of anxiety has affected the lives of individuals through diagnosis of disorders, along with lists of symptoms that make up each disorder. The list includes; Agoraphobia, Panic Disorder, Social Phobia, Obsessive-Compulsive Disorder, Posttraumatic Stress Disorder, Acute

Stress Disorder, General Anxiety Disorder and Substance Induced Anxiety Disorder. Beyond these major topics, you also can find combinations of anxiety disorders with other disorders, commonly referred to as a connection through co-morbidity (Lundberg, 1998). Also, it must be stated that many years have passed since researchers began studying anxiety and the reliability and validity of this research has been proven many times over.

Keeping this in mind, the question may arise, "Why look at anxiety as an emotional addiction?" Certainly, it has been studied as a disorder with remarkable results, and it is diagnosed as a disorder by psychologists, psychiatrists, mental health counselors, and others who perceive anxiety from the perspective of mental illness (Andreasen, 2003). This chapter tries to answer this question, precisely because anxiety has been so thoroughly studied from the perspective of mental illness (Wahl, 1995). The fields of mental health and addictions may gather another perspective by seeing anxiety as an emotional addiction. Such an approach does not, in any way, lessen the importance of the research on anxiety found in books such as the DSMIV. It augments this research with an understanding of anxiety as an addiction, where certain people have developed a pattern of anxiety that mimics other physical addictions.

The famous philosopher, Kierkegaard once stated that, "Life was like trying to walk through the raindrops of anxiety."(Beabout, 1996) and all of us have experienced anxiety, sometimes on a daily basis. It seems probable that we would accomplish very little in life without a moderate amount of anxiety. A certain level of anxiety helps us focus on those projects that we deem important. Anxiety has been researched as beneficial, based on this assumption (LaTorre, 2001). Keeping this in mind, we assume that life will hand us circumstances that cause anxiety, and our anxiety will remain beneficial until it disrupts our everyday functioning. In effect, disruption of everyday functioning by anxiety is the definition of an anxiety disorder. One example can be found in the anxiety disorder, Substance-Induced Anxiety Disorder (Brown, Kahler, Ramsey, Read, & Stuart, 2004). This is where the taking of a substance causes anxiety that disrupts our everyday living, and the DSMIV comprehensively covers the connection between substance abuse and anxiety.

However, what happens when anxiety is not connected to any substance, yet still follows a similar pattern as substance abuse? What if there are individuals who have had anxiety disorders and have not improved much beyond their diagnosis? What about those people who may consider anxiety as a way of life; even when, their anxiety disorders have been treated and reduced? Taken in this context, there may be people who are emotionally addicted to anxiety, and use it much like an addict uses a drug. Their anxiety may be an addiction that steers the direction they take in life through; addictive thinking, denial and withdrawal symptoms. These people may be suffering from an addiction to anxiety, and what keeps them addicted, is a pattern of behavior that they depend on and tolerate. For these people, it may be beneficial to look at their anxiety through the eyes of an addict. Such an effort, may give addictions counselors and mental health counselors a new perspective on diagnosis and treatment.

Case Study

Cathy spent most of her life taking care of others. Around the age of twelve, she was given the responsibility for her brothers and sisters. This was in direct response to the lack of direction coming from her alcoholic parents. Over the years, she did her best to keep her siblings healthy and protected, and by all accounts, her efforts paid off. Now at the age of forty, she still was taking care of people, especially her two children who were now her focus, as a single parent, mom. Cathy seemed as successful with her children as she was with her family of origin. However, the emotional price for both experiences left her with bouts of anxiety that seemed to linger as she made her way through life.

Most of the time, Cathy would distract herself when anxiety occurred. She had a way of coping that allowed her to be successful at jobs and social interaction. When she decided to start counseling with Barb, a mental health counselor, she made it known that anxiety had been with her for most of her life, yet she always seemed to find a way to keep going. This was in spite of the constant underlying tension she felt in her body. Yet, recently she was finding it hard to cope. Her anxiety was causing her heart palpitations and her professional life was suffering. Unfortunately, Barb's attempts at counseling Cathy seemed unsuccessful. Cathy refused to take anti-anxiety drugs and all cognitive and behavioral techniques to ride out the anxiety, did not seem to work. More importantly, Cathy seemed to be fighting against her recovery. Instead of practicing techniques that were proven to help with many anxiety disorders, she avoided practicing these techniques, and she refused to take medication. Cathy would sabotage her sessions with Barb and state that little could be done. However, she would constantly question Barb about, "How much longer will this go on?"

Barb started her counseling with Cathy by diagnosing her with general anxiety disorder. This was reinforced by a psychiatrist's evaluation where anti-anxiety drugs were recommended. However, as accurate as the diagnosis seemed to be, treatments considered under this diagnosis were not working. After much agreed upon frustration between Barb and Cathy, Barb decided to treat Cathy's anxiety as an anxiety addiction. She confronted Cathy and told her that she was in denial of her anxiety problem. The only time she wanted to face it was when she could not function. Yet, when this happened, she resisted treatment that was proven effective. Also, she treated her anxiety as though it was something that she must endure and learn to tolerate, and this belief seemed to lead to thinking that would not allow change. Since anxiety constantly seemed to be there, Cathy actually defended her anxiety as a part of her personality, and would argue with Barb when she suggested ways to change it.

The most noticeable event came when Barb somehow moved Cathy to the brink of recovery. For a number of weeks, Cathy seemed anxiety free, at least as far as it disrupting her life. During her sessions, she would tell Barb how uncomfortable she felt with the absence of any discernable anxiety, and this strange feeling seemed to cause her more anxiety. Barb pointed out that her behavior fit closely with symptoms of withdrawal found in addicts when they stop using, and that she seemed to practice an addictive form of thinking that guaranteed her beliefs would undermine her recovery.

For the next several months, Barb treated Cathy's anxiety as though it was an emotional addiction that included; denial, tolerance, dependency, withdrawal, compulsive behavior and addictive thinking. The change from perceiving her problem as an addiction; rather than a disorder, helped Cathy monitor her anxiety in an effective manner. For Barb, the change in treatment from an anxiety disorder to an anxiety addiction was most notably perceived in how Cathy viewed her anxiety problem. Instead of focusing on the symptoms that described her anxiety disorder, Cathy began to focus on an addictive pattern that allowed her anxiety to continue. Eventually, her understanding of this addictive pattern helped her to relieve the symptoms of her anxiety disorder.

The Experience of Anxiety

Many people confuse anxiety with fear; however, there are differences between the two. Fear is what we feel when threatened, and usually with fear, we are clear about what threatens us (Ladd, 1974). Because of this, we can take a stand when threatened, and if we overcome the threat, we can feel relief. Anxiety is different. We are not necessarily sure whether we are threatened or not, and it is that uncertainty where the seeds of anxiety begin to grow. Also, it is our uncertainty that stops us from taking a stand and eventually robs us of relief and release. However, when we do take a stand, successful or not, fearful or not, we clarify our position, and may have less anxiety about the unknown. In many respects, people who conquer their fears have begun to conquer their anxiety, (Taylor, 1999) and when we do not conquer our fears, it is the uncertainty of future events that can trigger one's anxiety (Figure 2). For example, in the case study, Cathy was called upon to take over responsibility for her siblings at a very young age. It seemed reasonable to perceive her experiencing uncertainty with both the care of her siblings, and the lack of support from her alcoholic parents.

Like the description of Cathy, in the case study, all of us have been in the position where we are uncertain whether our pursuits will be successful, but unlike Cathy, we may find ourselves taking a stand and working through our anxiety. Many of us learn to face anxiety and eventually to overcome it by taking such a stand. Actually, working through our anxiety may give us confidence whenever a similar pursuit presents itself.

Therefore, working through anxiety may make us more aware of the dangers we face in life, and give us the wisdom to understand our uncertainty. Working through anxiety may sharpen our ability to see problems, and make these problems more realistic and manageable. Using the metaphor of strings on a guitar, anxiety in our lives is like the strings on a guitar. Too much tension and the strings will break. Not enough tension and we cannot hold a tune. In life, too much tension can cause our anxiety to become a disorder. Not enough tension and we accomplish little, leading to the possibility of accumulating more anxiety. It is the moderate use of anxiety that seems most productive in our lives.

As human beings, we tend to be problem solvers (Davidson & Sternberg, 2003). So what happens with our uncertainty when we cannot solve a problem in life? Most of us find a way to face our uncertainty by narrowing our focus until some answer gives us clarity and direction. At this point, we may become afraid, but we are not anxious. We are now clear on how the problem presents itself, and we are now in a position to take a stand. Sometimes taking a stand is scary while other times it gives us the confidence to be assertive and bold. For example, two female students may experience anxiety when they have a test on Friday, and both feel anxious the Monday before they take the test. However, the one takes a stand by finding out what is on the test, and studies to pass it, while the other worries about it, and procrastinates until the night before the test is given. In the first example, the student takes a stand, and by studying, she gains confidence and expands her focus so that she can accomplish other things between Monday and Friday. However, the second student's focus becomes narrow, by constantly worrying about the test, and thinking about very little other than the test. We would say that the second student is moving more deeply into anxiety by having her, focus narrow (Figure, 2) but without actually taking a stand on studying for the test.

When people feel uncertainty and continue to narrow their focus, at some point, such a focus can be disruptive. The second student needed to narrow her focus, but her too narrow focus became confusing, and did not help her study for the test. Subsequently, her narrow focus went from being beneficial to becoming a problem. It is not the narrowing of one's focus that relieves uncertainty. It is taking a stand, and eventually expanding our focus, that changes the characteristics of how we face our uncertainties (Bourque & Cyr, 1982).

Constant
Worry

Sometimes, it is our inability to expand our focus and think of other things beyond our uncertainty, that puts us in a position to constantly worry about a problem (Figure, 2). For example, in the case study, Cathy was an adolescent who narrowed her focus, and tried to take care of her siblings while her parents were drinking. Even though, she was successful in raising them, she did not expand her focus and stop worrying about what was going to happen. We might say that even her success had not stopped her constant worry. Her successful caretaking of her siblings, and her successful caretaking of her own children, did not stop her from constantly worrying about them. It was not her ability to narrow her focus and face the problem of caretaking. She had successfully accomplished this, and her relatives were benefitting. It was her inability to expand her focus and feel successful, that brought her to counseling.

All of us have faced problems in our lives where we felt uncertainty and focused on it, in order to solve a problem. It seems that narrowing one's focus to face uncertainty does not necessarily create ongoing anxiety (Robertson, 2001). It may be our inability to expand our focus whether we solve a problem or not, that creates it. Stuck with a narrow focus and unable to expand that focus, may cause us to worry. In the case study, Cathy constantly worried; even though, she seemed successful. It was her inability to expand her focus and "let it go" that haunted her most of her life. Her anxiety was always there, regardless of her success.

This may be an appropriate time for us to separate worry from concern. Most of us, when we narrow our focus to solve a problem, and then expand it when the problem is solved, probably practice some level of concern. However, when we narrow our focus to solve a problem and stay there, it may be that our concern has changed to worry. Concern is our ability to focus on a problem until we solve it or let it go. Usually, we are quite specific about our concerns, and do not generalize them to our entire lives. Worry is different. Somehow we narrow our focus on a specific problem and somewhere in solving it, the problem becomes more all-inclusive. In other words, we worry about more than just that problem, and our generalized worry stops us from expanding our focus and moving on.

Symptoms
Develop

Our inability to expand our focus and to move on leaves us vulnerable to the development of symptoms such as, ulcers, sweaty palms, heart palpitations and the list goes on (Figure, 2). Our narrow focus has eliminated all those coping mechanisms that we once used to avoid these symptoms. For example, if I narrow my focus and believe that being fired from a job will be the downfall of my professional existence, then I might constantly worry about being fired, and develop symptoms around this worry. However, if I narrow my focus and believe that my job is manageable, but I could do other things, then I might be concerned about it, but may not constantly worry and develop psychosomatic symptoms over it. I might show concern but not to the point of constantly worrying. When any of us constantly worry about some problem, there is a high probability that symptoms will develop around this worry. For, example, in the case study, Cathy developed heart palpitations when her constant worry reached a "critical mass." Unable to expand her focus regarding care for her relatives, Cathy's underlying pattern of worry seemed to create physical symptoms that she could not ignore.

In our society, we have a multi-billion dollar industry devoted to relieving constant worry and the symptoms associated with it (Blumstein, 1995). In some cases, we use anxiety medication to help expand our focus and minimize our worry. However, most of this medication focuses on our symptoms, and not the patterns we develop leading to these symptoms. For example, Cathy had symptoms of underlying anxiety for most of her adult life. It was only when she experienced heart palpitations that she sought counseling. Yet, symptoms are important. It may be our body's way of telling us that uncertainty is affecting our lives. The premise for obtaining treatment for anxiety could be based on these symptoms. However, panic attacks, post-traumatic stress, agoraphobia, et al. focus more on symptoms and causes, than the underlying pattern of anxiety. Understanding the underlying pattern of anxiety, may help reduce our symptoms.

Crisis Mode

This is not to say that treatment for the symptoms and causes of anxiety are not important; some causes may be genetic while others may be learned. In most cases, we treat mental health disorders by finding causes and by treating symptoms. Yet, understanding how we experience anxiety may also be important. For example, most people may seek treatment when they reach a noticeable level of crisis (Figure, 2). One definition of this phenomenon is called, crisis mode. Here is where an anxious person seems to be in crisis, most of the time. All of us, may have experienced being in crisis, and have weathered the anxiety created by the crisis. However, an anxious person in crisis mode, might experience overwhelming anxiety; or possibly, anxious symptoms regardless of whether the crisis is ongoing or has ended. It is a frame of mind where, no matter what you are doing, living seems more dangerous and uncertain.

In the case study, we could argue that Cathy was in crisis mode most of her life. It was not acute crisis because she was able to function and be successful in raising her family. However, there seemed to be an underlying sense of crisis that kept her focus narrow and created constant worry. It was only when her symptoms became acute that she sought help. How many years did Cathy spend in crisis mode, never free of its worry, and where anxiety played such a major role?

Accumulate Uncertainty

Anxiety seems to be one of most accumulative emotions that we experience. Anxiety will build up over time until it accumulates into something that can ride on its own momentum. In other words, accumulated anxiety can create more uncertainty and more uncertainty can lead to the accumulation of more anxiety. (Figure, 2) In the case study, Cathy accumulated low grade anxiety throughout her adolescent years and into her adult life. It appeared in counseling, that her successful caring for her family of origin and eventually her own family, had not given her a sense of accomplishment, or had it relieved her ongoing anxiety. She seemed to have accumulated a large reservoir of anxiety that had implications for how she conducted her everyday living. It is almost as if, this accumulated anxiety would not let her move on from her goal of successfully caring for people. She seemed unable to accept that she had been successful and allow herself to enjoy life. Her accumulated anxiety bogged her down, eventually creating more uncertainty. She had entered a vicious cycle of anxiety where anxiety seemed more like an addiction than a disorder.

How an Anxiety Addiction Works

The field of mental health has demonstrated the many facets of anxiety through treating disorders that disrupt the lives of countless people. It would be hard to imagine treating anxiety without the knowledge given in such works as the DSMIV and others (Austrian, 2000). In fact, a whole professional system of diagnosis, treatment and insurance reimbursement has focused on the many facets of anxiety such as, agoraphobia, panic disorder, post-traumatic stress disorder, just to name a few (McLean & Woody, 2001). However, most of the treatment of anxiety seems to dwell on its causes, and most professionals differentiate disorders by their symptoms.

However, when we look at anxiety as an addiction, symptoms and causes take a secondary role. Understanding how someone forms a dependency on anxiety, and has withdrawal systems when attempts are made to let go of it, are different than the issues demonstrated in an anxiety disorder. Looking at anxiety as an emotional addiction, may help us understand more than symptoms and causes. It may give us a different view of how we experience anxiety, and it may help in understanding the ways we *live with* our anxiety. The following describes a pattern of anxiety that shows addictive tendencies:

Uncertainty and Dependence—Many of us feel uncertainty in our lives, and our uncertainty may lead to feelings of anxiety. Furthermore, it appears that anxiety begins with uncertainty about some life problem that is not completely clear to us. In other words, we all have the potential to feel anxiety about the unknown. As stated in the last section, all of us have moments of anxiety and such moments may continue anytime we are concerned about a conflict where we have little clarity or control (Maresfield, 1988). However, most of us are not closely aligned with our uncertainty and overcome it; rather than, remain in a state of uncertainty.

This does not appear to be the case with people who have an anxiety addiction. Subtly, and possibly without their knowledge, people learn to depend on uncertainty. It sets the tone for their future, thinking, feeling and behavior. For example, in the case study, Cathy remained uncertain even after accomplishing overwhelming odds in raising her family of origin and her two daughters. Her thinking reflected uncertainty, and she believed that life was filled with it. Her feelings of anxiety never completely left her; even though, she had numerous opportunities to gain confidence and feel more certain. Furthermore, her thinking and feelings were reflected in her behavior. She seemed to lack confidence and she remained uncertain about her life, regardless of her successes

Professionals may argue that Cathy's uncertainty is just a part of her genetic personality, and some of us are more cautious than others. However, not all traits can be contributed to genetics. For example, in the case study, it appears that Cathy developed a dependency on her uncertainty and it set the tone for her personality. Who is to say, how much uncertainty was established in Cathy's personality when forced to care for her siblings at a very young age? And, who is to say how much she depended on uncertainty to proceed from that moment on?

Narrow Focus and Addictive Thinking—It may be the unchecked assumption that, "Life is filled with uncertainty and there is little you can do about it", that influences people addicted to anxiety. As stated previously, narrowing our focus to solve problems, for most of us, is a commitment to overcoming our uncertainty. Most successful problem solvers will narrow their focus and use their skills to face a problem, and most of these people will reflect a sense of accomplishment when a problem is solved (Brown & Walter, 2005). And, if they do not solve a problem, most likely, they will seek out other ways to regain certainty in their lives. This does not appear the case in the addictive thinking found in an anxiety addiction. For example, many drug addicts who suffer from Substance-Abuse Anxiety Disorder may continue to have anxiety; even though, their anxiety was diagnosed as being directly connected to drug use (Langone, 1995). They may continue feeling anxious long after they have stopped using the drug that caused their anxiety. Successfully controlling the substance causing their anxiety may not stop it. In effect, they may have learned to depend on uncertainty as a way of life, and their addictive thinking may not accept successful recovery.

Cathy, in the case study, made a point to use addictive thinking when talking about her life. Even when confronted with ways of coping with her anxiety, she had difficulty expanding her focus and fought her counselor's efforts. Her addictive thinking became complacent to the belief that, "Little can be done to change a person's uncertainty." In other words, she did not have uncertainty rather uncertainty had her. She openly stated that she wanted to be rid of anxiety yet her thinking did not allow her to wholeheartedly make attempts at reducing it. As she narrowed her focus to follow the information given by her counselor, her addictive thinking began to reject it. Her dependency on uncertainty and her addictive thinking about solving her anxiety problem caused Cathy to sabotage treatment before it had an opportunity to help her.

Constant Worry and Compulsive Behavior—Let us continue with the example of Cathy, from the case study, and her attempts in counseling to relieve her anxiety. As stated above, Cathy had difficulty thinking about reducing her anxiety; even though, her counselor gave her numerous cognitive behavioral techniques (Beck, Emery & Greenburg, 1985). The combination of, depending on uncertainty to be there no matter what she tried, and the addictive thinking that lowered her enthusiasm to face anxiety, led her in a different direction.

So, what direction did Cathy discover within her anxiety addiction? Instead of making concerted attempts at reducing her anxiety, Cathy began to constantly worry about it. She continually asked Barb about how long her anxiety would last. We can probably visualize Cathy leaving Barb's office and continue to worry. She may even have anxiety about her anxiety. Instead of making serious attempts at reducing her anxiety, Cathy may find her anxiety popping into her consciousness compulsively and without warning. She may compulsively worry about when it will return, or compulsively worry about when it will end.

In an anxiety addiction, it may be the compulsive worrying that most frightens those involved in this addiction. Much like an alcoholic compulsively reaches for alcohol; even though, they know alcohol is killing them, people with an anxiety addiction compulsively worry; even though, they realize their worry will only make things worse. For those caught in an anxiety addiction, their worry has gone far beyond any form of concern. Actually, their compulsive worrying has little to do with concern. In the case study, a concerned client may have practiced the cognitive behavioral techniques presented in counseling, no matter how anxious or afraid they were feeling.

Symptoms Develop and Denial—In an anxiety addiction, a person depends on uncertainty as a way of life, much like an alcoholic depends on alcohol as a way of life. In an anxiety addiction, a person sabotages recovery through their addictive thinking, much like an alcoholic sabotages recovery through their addictive thinking. In an anxiety addiction, a person practices compulsive bouts of worrying much like an alcoholic practices compulsive bouts of drinking. Yet in both cases, it seems that recovery becomes problematic as long as people remain in denial. So, what seems to be the motivating force that will bring alcoholics or anxiety addicts to a point where they stop denying their circumstances and begin confronting problems? Usually when their symptoms become a bigger problem than their addiction problem, both groups may seek some form of help. If you are an alcoholic and drink to excess, but still function effectively in everyday life, it is far easier to remain in denial of your alcohol problem. It may be the development of symptoms as discussed in the DSMIV that may shake an alcoholic out of denial and help a person face alcoholism (March & Ollendick, 2004). However, even with knowing and understanding one's symptoms there are no guarantees that an alcoholic will stop denying their behavior.

It appears the same assumptions may hold some validity in an anxiety addiction. For example, in the case study, Cathy spent most of her adolescent years and her adult life filled with low level anxiety. She based her anxiety on feeling uncertain and the addictive thinking that accompanied it. It was only when she developed heart palpitations that she sought help. Yet, this debilitating symptom still did not wrench her loose from her denial. Consciously, she told her counselor that anxiety was ruining her life, but unconsciously she was sabotaging any effort to prevent it. It was almost as if, she trusted her addictive thinking more than the thinking of her counselor. Developing symptoms that bring anxiety to the surface may be a person's best chance at facing an anxiety addiction; however, there are no guarantees facing one's symptoms will force someone out of denial.

Crisis Mode and Withdrawal—Many experienced addictions counselors will tell you how strongly addiction can play in the decisions and behavior of addicts. To the lay person, it may seem that, "Tell the addict to just get over it!" should be enough to create change. However, experienced counselors know addiction takes more than conscious free will for change to take place (Donovan & Marlatt, 2005). This seems to hold true whether we are speaking about a physical addiction or an emotional one. Withdrawal symptoms may be present, that stop an addictive person from changing their future, and these withdrawal symptoms are usually powerful phenomena affecting one's life. For example, such organizations as Alcoholics Anonymous have paid considerable attention to helping alcoholics deal with their symptoms of withdrawal. They even designate a sponsor for those times when withdrawal symptoms seem to be getting the better of someone who is trying to stop drinking.

In the area of an anxiety addiction, withdrawal symptoms seem to occur much like in a physical addiction. Uncertainty, addictive thinking, constant worry and the arrival of physical and emotional symptoms have a tendency to put an anxiety addicted person into crisis. One might call this state, being in crisis mode. In the case study, Cathy seemed to live her life in crisis mode. No matter what she accomplished, her life was perceived as in crisis, and even when she obtained counseling, the crisis did not subside. The question may arise as to why Cathy, seeing herself in crisis, did not work harder at controlling her anxiety? One possible reason may be that every time she attempted to work on herself, withdrawal symptoms of compulsive worrying and resignation through addictive thinking stopped her from feeling that she was out of crisis. It was only when Barb, her counselor, told her that she was addicted to being in crisis, and her symptoms of withdrawal were inhibiting her progress, did Cathy begin to improve. Cathy, eventually, saw that her underlying uncertainty and compulsive worrying were withdrawal symptoms that kept her in crisis mode. Beyond her symptoms of anxiety, Cathy now could take a stand in stopping withdrawal symptoms based on experiencing underlying uncertainty and compulsive worrying.

Accumulating Uncertainty and Tolerance—It seems that anxiety and resentment appear to be two emotions that can accumulate over time, with resentment accumulating frustration over time, and anxiety accumulating uncertainty, over time (Ladd, 2005). Regarding anxiety, it may the accumulation of uncertainty that eventually puts an anxious person into crisis, and it may be staying in crisis that eventually accumulates more uncertainty. However, it may be accumulating more uncertainty that leads to an accumulation of more anxiety. At this point, we have the phenomenon of an anxiety addiction not needing outside uncertainty to create more uncertainty. Anxiety addiction seems to generate its own uncertainty by accumulating it over time.

For example, a client went to a mental health counselor desperate about her condition. She stated that she had been to numerous psychologists, psychiatrists and mental health counselors. She said that she had taken most of the anti-anxiety and anti-depressant drugs available, yet she still had ongoing anxiety. Finally, her counselor asked her, "Has anyone explained to you how anxiety works?" Her answer was, "No!" After her counselor explained how it worked and pointed out such things as, uncertainty, compulsive worrying, and being in crisis mode, she commented, "At least now I know what is bothering me." In effect, she was having anxiety about having anxiety. The more accumulated uncertainty she experienced, the more it reinforced a pattern of anxiety that was moving on its own momentum. It became apparent that she had developed a tolerance for her an anxiety addiction.

Emotional Connections
The connection between anxiety and specific medical conditions can be studied in the DSMIV (Barber & Crits-Christoph, 199) where comprehensive

descriptions of anxiety and such diseases as, hyperthyroidism, high blood pressure, diabetes and others are referenced for the use of professional counselors. Furthermore, the DSMIV covers anxiety and its connection with different substances such as, cocaine, stimulant drugs, nicotine and others. The approach taken in this section is not to repeat this excellent work, but to refocus it on anxiety as an emotional addiction. For counselors, the connection between anxiety and fear are two phenomena that can be confused when treating someone for anxiety. Fear plays a different role in many counseling sessions, even when the main focus is one's anxiety.

This section, also, will consider the connections between anxiety and trying to be perfect. In today's world, the striving for excellence can affect all of us. We will compare the pattern found in an anxiety addiction with the pattern found in perfectionism. In many ways, these patterns are similar, and it is no wonder that some people who try to be perfect end up experiencing anxiety.

Anxiety Addiction and Experiencing Fear—We have briefly covered some of the differences between fear and anxiety, earlier in this chapter. However, it may be important to continue the discussion, especially regarding how fear is experienced when being treated for an anxiety addiction. Let us start by focusing on one myth that seems to dominate many counseling sessions, where reducing anxiety is the goal. Namely, "By getting rid of anxiety, I will then feel safe and secure." In the course of counseling, that may be one's ultimate goal, yet many times, it is not what a client experiences when they start to successfully face their anxiety (Massr & Tuma, 1985). It may be important for counselors to allow a client's anxiety to turn into fear. Here are some reasons for making this assumption:

- With anxiety, the threat is unclear. With fear the threat has been clarified.
- Anxiety may turn to constant worry when a client cannot take a stand.
- Helping a client take a stand with their anxiety may cause fear.
- Dealing with clear threats is more workable for both the client and counselor, than dealing with client uncertainty.
- By clarifying the threat and taking a stand, the client is put in a more favorable position to risk. It becomes difficult to risk when a client is experiencing uncertainty.
- The risk found in experiencing fear, increases the client's chances for eventually feeling relief or emotional release.

Example — Fred entered counseling with the hope of finally getting over the constant low level anxiety he was feeling for the last ten years. Peter, his counselor, listened intently while Fred described years of uncertainty and

merous occasions, Fred would comment that he looked forward
hen he could wake up in the morning and feel secure. His con-
_____ about each new day set the stage for uncertainty. It was an insecurity that had dramatic effects on his relationship with his wife, and his performance at his place of employment. Fred was looking for the cure that
would make him an all around better person, and his expectations regarding
counseling focused on that assumption.

Unfortunately for Fred, the more he talked about his anxiety the worse
it seemed to become. He would ask Peter, whether he knew what he was doing. He would make remarks such as, "When I leave counseling, I feel
worse, and I thought my goal was to feel better." Peter would comment to
Fred that, "Whatever is causing this underlying anxiety seems hidden, and it
is resisting being revealed." Fred would acknowledge that something must
be there but he was having trouble facing it. Finally, Peter told Fred that
maybe facing his anxiety would not, at first, feel safe or secure. Maybe facing it would require Fred to experience fear. From that point on, Peter would
continuously ask Fred, "What is it that you are afraid of?"

Basically, this scenario went on for a number of months where Fred
seemed anxious about something, and Peter would ask him what might be
causing such ongoing anxiety. The session where Fred's anxiety was revealed seemed uneventful until he expressed the overwhelming terror he felt
when telling Peter about what he feared most. At this point, Peter told Fred
that it was important to feel afraid, and just as important to face his fear. Fear
was not the enemy, as much as, the underlying anxiety that was robbing him
of a productive life.

Fred told Peter that most of his life he had been living in the shadow of
his father, who everyone thought was a great man. Some would actually call
him a, "Man's Man." However, Fred for all of his gifts was nothing like his
father. He enjoyed the arts more than sports. He was interested in his community; not in making a mark on the national stage. Fred's anxiety came
from his realization that he would never be his father, and the disappoint-
ment he felt from such a realization. However, Peter saw the situation differently. Peter explained to Fred that trying to meet an expectation that is unob-
tainable would give anyone low level anxiety, and unattended that such
anxiety could develop into an addiction. Peter told Fred that his anxiety may
be working as a drug, keeping him unaware of his real fear. Peter told Fred
that his anxiety may be keeping him from facing the fear of being, himself.

Later in counseling, Fred seemed acutely afraid; although, his fear
helped him to eventually take a stand and find himself within the counseling
sessions. Fred finally realized that he was comfortable with being himself,
and when his anxiety was over then his fear was over. Now Fred could go on
with life feeling normal fears and anxieties, like the rest of us.

Summary—During counseling, Peter focused on getting rid of Fred's anxiety. Fred went from underlying anxiety to taking a stand on a problem that kept him emotionally addicted and insecure. Anxiety was the drug Fred took as a way of denying his fear. Constant worry was the behavior he practiced as a substitute for taking a risk. Fred used anxiety as a way of avoiding his underlying problem. Similar to an alcoholic drinking to avoid taking a stand on problems; Fred remained anxious to avoid facing the fear of not being like his father.

In Fred's situation, it might be more common to diagnose him with having General Anxiety Disorder (DSMIV). He may be treated with anti-anxiety drugs and anti-depressant drugs, and who is to say, whether these drugs would not have had a positive effect on Fred' symptoms? He may have been treated with Cognitive Behavioral Therapy, and realized that his expectations were unreasonable, and that being himself was far more productive than trying to be someone else (Dryden & Neenan, 2004). Again, who is to say that such counseling would not be productive? However, Peter treated Fred as though he used anxiety as an addiction, and when Fred faced his fear, he would be in a position to take a stand and risk overcoming this addiction.

Treating this problem from an emotional addiction perspective did not limit Peter's ability to help Fred. He still could have used Cognitive Behavioral Therapy and, through working with a psychiatrist, could have administered anti- anxiety and anti-depressant drugs. However, Peter's thinking was that, before Fred could start thinking and behaving differently, he still had to "face his fear" as a remedy for his anxiety addiction. In our attempts at helping our clients, who is to say what treatment will work — one of them, two of them or all treatments. Treating Fred for anxiety addiction should, at least, be considered as one of them.

Anxiety Addiction and the Experience of Being Perfect—

Perfectionism and an anxiety addiction seem to have many similar connections. For example, both require a certain level of dependency, both practice addictive thinking, both demonstrate compulsive behavior, both show withdrawal symptoms and both develop a tolerance over time. Let us now try to describe these connections:

- People with an anxiety addiction depend on anxiety to explain problems in their lives. People practicing perfectionism depend on being perfect to evaluate accomplishments in their lives.
- People with an anxiety addiction practice addictive thinking that keeps them focusing on their uncertainty. People with perfectionism practice addictive thinking that keeps them believing they need to be perfect.

- People with anxiety addiction can compulsively become anxious whenever uncertainties arise. People with perfectionism compulsively can be anxious whenever they cannot be perfect.
- People with anxiety addiction can sabotage recovery by experiencing symptoms of withdrawal when forced to face problems. People with perfectionism can experience withdrawal symptoms whenever they have problems.
- People with an anxiety addiction can develop a tolerance for anxiety. People with perfectionism can develop a tolerance for anxiety whenever they perceive themselves as imperfect.

In all of these comparisons, it may be important to keep in mind that perfectionism is different than idealism. The idealist may have high goals which he or she, strive to obtain, however they are able to put into perspective the imperfections that accompany being human. On the other hand, perfectionists, also have high goals which they strive to obtain, but are unable to put into perspective the imperfections that accompany being human.

Example—Frances seemed to have it made. She had a marriage that everyone who knew her, commented on how lucky she was to be in such a perfect relationship. At work, she seemed to rise to the pinnacle of success, and was the envy of all of those competing in the company where she was employed. She raised successful children and was well liked among her friends and family. From the outside, it would be easy to say, that Frances had a perfect life. However, this was not the case inside. She seemed to be constantly plagued with anxiety, and even though she was a success in many areas of her life, she did not feel successful. Actually, she was quite disappointed in how her life was going.

Getting Frances to see a counselor might have been one of the true success stories in Frances's current lifestyle. She was against counseling, and felt those who went to counseling were probably weak, and had not totally applied their abilities. The only reason she agreed to go was because her anxiety began to threaten how others perceived her both at work and at home. She was a "nervous wreck," and this was the attitude that faced her counselor, Justin, when Frances entered his office. Frances said that she was just fine, and if he could give her medication to relieve her anxiety, that she would be on her way. Justin said that he was connected to a psychiatrist who could evaluate her and, possibly, she could obtain medication. Frances said, "Well, thank you for your time. Give me the name of the psychiatrist and I will leave you alone."

Six months later, Frances was, again, at Justin's door stating that the medication did not seem to help. She still had nervous feelings, and she was not sick, so why take medicine. She was nervous, and just needed someone to take away her nervous feelings. She commented that the psychiatrist said she had some form of mental disorder, and that is when she quit. She wanted to know how the psychiatrist could believe there was something wrong with her when she had been so successful in her life.

Justin commented on two points. First, you have been successful in many facets of your life, and that is quite an accomplishment. Secondly, you still have ongoing anxiety, in spite of your accomplishments. Maybe your anxiety stems from believing your accomplishments are not enough or are not good enough. Maybe not being good enough is directly connected to your anxiety. Over the next six months, Frances focused on why her success was not good enough, and why she seemed to have anxiety based around this belief. With time, she realized that believing, she was not good enough, caused her anxiety, and having anxiety meant she was not good enough. In the end, she realized that she did not need to be anxious or perfect. Somehow, she had fallen victim to becoming addicted to both.

Summary—Frances's problem was twofold. She had become dependent on perfectionism as a monitor for whether her life was successful or unsuccessful, and since she could not be perfect, she believed her life was unsuccessful. Furthermore, she had become dependent on anxiety as a way of verifying her lack of success in life. In effect, she needed them both to justify her beliefs about life.

When treated only for anxiety, the treatment lacked a complete understanding of her problem. Yes, she did have anxiety and it was disrupting her life. However, diagnosed for an anxiety disorder and given medication to treat it, worked against her beliefs about, herself. How could a perfect person accept that she was imperfect? The question would eventually lead her back to Justin, her mental health counselor. Treating her anxiety without treating her perfectionism seemed to solve only half the problem. Frances needed to realize that both were connected, and both were difficult to resolve because they showed the characteristics of an addiction. Beyond any anxiety disorder that she may have possessed, was a pattern of addiction where perfectionism and anxiety where intertwined within this pattern.

In the treatment of anxiety, sometimes treating only the disorder, may limit one's ability to help clients face their anxiety. In treating anxiety as an addiction, it may allow a counselor to treat parallel patterns of addiction, such as perfectionism. Many phenomena in living can have addictive patterns associated with them, not just those found in physical addiction. Looking at anxiety and perfectionism from the viewpoint of addiction, may open another way of treating these problems.

Potential Counseling Solutions

- There seems to be consensus that cognitive behavioral therapy and some form anti-anxiety and anti-depressant medication can be beneficial for the treatment of anxiety (Baer, 2002). However, neither of these treatments helps describe the specific pattern of anxiety that a client experiences. It may be important to consider treating anxiety as an addiction, where a specific pattern can be explained to the client.

- It may be important to point out the power of addictive thinking, especially when treating a client for anxiety. Much of anxiety is created by how a client views his or her belief system. Our beliefs lead to our behavior and if we believe that we are out of control and nothing can be done, then the probability for anxiety increases

- It may be important for clients to have a thorough understanding of the differences between anxiety and fear. Sometimes when clients become afraid, they are actually overcoming their anxiety. Anxiety is fear of the unknown. The ability to use one's fear to clarify threats and to take a stand can make fear an ally in overcoming anxiety. However, if a client does not understand the difference between them, fear could be a signal to the client that he or she is getting worse.

- One area that seems to have bearing on a person recovering from an anxiety addiction is to be aware of withdrawal symptoms, when a client begins to improve. Common knowledge would indicate that when a client with anxiety has less anxiety, then they would begin to feel better. When looking at anxiety as an addiction this may not hold true. From an addictions point of view, letting go of anxiety, might be as traumatic as letting go of alcohol, where both have symptoms of withdrawal (Wainrib, 2006).

- Many clients suffering from an anxiety addiction may be looking for a quick fix, making medication a popular remedy. Primarily, medication treats symptoms and helps one cope effectively with life. If coping with anxiety is a person's major approach to treatment, then medication will work effectively (Leaman, 1992). However, if a client is more interested in shorting out an underlying pattern of anxiety, then medication will be less effective.

Anxiety Addiction Short List

- Uncertainty can be the beginning stage in an anxiety addiction.

- Check to determine whether a client knows the difference between fear and anxiety.

- Map out an anxious person's expectations and how reasonable they appear.

- Remember that a client's belief system has an impact on anxiety.

- Remember how important the issue of control enters into treating anxiety.

- Look for underlying causes creating symptoms of anxiety.

- Remember that moderate anxiety may be helpful in solving problems.

- Anxious people have more difficulty letting go of solving problems than actually solving problems.

- Remember when anxious clients become afraid, it may be one of the first signs, they are facing their anxiety.

- Remember that letting go of anxiety may create withdrawal symptoms of feeling more anxious.

- It may be important to use both mental health diagnoses and medication to completely treat an anxiety addiction.

- Anxiety addiction may be closely associated with other addictions such as, addiction to stimulants, cocaine and other hyperactive drug symptoms.

- Consider the connection between anxiety and perfectionism. It seems impossible not to have anxiety if you need to be perfect.

Format for Other Emotional Connections

This is an opportunity to develop a connection between an anxiety addiction and some other real life experience. This could mean making a connection between an anxiety addiction and some form of physical addiction, or a connection with another process oriented addiction. Also, this could be a connection between an anxiety addiction and a mental health disorder. Finally, this could be a connection between an anxiety addiction and an everyday life experience where an anxiety addiction makes an impact on this experience:

Briefly describe the connection between an anxiety addiction and your chosen phenomenon:

Write an example of how an anxiety addiction is connected to your chosen phenomenon:

Summarize your thinking on this connection:

Chapter 3: Apathy Addiction

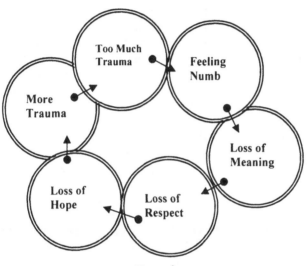

Figure 3

Background

Anytime people experience too much trauma, the phenomenon of apathy may loom heavily in their thoughts and behavior (Greenberg, 2003). Our most recent and dramatic examples of this phenomenon happened on September 11, 2001 where thousands of people were killed at the World Trade Center in New York, leaving friends and relatives behind, to attempt some form of understanding for this barbaric event. And, in 2009, a number of these survivors are still facing fallout from this tragic disaster, through experiencing the ongoing apathy caused by attempts at regaining meaning in their lives.

Similar events have been recorded throughout history, but with little descriptions of the effects these tragedies had on people (Berson & Berson,

2008). It was only at the end of the Nineteenth Century that the academic community began to study trauma in a more systematic way (Young, 1995). Today, we have a continued interest in forms of traumatic stress and the apathy that seems to follow it. The latest emphasis has been on the post traumatic stress experienced by some Vietnam era and Iraq and Afghanistan War veterans who have come home from these wars feeling numb, hopeless and cynical about their futures (Harpriva & Schmetzer, 2007).

In a world where large traumatic events have finally given attention to such a disorder as post-traumatic stress, there seems to be an opportunity to understand more fully the phenomenon of apathy. First of all, both apathy and post-traumatic stress begin with experiencing too much trauma (Ladd, 2005). However, *how* these traumatic experiences are formed may shed some light on their differences. For example, post-traumatic stress usually develops from a dramatic, overwhelming trauma that can cause nightmares, flashbacks and other forms of hyper-vigilance to people experiencing it. On the other hand, apathy can be caused not by one dramatic trauma but by hundreds of small traumas that inflict similar symptoms of feeling numb and being "out on the edge." Many times, people refer to this experience as "burn out: or being "burned out" (Lambie, 2006) and many of us can say that sometime during our lives we either pushed ourselves too hard, or had too many traumas in a short period of time, and found ourselves in this condition. Therefore, apathy seems to be a subtle yet different phenomenon than post-traumatic stress; even though, they both originate from too much trauma. For example, in our modern information age, the constant flow of information may cause all of us to experience some form of apathy, especially regarding the constant bombardment of information about trauma happening around the world. Within this example, we may see how apathy could easily go un-noticed, or be classified as anxiety or depression. Some may even say that we live in an age of apathy where trauma is unavoidable (Dilulio, 2006) and much like anxiety, there is no reasonable way to escape it.

Yet, there seems to be conclusions made by certain people that the constant experience of small traumas is too overwhelming, yet for these people, being apathetic may appear to have its advantages. Apathy may be a way of coping with a traumatic world, and the thought of giving it up may bring on withdrawal symptoms where being open to one's feelings seems a frightening possibility. People in this frame of mind, may decide to embrace apathy as a life style, making their lives devoid of deep feelings or investment in strong commitments. For these people, apathy stops becoming the experience of too much trauma in peoples' lives. It can evolve into an emotionally addictive approach to life that allows certain apathetic people an opportunity to avoid involvement, commitment, and an intentional search for meaning (Frankl, 1997).

Case Study

Since elementary school Tammy suffered from one crisis after another. Though she was very intelligent and highly social, she performed poorly according to her teachers. Some teachers openly called her lazy. After being tested, it was determined that she had the learning disability, Attention Deficit Disorder. However, this did not stop her from being labeled as lazy throughout her public school education. Two important crises stood out the most. In ninth grade, Tammy lost all of her close friends at school. Her friends were the smartest in the class; however, in ninth grade she was separated from them, and from that point they paid little attention to her. The second incident happened when she went to college. Tammy had worked hard to get into a prestigious school, but soon realized that others could perform far beyond her abilities. An accumulation of these and other traumas caused her to eventually leave college with her decision that education was a major portion of the problem.

She openly avowed that she would never go back, and that she would find other ways to be a success. Tammy returned to her home town and found the only people her age left were in some form of trouble themselves. Unfortunately, this led to a series of small incidents with law enforcement, and as in public school, she was labeled again, only this time as trouble maker by local law enforcement agencies.

However, constant failure had changed her. After high school, she was still hopeful and optimistic about her future. She conveyed this to her parents and other relatives. Tammy thought education meant something, and she wanted to be like her educated parents and friends. But, the countless failures over the years and the embarrassment attached to them, had taken their toll. After leaving college she spent time in and out of problems with the law. Though she never took hard drugs, she would be picked up for underage drinking, speeding violations, and holding parties when her parents were out of town. All of these incidents seemed to drain her of any purpose or goal. She was once an intelligent hopeful person but had become a cynical observer of a world that she did not care about. The only people who she seemed comfortable with were her friends, yet they repeatedly abandoned her when she got into trouble. Her parents became desperate and sought help before she destroyed the rest of her life.

Luckily, she was directed to a female addictions counselor to help Tammy face her problems — at least to stop her drinking. When Tammy entered Mary's office, she stated that, "I am only here for my parents and really do not have any problems." Quickly, Mary realized that Tammy saw little hope, and that alcohol was not the major problem she was facing. Some may have diagnosed her as having Attention Deficit Disorder combined with an alcohol addiction; however, Mary saw it differently. Both ADD and alcohol were a part of the problem but Mary's immediate concern was something else. She believed that Tammy was now focusing her life around the emotion of apathy, and that it was the major reason for much of her behavior. She assumed that Tammy continued to fail because, she believed, she was supposed to fail, and that success and feeling any form of high self-esteem were unreachable goals. For Tammy, it was much easier and made more sense to just to give up and not care what happened. Mary also realized that Tammy's drinking problem and ADD were secondary to her beliefs about herself. She had gone from a hard working hopeful young person to a burned out, apathetic victim of the system. Mary realized that Tammy's addiction was more emotional than physical, and that she was addicted to a life filled with constant crisis and trauma, where being numb and not caring had become an addictive pattern of living. Mary decided to help Tammy face her trauma and begin to restore meaning in her life.

The Experience of Apathy

Apathy begins with too much trauma. Many of us have experienced times in our lives when traumas piled up, hitting us all at once. For example; unease with the behavior of a loved one, followed closely by the loss of a job promotion, and possibly the experience of social embarrassment, and all happening one after the other, may be responsible for an apathetic experience. It is a series of collected small traumas that sets the stage for apathy, and it is the accumulation of these traumas that eventually may force traumatized people to slowly close down (Figure 3). One of the dangers of accumulating too much trauma is that it can catch up with you, and sometimes one feels overwhelmed and confused. It seems that apathy reaches a point where the body and mind unconsciously make a decision that enough is enough and both begin to shut down.

Similarly, we see this happening in post traumatic stress, yet the shutting down happens more quickly and dramatically. Unlike apathy, post traumatic stress usually has tragic and dramatic life events initiating the shutdown process, and in any post traumatic stress debriefing it becomes clear to most counselors which traumatic incident must be faced (Hugdins, 2002).

However, this is not always the case with apathy. Small accumulated traumas are not necessarily dramatic nor does it seem evident when a client has become overwhelmed. For example, in the case study, at some point Tammy seemed to become overwhelmed with her life experiences and gave up, yet this was not caused by some large definable trauma; but rather, a critical mass was reached somewhere between going to college and leaving college. Apathy is a subtle accumulation of trauma where a moment is reached, and people openly begin to shut down many of the emotional and psychological beliefs and skills they previously possessed.

Feeling Numb

Why do people experiencing critical traumatic events turn off emotions and become numb? Why do people experiencing accumulated trauma become numb? Studies have been done with post traumatic stress to answer the first question (Balrama, Bux, Hahn., Wallace, & Volpicelli, 2004) where the answer lies in a physiological response by the body to the traumatic impact of tragedy, and the body protecting itself by shutting down. Yet, there seems to be little research pointing to the second question of becoming numb from accumulated traumas. The answer to why people become numb after experiencing too many subtle traumas may not be too surprising for those who want to understand apathy. In effect, trauma is trauma whether it happens dramatically or accumulates over time. For example, let us use the analogy of water in a glass, where the water is a metaphor for trauma, and when the water reaches the lip of the glass, people have experienced too much trauma and begin to shut down. In post traumatic stress, the trauma reaches the lip of the glass quickly and dramatically and to protect themselves, people begin to become numb. Apathy may take longer but eventually the trauma may reach the lip of the glass, and the numbing process may begin similar feelings of numbness as post traumatic stress. For example, some people who have had constant trauma at work may come to a counselor and say, "I feel numb. I go to work but I am on 'auto pilot' and feel little emotion for my work." These people may have experienced too much trauma over time, and are beginning to shut down emotionally (Figure 3). One of the symptoms for too much trauma is to feel numb whether it is a large disaster or a series of subtle small disasters.

Loss of
Meaning

With subtle increases in trauma over time, people experiencing apathy will care less about those important themes in their lives, and will begin to lose the commitment and meaning that goes along with these themes (Figure 3). For example, in the case study, Tammy tried to overcome her ADD yet in the end, controlling her condition meant less to her as accumulated trauma increased in her life. At some point, she became numb, eventually leading to a loss of meaning about her aspirations to get a college education. In some respects, loss of meaning in apathy is a result of overall emotional numbness spreading from the emotions to one's thoughts, where feeling numb creates a state of thinking less about prior meaningful behavior.

However, this phenomenon of "not caring" has affected most of us at some point in our lives. Here is a brief example of this:

> John was a counselor who worked diligently within a community counseling center for adolescent boys. One day he went to his mentor and said, "I am going to quit counseling because when I look at my clients' faces, I want them to shut up and leave me alone." His mentor replied, "Congratulations John! You will most likely make a great counselor some day. Getting involved with these kids will cause you to experience a certain amount of trauma. What you need is a break, not a new job."

All of us who have committed ourselves to taking risks have experienced trauma, and are open to loss of meaning and periods of not caring. It comes with the territory of getting involved, and it may be the reason that some people choose not to get involved. Apathy begins with too much trauma where we protect ourselves by becoming numb, and eventually we come to the conclusion that, we do not care anymore. However, our test for any form of apathy addiction may come when trauma is reduced, and at that point, do we still not care?

Loss of
Respect

Counseling people who do not care and have lost meaning in their lives can be an experience filled with cynicism, disrespect and pain (Deluca, 1995) (Figure 3).The question may be asked, "Why would loss of respect follow a loss of meaning in the lives of apathetic people?" The case study may give us clues to this phenomenon. Tammy believed her parents that getting an education was a meaningful part of growing up. However, when in college her trauma seemed to reach a breaking point where education lost its meaning. At this point, she returned to her home, disillusioned about education as a life project, and the value of her education was drastically diminished. In a sense, she had lost respect for it, setting her up for future trouble with law enforcement. Her loss of respect for education, transferred to a loss of respect for other portions of her life. She experienced a loss of valuable meaning in her life and the respect that accompanied it.

We may have experienced similar events at some point in our lives where we invested much of our time and effort into something we valued, only to lose meaning and respect for it, at a later date. For example, Couple's Counselors have reported the lack of meaning and respect demonstrated by some couples when their marriages have ended and apathy has set in. Many of these couples show a level of apathy that may be characterized as "business like" in their behavior. For these couples, too much trauma may have led to feeling numb, followed by a loss of meaning and respect for their relationships. It may be argued that apathy holds a significant role in the separation of couples who have been traumatized by their relationships (Turell, 2003).

Hope and apathy seem significantly intertwined. When there is a loss of hope, apathy can be a common symptom (Figure3). Conversely, too much trauma can move through the stages of apathy until people experience a loss of hope. However, at this point it may be important to differentiate hope from optimism. These are two phenomena that are commonly confused. Optimism is the conscious act of deciding to be positive about life, and to keep a confident outlook toward living (Davidson, 2004). Hope is the ability to transfer energy from a failed project in life to another project that has the potential for success. In this regard, hope is based more on realism than optimism (Churchill, 2004). For example, in the case study, Tammy lost hope based on a loss of meaning and respect for aspirations in her life. If she could have transferred her energy into some meaningful project other than a college education, she may have sustained hope. However, her response was to be overwhelmed with trauma, experience being numb and subsequently lose hope in a life long dream.

Loss of hope is our inability to transfer meaningful energy from one failed project to another more "hopeful" project (Wong & Prem, 1998). When we see adolescents unmotivated by opportunities in their lives, it may be a symptom of apathy and the loss of hope. Taking drugs, illegal behavior and other societal maladies may be their resignation to a loss of hope through the experience of apathy.

Unfortunately, people experiencing apathy may become susceptible to increased trauma in their lives (Figure 3). When you see the world as a hopeless place it becomes far easier to be drawn to traumatic experiences that lead to a loss of meaning, respect and hope. In the case study, it appears that Tammy was plagued by bouts with law enforcement. We may ask ourselves, "Why doesn't she listen to her parents and regroup, and find more positive outlets for her energy?" The answer may be found in the simple quote, "Life is either feast or famine." In some respects, Tammy had been set up for famine. She may have become a self-fulfilling prophecy. By seeing the world as hopeless, Tammy was more likely to be drawn to trauma than to positive factors in her life. In the experience of apathy, too much trauma may lead to increased trauma where the possibility for an emotional addiction has fertile ground to develop.

How an Apathy Addiction Works

Our world in the 21st Century seems filled with trauma. We are constantly being bombarded with information through the media depicting one trauma after another. Added to societal trauma is our personal traumas — our daily losses and shocks; losing a job, death of a relative, interpersonal problems, and so on. It seems hard to believe that any of us are completely immune to one or more of the stages of apathy. The experience of feeling overwhelmed or numb to emotions, added to the possibility of losing meaning, respect, or hope can be moments that we may look back on with vivid memories.

Yet, there may be those people who have become so overwhelmed with trauma, or have had a constant and lengthy history with it that other more positive emotions seem unachievable or foreign. These people may have accepted trauma and its symptoms as a way of life, a pattern of life. For these people, addiction may be a substitute for positive growth where drugs and alcohol help to numb a negative outlook for the future. Those who have stopped some form of physical addiction may still feel hopeless and lack meaning and respect for a comfortable future. These people may be experiencing an apathy addiction where a dependence on apathy inhibits future growth and function. The following are guidelines for understanding this form of emotional addiction:

Too Much Trauma and Denial—Experiencing overwhelming trauma and being aware of this experience are different phenomena. Some of us find ourselves experiencing overwhelming trauma by physically becoming ill or feelings of exhaustion while others may cut back on taking risks or starting new projects that require large amounts of emotional energy (Herman, 1997). For these people, something is telling them, "You are experiencing too much trauma." in one form or another. For example, a person that dedicates time and energy to a certain cause may become aware that, at some point, they need a rest where they can regroup to recommit to their goal. People like this may have experienced too much trauma, and realize that they have to pull back and balance out their lives.

However, there are people who have experienced too much trauma and seem completely unaware of this experience. They act as if the trauma is not a major problem in their lives, and they continue without acknowledging it or facing it. For example, the term "workaholic" may stand for someone who is driven to work regardless of the impact it may be having on his or her personal wellbeing, or on the wellbeing of family and friends. In a sense, these people are in denial of overwhelming trauma while accepting a life style that may lead to later stages of apathy. In counseling, such people may openly argue with the counselor regarding their physical and mental deteriorating condition. They may be in denial that too much trauma needs to be addressed at some level of their awareness. For these people, denial of trauma may be the first stage in the development of an apathy addiction.

Feeling Numb and Tolerance—As stated in the last section, we all may have the experience of feeling numb after extended bouts of trauma. Yet, those people who experience a possible apathy addiction are usually in denial of the numbness, and have developed a tolerance for living a life devoid of emotional incidences that require an expression of emotions. For counselors, this may be one of the first indications of apathy addiction. In some respects, people addicted to apathy have difficulty turning emotions on. They seem numb to experiences that require sadness, joy or even anger.

In professional life, there are numerous occupations that require a certain level of being numb, or reserved feelings while performing one's tasks or duties. Trauma nurses, EMTs, crisis counselors, emergency room doctors, all need a certain amount of keeping one's feeling in reserve while completing the tasks at hand. Yet, hopefully, these same people can go home, be with their families and experience open emotions with the people they love.

This does not seem to be the case with people experiencing an apathy addiction. In many respects, they have developed a tolerance for such traumatic events, and the tolerance seems to extend beyond any similar traumatic incident. It seems the switch, to turn emotions back to full capacity after the trauma, has been broken. For example, some newly trained social workers are shocked at the lack of emotion demonstrated when investigating cases of abuse. Daily trauma has made some abusers tolerant to the outcries of their children to the point where, what is shocking to a social worker may be simply numbing to the emotions for the abusive party. Within a tolerance for numbness, abusers may be insensitive to further abuse. However, this is not only seen with abusers. In the case study, Tammy seemed to have developed a tolerance for feeling numb after her failure at college. She seemed to have developed a tolerance for failing where further failures became less emotional.

Loss of Meaning and Dependency—In an apathy addiction, denial of trauma leads to developing a tolerance for being numb, and tolerating numbness sets the stage for a loss of meaning, or more commonly stated — not caring anymore. Most of us have had the experience of being "sick" of some project and stating, "I don't care whether this works or not. I am sick of it." Yet, at a future date, we resume caring by regaining our commitment. In an apathy addiction, the opposite seems more prevalent. For example, teenage drug addicts who have stopped using drugs may still not find life meaningful, and may immerse themselves in not caring. Addictions counselors sometimes face these clients where getting off drugs remains only part of counseling. For these clients, a dependency on not caring may be a part of an apathy addiction where they, from their point of view, cannot afford to care, and find comfort in not caring. Unfortunately, for some, depending on not caring may eventually lead back to further drug abuse.

Within the behavior of drug addicts, a whole culture may have been formed around not caring. A dependency on making life less meaningful may be a way of justifying further addictive behavior. Addiction's counselors state that one predominant problem in their work is to get addicts to care about themselves, and not to depend on a lack of meaning to hide from further growth and responsibility (King & Shearer, 2001). Yet, dependency may be viewed differently from the perception of a person addicted to apathy. For example, drug addicts develop a dependency on cocaine or alcohol where the drug becomes one of the major meaningful events in their lives. With an apathy addiction, ironically, it is the lack of caring that may form a dependency. For addiction's counselors, understanding the dependency on "not caring" may be a clue to helping those afflicted with an apathy addiction.

Loss of Respect and Addictive Thinking—It may be that losing respect is a way of reacting to a dependency on not caring. Respect, in its own right, designates becoming involved, and acknowledging and appreciating the world around you (Ladd, 2005). However, apathy signifies the opposite of respect, and that may be why some addicts find respect for self or others, a behavior devoid of meaning, and this may be connected to addictive thinking in general. Loss of respect may be why addicts have such a difficult time making healthy decisions on their own behalf (Twerski, 1990). In an apathy addiction, denial of trauma, leads to tolerance for feeling numb, and such a tolerance may cause a dependency on not caring, and not caring may lead to addictive thinking where loss of respect for self and others becomes a form of personal destruction (Ladd, 2005). For example, in the case study, Tammy seemed to have fallen into an addictive form of thinking based on loss of meaning and respect. Mary, her addiction's counselor, focused more on her addictive thinking and lack of respect, than on her alcohol use. She realized that Tammy was not a hardened criminal who was dedicated to a life of crime. She was more a client who had lost respect for herself, and Mary focused on the addictive thinking that accompanied this lack of respect.

For many people addicted to apathy, we may see this manifested in cynical behavior. Cynicism seems to be the language of those addicted to apathy. Within this thinking, may be the assumption that, "nobody cares" and it may be the first step for counselors to establish that someone does care. This seems the case if addictions counselors are going to successfully counsel this form of emotional addiction. Cynical behavior is not the exclusive realm of apathetic people, yet for those with an apathy addiction, it may have a significant impact on their thinking.

Loss of Hope and Withdrawal—Hopelessness may be the end product of loss of meaning and respect for people suffering from an apathy addiction. Certainly, we find this in numerous examples from the world of physical addictions where lacking hope becomes a major priority of homeless addicts, and others who have reached the edge of desperation from long

standing trauma (Elliot, 1994). Yet, in an apathy addiction, attempting to instill hope may cause withdrawal symptoms. The lack of hope may seem
more acceptable to those who are numb, do not care, and have lost respect
for themselves and others. Furthermore, attempting to feel hopeful may be a
threat to a lifestyle where cynicism far outweighs optimism. For example, in
the case study, Tammy's counselor, Mary, may have to consider a gradual
attempt to instill hope back into her life. Tammy may experience withdrawal
symptoms if the counseling moves too quickly. It is conceivable that Tammy's parents and friends have already reminded her of all of the loving and
nurturing that she has received, and explanations for why she should not give
up on herself. However, what may be missing is overlooking the withdrawal
that she may have experienced by trying to be hopeful without initially
restoring meaning and respect back into her life. Countless examples could
be mentioned where "pep talks" do not work, and may cause withdrawal
symptoms for those experiencing an apathy addiction.

In an apathy addiction, too much trauma may eventually lead to a loss of
hope. It may be important to remind counselors that accumulated trauma,
over time, may cause numbness, loss of meaning and possibly a loss of respect within the client addicted to apathy. It may take a rebuilding of meaning and respect and a rekindling of emotions before hopefulness can be an
acceptable experience.

More Trauma and Compulsive Behavior—Unfortunately, fear of
withdrawal symptoms from attempts at regaining hope may cause more
trauma and this form of trauma may be self-induced. People addicted to apathy may compulsively create their own trauma. For example, apathetic people who are numb, lack meaning, respect and hope, may make decisions that
are more compulsive than calculating. Such decisions may draw these people
into future traumas, generating the apathy cycle to further continue. For example, someone who has lost meaning and hope may turn to drugs and alcohol to deal with these lost feelings. They may compulsively use these remedies as a solution for their problems. In some respects, an emotional addiction to apathy may cause similar compulsive behavior without the use of
drugs or alcohol. Apathetic people may create trauma by compulsive acts
based on a loss of hope, leading to further overwhelming trauma in their
lives. Much in the manner of an alcoholic compulsively drinking; a person
with an apathy addiction may compulsively create more trauma. It could be
argued that numerous inmates now serving time in our correctional facilities
are the victims of their own apathy, and the compulsively induced trauma
that accompanies it, or recidivism rates would not be so high (Chin, 2003).

In an apathy addiction, compulsive behavior leading to increased
trauma may be what separates an everyday apathetic experience from an apathy addiction. When a phenomenon that begins with the experience of too

much trauma ends with the same experience, then a vicious cycle of addiction may be born. When too much trauma creates an apathetic experience that eventually generates more trauma; the chances of an addiction to apathy may be increased.

Emotional Connections

It has already been discussed in the opening remarks the connection between post traumatic stress and apathy, but further connection can be made, and in this section, a more in-depth analysis of how they directly connect to counseling will be explored. Also, the crossover connections between addictions counseling and mental health counseling can be demonstrated in the similarities and differences between an apathy addiction and depression. It may be of interest to both addictions and mental health, how both of these phenomena can be treated in a counseling setting. The following are two examples where apathy may be an alternative phenomenon to consider when treating both post traumatic stress and depression:

Apathy Addiction and Post Traumatic Stress Disorder—

Post traumatic stress is an anxiety oriented disorder that has symptoms of; hyper-vigilant behavior, flash backs, difficulty in sleeping, and certain cues leading to disruptions in the lives of traumatized people (Sommer & Williams, 1994). It usually is brought on by some drastic event in one's life that is so disruptive that impressions of the event linger in the minds of its victims. It may be the passage of time that makes post traumatic stress so painful, and it may be time that enters as a connection between post traumatic stress and an apathy addiction. Beyond the drama of this disorder may be the fallout in apathy that seems to follow with some traumatized people.

At first glance, both of these phenomena seem similar. They both are caused by too much trauma with one being dramatic and acute and the other more subtle over time. Also, feeling numb may be symptoms that both exhibit, and for similar reasons. People with post traumatic stress disorder may feel numb as a defense against flashbacks and traumatic cues (reminders) experienced in the course of living. Conversely, people with an apathy addiction may defend themselves by becoming numb, in order to protect themselves from a barrage of small traumas experienced over time. However, here is where differences seem to develop between the two. People with post traumatic stress are chronically brought back to the anxiety that originally caused the trauma, while in an apathy addiction it is the future that seems most affected. A loss of meaning, respect and hope seem to occur with little reference to the original traumas. In fact, there may be a denial that original traumas exist. However, post traumatic stress disorder and an apathy addiction may be connected in that apathy may be the "fallout" from constant bouts of PTSD.

Example—It was 2005 and Jerome had done his best in Iraq and like so many of his fellow soldiers had returned home after extended tours in combat situations. On his return, it became obvious that Jerome needed to talk with someone about his nightmares and flashbacks, and for a year he received counseling and psychotropic drugs to reduce his symptoms. During this time, his counselor saw improvement and through weekly meetings, Jerome's symptoms began to subside. However, Jerome's understanding of PTSD made him aware that it was a disorder that could resurface at a future date; especially when some trigger could set it off, unknowingly.

It was under these circumstances that Jerome returned to counseling two years later. At first, his counselor began focusing on counseling for PTSD yet it seemed, this time, the therapy was having little effect. Jerome appeared much more cynical and disrespectful of his life as opposed to anxious. He still felt numb to many experiences, yet he now did not care as much about lack of feeling, as he did when fighting his PTSD. Actually, Jerome was losing meaning in most of those areas that brought him joy. Depression was one of the first thoughts to enter his counselor's diagnosis, but he seemed more emotionless than desperate or trapped. His family believed that Jerome was drifting away, and reaching him continued to be a problem.

It would have been easy for Jerome's counselor to continue treatment for post traumatic stress disorder, many of his colleagues took this path. Yet, Jerome's counselor believed his behavior acted more like an addiction, and tried to restore meaningful energy back into his life. He treated him for a dependency on "not caring" and how his addictive thinking had caused a loss of respect for himself and others. He talked about the withdrawal symptoms Jerome demonstrated when the theme of hope was discussed. Over time, Jerome started to regain meaning in his life. Though the flashbacks had ended in the first year of his recovery, it took a longer period to overcome an addictive lifestyle based on apathy.

Summary—The case of Jerome may shed some light on why some counselors treating post traumatic stress disorder are more successful than others. In the case of Jerome, experiencing the horrors of Iraq was only part of the problem. Too much trauma controlled his present day activities through horrors from the past, but over time, these horrors began to affect his future. The constant onset of trauma continued to make him numb about the future, and it was thoughts of the future that brought him back to counseling. It appears that an apathy addiction can rob a person of their future by creating an environment of lost meaning, respect and hope. Subsequently, Jerome's counselor needed to refocus his counseling away from bouts of PTSD, and towards Jerome's reliance on apathy. He treated his apathy as an addiction much like a counselor would treat alcoholism as an addiction following a major experience of post traumatic stress disorder.

The connection between PTSD and an apathy addiction seems a natural one. Both begin from too much trauma and both are defended by feeling numb. However, it appears that each takes on a different meaning with post traumatic stress being a disorder from too much trauma from the past, and an apathy addiction stemming from too much trauma blocking a productive future. The treatment of PTSD, from a mental health perspective, may benefit by looking at it from the position of addictions counseling. Within such observations, both addictions and mental health counselors may find the emotional addiction of apathy.

Apathy Addiction and Depression—The connection between an apathy addiction and depression may be found in the misdiagnosing of one for the other. The diagnosis for depression stands as one of the most ubiquitous labels used when someone seems to have despair about the world around them, and especially in the manner that others expect from them. There is no question that a diagnosis for depression may be warranted when experiencing unresolved grief, or a chemical imbalance, or when feeling trapped with overwhelming emotion. Yet, a different diagnosis may be equally important to consider. For example, teenagers who are constantly being singled out for not caring are not necessarily depressed. They may appear depressed because of their lethargy or silence, yet they also may be apathetic where their symptoms reflect more a sense of not caring, rather than being trapped. It may be that numerous other cases diagnosed as depression may be more closely aligned with an apathy addiction.

So, how do we tell these two phenomena apart? In simple terms, we may say that, "Depression is the experience of caring too much, and apathy of caring too little." However, the connection between these two may come when depressed people have had enough, and let apathy set in, where apathy may be the "fall out" from depression when someone has cared too much and yet does not improve his or her state of despair.

Another point to consider is that apathy and depression may be connected, but it does not mean they require the same treatment. It may be that recent research showing suicidal tendencies in giving anti-depressants to adolescents (Arias & Laughren, 2007) may be the outcome of confusing apathy with depression, where the drugs may actually increase adolescent symptoms such as, loss of meaning and loss of hope. Anti-depressant drugs cause a leveling effect for those who are overwhelmed with caring too much. Giving these drugs to people who care too little may not help level imbalances in the brain but may create further imbalance.

Example—Margo had experienced bouts of chronic depression for most of her life. During therapy, she reached the conclusion that some form of unresolved grief, resulting from childhood sexual abuse was causing her these ongoing symptoms. For a number of years, she had been taking anti-depressant drugs in her struggle to keep her head above water, in what she considered a sinking ship. Yet, her depression seemed overwhelming, especially when she tried to live a normal life around her family and friends. She remarked how much she felt like a failure when her symptoms would wreck a family gathering, or when her depression forced her to leave numerous jobs. In counseling, this was all she talked about — being sensitive to all her failures. On her first attempt at suicide, she seemed to take the stance that no matter how hard she tried, nothing seemed to work, and life had become too painful. Under these conditions, her dosage of anti-depressant drugs was increased, and her therapy took on a more rigorous approach.

However, her second attempt at suicide seemed different, especially to her family and her therapist. She seemed resigned that her symptoms of depression were going to continue haunting her throughout the rest of her life, and that trying new anti-depressant drugs would not work. Her resignation to live a life of despair began to dominate her thinking over the next few years.

In desperation, she tried talking to an addiction's counselor, mainly because of her concern for the number of years she had been taking anti-depressant drugs. What happened to Margo over the next six months was remarkable. Her counselor acknowledged that depression was a driving force in Margo's thoughts and emotions; however, her counselor believed another driving force may have taken over. Her counselor pointed out that something other than depression was at work. She stated that, Margo seemed filled with apathy to the point that any recovery from her depression was sabotaged by this form of emotional addiction. Her counselor pointed out that when she was diagnosed for depression, Margo was highly sensitive and seemed to care too much. Now she seemed numb and appeared to care about very little, and taking anti-depressant drugs, at this point, may be having a counterproductive effect on her recovery.

Over the next six months, Margo and her counselor consulted with Margo's psychiatrist and decided to reduce her anti-depressant drugs, and increase a focus on new projects in her life. With time, Margo's thinking shifted from thoughts about the past to thoughts about the future. Her successful attempts at controlling her apathy helped her eventually control her depression.

Summary—Margo's case may exemplify why psychiatrists, addiction's counselors and mental health counselors should work together when someone is battling depression. It may be that what is viewed as depression by one can be seen as some form of emotional addiction by the other. And, even when it seems a person's disorder is clearly depression that is not to say that apathy could not be connected to constant bouts with it, especially when clients are demonstrating suicidal tendencies.

In the circumstances surrounding Margo, this appears to be the case. Her counselor made a shift away from her focus on caring too much and the despair accompanying it, and refocused on Margo's intentions not to care as much. To some, symptoms of despair and not caring anymore may seem the same phenomenon, and they may appear as different nuances of depression; however, to Margo's counselor, caring too much was quite different than caring too little. In some circles, professionals may even state that caring less may be beneficial for those going through bouts of depression. (This also may be true with anxiety. Yet, in Margo's case, it appeared that caring too little after experiencing the despair of caring too much, may have been responsible for her suicidal tendencies.)

The disconnect between depression and apathy may be when professionals treat depression without considering how some depressed clients may become addicted to their apathetic feelings, and treating *only* depression may not be comprehensive enough.

Furthermore, it may be important for counseling professionals to diagnose apathy and depression differently. Primarily, they seem to be heading in opposite directions, with one phenomenon caring too much and the other too little. Added to this may be the direction both take in the life of a client going through desperate times. Depression, for the most part, seems to be a disorder that focuses on the past while apathy's major focus seems to be on the future.

Potential Counseling Solutions

- More free association (Hook, 1959) may be needed to combat the trauma that appears a part of an apathy addiction. The more clients talk about their traumas, the better chance of not accumulating them over time. One of the major problems in working with apathetic clients seems to be in getting them to verbalize their feelings. Being overwhelmed with trauma does not create the optimal climate for emotional conversation.

- It may be important to point out how being numb is a common experience when people feel overwhelmed with trauma. Being numb can be a defense mechanism (Clark, 1999) that should be taken seriously. With apathy, a counseling problem can arise when the counselor sees being numb as a problem in itself. It is not being numb that is the problem. Many times it is the client's inability to stop being numb that can bring on an apathy addiction.

- *Active Listening* (Ihde, 1976) may seem a less pro-active technique, yet apathetic people suffer from a loss of meaning, and listening for meaning can increase acceptance of personal projects in one's life. It, also, may be important to allow ample time for meaning to come out in counseling. Feeling traumatized and numb are two experiences that are not easily turned around.

- Much of the language found in an apathy addiction has cynicism as a driving force. The use of some form of Solution Focused Brief Therapy (Lewis & Osborne, 2004) may be effective when dealing with clients who have either lost respect for themselves or others. Focusing on solutions can redirect clients away from being cynical about a world filled with problems

- It may be important to stop the compulsive nature of cynicism when treating an apathy addiction. Cynicism can be habit forming. Giving cynical answers even to the most objective and logical questions shows how apathy has little respect for meaningful dialogue. Make attempts to short out a client's compulsive, cynical remarks by being assertive and talking in specific terms.

- Loss of hope, with clients suffering from an apathy addiction can generate an accumulation of increased trauma. The irony of this form of emotional addiction is that apathy appears to be created by too much trauma and the act of experiencing apathy may add to one's trauma.

Apathy Addiction Short List

- Being overwhelmed with trauma can be the beginning stage in apathy.

- When becoming numb from too much trauma, make sure that you can turn off being numb when the trauma is over.

- Do not focus on what apathetic clients are saying. Focus on what they mean.

- Apathy is more difficult to practice when others are showing positive regard.

- Do not fall into the trap of taking the cynical language of apathetic people too literally.

- Disrespect, in some form, can be associated with an apathy addiction. Counter balance disrespect with some expression of respect.

- Help apathetic clients believe in something meaningful in their lives, no matter how unimportant it may appear.

- Watch out for the addictive, negative thinking that seems to accompany most experiences with apathy.

- Apathetic clients may develop a tolerance for negative behavior. Show how a tolerance for apathetic behavior can produce increased trauma.

- Understand that attempts at suicide for people suffering from depression, may also be signs of people suffering from an apathy addiction.

- Remember when people say they are "burned out." They may be experiencing symptoms of apathy.

- Remember that being numb to your feelings can make those around you, numb to their feelings.

Format for Other Emotional Connections

This is an opportunity to develop a connection between an apathy addiction and some other real life experience. This could mean making a connection between an apathy addiction and some form of physical addiction, or a connection with another process oriented addiction. Also, this could be a connection between an apathy addiction and a mental health disorder. Finally, this could be a connection between an apathy addiction and an everyday life experience where an apathy addiction makes an impact on this experience:

Briefly describe the connection between an apathy addiction and your chosen phenomenon:

Write an example of how an apathy addiction is connected to your chosen phenomenon:

Apathy Addiction

Summarize your thinking on this connection:

Chapter 4: Egotism Addiction

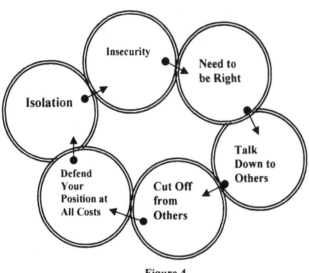

Figure 4

Background

Egotism may be viewed as more than just an emotion. For example, we say that we feel angry or we feel guilty. We do not say that we feel egotistical. However, the more closely we look at egotism the more it aligns itself with emotions such as, isolation and insecurity. When you combine these emotions, with a state of mind that is inflexible and condescending, only then do we begin to understand how it must feel to be an egotist. Keeping these characteristics in mind, we define egotism as a feeling of false confidence with one's self and with others. Some Latin countries might call this phenomenon, machismo, where males take on an air of confidence, and do not want to be seen as weak or less a man (Abalos, 2002). Others may define people who act egotistical as bullies, where the egotistical person needs to be right, and will use force to get his or her way (Randall, 2001). The terms braggart, blow hard and other more vulgar expletives, sometimes enter into our vocabulary when trying to define an egotistical person.

However, these terms are defining what we perceive as constituting an egotist's behavior, not how they feel inside. Feelings of isolation, insecurity and defensiveness bring us closer to the makeup of an egotistical person. The contrast in an egotistical person, between what is being outwardly displayed in behavior, and what is inwardly displayed in feelings, gives us an idea of what it means to be egotistical. Usually, egotism starts with feelings of insecurity, and sometimes ends with feelings of more isolation and insecurity. Yet, it is the need to not appear isolated or insecure, that makes us question an egotistical person's contradictory behavior. For example, we may have had a boss at work that over-reacted with force when his or her directives were not followed. The boss may appear, on the surface, as a forceful tyrant while inside he or she may harbor feelings of insecurity. In many ways, it is the struggle between insecurity on the inside and over-reaction on the outside that makes these people act egotistically.

Many of us have had moments where our insecurities made us pull back within ourselves, and defend our positions regardless of whether we were right or wrong. Most of us have had times when we became defensive and intractable in our positions. As human beings, it would be unbelievable if, in our own way, we did not occasionally feel insecure yet acted as if we were the opposite. Putting on a false-face sometimes may even be required in order to make sure we do not become too vulnerable to our feelings (Parker, 1989). When such events happen, most of us find a way to be less egotistical, even if it means acting one way at work and another at home. Usually, we do not have to keep up appearing forceful and in control, all of the time. Sometimes we may even have to apologize for acting egotistical, and sometimes we hope that others forget our self-centered behavior.

However, there may be those people who cannot let go of moments when they are putting on a false front. There may be people who believe they need that false front in order to survive. These people may believe that showing no weakness is mandatory if you are going to function in a highly competitive world, and some of these people may be correct (Bielski, 2002). Unfortunately, using egotism in such a manner can harbor addictive tendencies. Sometimes, a person's true feelings can be lost in making sure no one discovers what is happening inside. Sometimes, people may depend on their egos to get them through the day much like a drug addict depends on their drugs, for the same reasons. And, sometimes an egotist will take certain drugs such as, cocaine to assure their egos remains intact.

Case Study

Doug prided himself as a tough administrator. His staff feared him and his behavior reflected their fear. In Doug's personal life, he demonstrated similar behavior with his wife and children. In many ways, he dominated them in the same fashion to his domination at work. However, Doug's behavior was not always like this, and his behavior was not always so defensive. To understand him, one needed to understand his life while growing up. In his youth, Doug was physically abused by an alcoholic father and a mother who avoided any form of intimacy. Over the years, Doug believed that he had a choice. Either he fall apart and become drowned in an abusive dysfunctional family, or become meaner and more self-centered than those around him. Doug chose the latter, and became an alcoholic who would be considered a mean drunk.

Yet, with the passing of years, Doug was able to rehabilitate himself by going through Alcoholics Anonymous and other treatments. After ten years of struggling with his sobriety, Doug became the administrator at a drug and alcohol inpatient facility, where he ruled with an iron hand. Many of those who disagreed with him were forced to leave. Their disagreements with any of his policies or decisions were unacceptable. It was either Doug's way or the highway, and everybody knew it. The saving grace for those who did disagree with him was found an assistant director named John. Many times, he would act as a mediator between Doug and the rest of the staff, and John had a way of keeping Doug's ego in check when talking to others. Unfortunately for everyone, John found a new job on the other side of the country and it wasn't long before major confrontations occurred between Doug and some of the senior members at the facility.

One day, Doug attacked the most senior member of the staff on ethical behavior, where he accused the staff member of becoming too involved with her clients. For Lucy, this attack bordered on harassment, and had little to do with any issue of ethics. From Lucy's point of view, it was more closely connected with Doug's defensive behavior when she criticized some of his procedures. From her point of view, it was he who demonstrated unethical behavior. According to Lucy, Doug would harass the patients at the facility. He would threaten them with being let go if they didn't hurry up and complete their recovery. Even though the facility had a designated number of weeks to give these patients an opportunity to recover, Doug began telling some of them to leave when he did not like the answers they gave to his questions.

A confrontation between Lucy and Doug seemed inevitable, but before it happened, Doug fired Lucy for insubordination. However, Lucy decided to go to the Facility's Board and grieve Doug's decision. The verdict they decided was that Doug was suspended, and needed to seek help as soon as possible. In order to get reinstated, Doug was ordered to counseling. When

Doug showed up for his first day of counseling with Mary, a drug and alcohol counselor, the tension was thick within the room. Doug viewed the whole procedure as unnecessary, and it was others who had the problem, not himself.

Mary knew that Doug would be a resistant client, and decided not to talk about Doug's problems but his solutions to his problems. She commented on how he seemed to defend his point of view regardless of whether he agreed or disagreed with another's point of view. She pointed out how isolated and alone he had become from his family and those at work. Mary believed, in Doug's way of thinking, that his behavior seemed justified.

After much discussion, Doug began to let down his guard and tell his story. He described how he had to be tough in order to survive a family that abused him and did not care about him, and that it was his toughness that helped control his alcohol abuse. He firmly believed that life was tough and you could not let down your guard and show weakness. Mary discussed that she accepted his way of thinking but only partially. She told him that he could be; tough, gentle, objective, compassionate, and any other way that was called for. She also stated that sometimes the method that gets you to a certain place may not be the method that keeps you there.

Doug had a difficult time accepting any of Mary's statements. He seemed to break out into a sweat when even considering changing his behavior. It seemed his whole personality was riding on remaining tough. Finally, Mary discussed something that Doug knew a great deal about. She told him that he was familiar with addiction to alcohol, and how difficult it was for him to stop drinking. She asked him to consider that he might be addicted to something else other than alcohol. His addiction may now be centered on being tough and being unable to act in any other way. After countless discussions about Doug's ego, he slowly considered that maybe he could change, but this was only when Mary allowed Doug to think it was his idea.

The Experience of Egotism

When speaking about the experience of egotism, it may be important to consider culture as one of the reasons for people appearing stronger than how they are feeling inside (Figure, 4). Many cultures expect their people to show strength; even though, inside they may be experiencing insecurity

(Christian, 2004). For example, in some cultures young men grow up with the expectation that they must act as, "men" and not to become emotional or show their true feelings to outsiders (Raeburn, 1984). Also, some people hide their insecurities for personal reasons beyond culture. For example, in the case study, Doug was left feeling insecure over the treatment he received from both of his parents. His looking strong to others covered his insecurity and, at first, helped him in surviving many of life's traumas. It was only later in his life when combining his need for a strong ego, and his need for alcohol that it caused him personal problems and more conflict.

Like Doug, many of us have felt periods of insecurity, and have hidden it behind the mask of our egos. In psychology, we might call such behavior a reaction formation (Clark, 2007), where we defend ourselves by forming a reaction that is different than how we feel inside. In the course of our lives, who can predict whether such behavior is beneficial or will cause serious problems?

However, when we hide our insecurities behind our egos, a certain phenomenon may develop that protects us from disclosing our inner insecurities. Some of us have a tendency to defend our points of view against the opinions of outsiders by hiding them in some "sound bite" that ignores our true feelings. When feeling insecure, we may be less open in admitting certain thoughts and behaviors, and we may present ourselves to others as inflexible (Tinder, 1997). Even when questioned about our thoughts and behaviors, we may need to be right (Figure. 4), leaving little doubt about our intentions. For example, in the case study, Doug spent most of his career as an administrator, needing to be right even when proven wrong. His appearance of toughness was more important to him than solving problems at the drug and alcohol facility.

Like Doug, some of us have had episodes with egotism where we needed to be right, in order not to lose "face" even when proven wrong. Such behavior seems to fall within the category of our own human frailty where hardly anyone wants to expose certain insecurities to an outside world. Under these circumstances, needing to be right is our way of defending our insecure feelings by appearing confident and of course, right (Figure, 4). Even in counseling, we might find our clients putting on a false front in order to protect themselves (Barnes & Moon, 2006). If you think about it, why would they be coming to counseling if they could get in touch with their true feelings while showing no inhibitions or insecurities?

The next step in practicing egotism may be in the way we talk to others. If you have gone as far as needing to be right in order to hide your insecurity, then talking down to others may feel like a natural next step (Figure, 4). Needing to be right, unfortunately, may put egotistical people in a position of either winning or losing, but hardly ever in a position of compromise. For example, in the case study, Doug's position of needing to be right made his condescending behavior an expected event with his staff. In Doug's mind, he could not afford to appear weak in front of staff members, so he condescended to them. He wanted to make the statement that he was in control; however, Doug confused power with force. By talking down to his staff, he forced himself on them and lost power. Power includes the ability to influence people, and Doug's egotistical behavior caused him to lose influence and respect. Sometimes, force may make people comply, but it does not necessarily create motivation or influence over the same people (Schwarzer, 1986). Ironically, even if Doug did not believe that talking down to his staff gave him the appearance of strength; he still may have condescended in order to convince himself of his own strength.

When we become insecure and begin lecturing, advising, analyzing, or judging others, we run the risk of appearing egotistical. Since insecurity in life does not appear to be disappearing anytime soon, all of us may, on occasions, find ourselves condescending to others. Being egotistical may mean that we appear self-righteous, even when we have no idea of what we are talking about.

It is no wonder that some people who have encountered egotistical behavior become angry and resentful. Bragging, boasting and patronizing behavior do not seem to attract many true believers to one's cause. In some cases, the opposite may be more the reality. How many people want to be around someone who is; self-centered and self-serving, who has a need to be right, and who talks down to others (Figure, 4)? Outside of other egotists or people afraid of egotistical behavior, the number may be minimal.

You would think that an egotist, who is cut off from others, would realize they may have a need to rely on others. Yet, the opposite seems more the case. Being cut off from others appears to reinforce an egotist's need to be right. Yet, paradoxically, being cut off from others rarely makes an insecure person feel more secure, no matter how much it may reinforce a need to be right.

When the stakes are high and we find ourselves condescending to others to protect our insecurities, and when we do not want to connect with others either personally or emotionally, it may be at this point we rely on egotism to justify our behavior. Cutting ourselves off from others may be the only way we can hide our insecurities, and satisfy our need to be right. In the case study, Doug is not concerned whether he makes friends with his staff. His need to be right is more important than his need to be friendly.

Many of us, who have reached a point of being obnoxious, condescending or stubborn, may admit our insecurities, at some point, and try to reconnect with those around us. However, there are those people who cannot let their insecurities go, and cannot work at a level of frankness or personal self-disclosure that would be conciliatory. Even when they know their actions are wrong, they may defend their positions at all costs (Burgess-Jackson, 2003). For example, in the case study, Doug would not consider the opinions of senior counselors at the rehabilitation facility. He defended his position at all costs, until he was suspended from his job. How many people can you think of who have let their egos interfere with their marriages, jobs, friendships and their health by defending their positions at all costs?

Defending one's position at all costs can be risky business for all of us, even when one is right. Sometimes we can be right and wrong at the same time. We can be right on a particular point of view, but our delivery may be so condescending that it ruins our chances at influencing others (Rippin, 2004). How many people have given correct answers in their jobs or in their relationships, yet have isolated themselves because hardly anyone wants to listen to them?

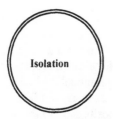

Isolation

Needing to be right, being condescending to others, cutting yourself off from others and defending your position at all costs, seems a recipe for spending much of your time, alone. In egotistical behavior, isolation can be one of the serious by products of covering up one's insecurities (Bashford & Strange, 2003). For example, in the case study, Doug had trouble even developing a relationship with his counselor, Mary. During counseling, he admitted to being alone in his point of view, but he believed that being suspended was an unfair set of circumstances. Even though he was isolated and alone, he still believed he was right in the manner in which he ran the rehabilitation facility, and he defended his position by arguing with Mary. Fortunately, Mary recognized that his defense was isolating him from confronting his problems. Her concern was that his isolation could generate more insecurity, thus setting the stage for another round of needing to be right, condescension and defending his position at all costs. Doug ran the risk that most egotistical people have to contend with, namely, "Acting egotistically, in order to deny insecurity, may actually generate more insecurity."

Some of us, who have felt insecure in our lives, may have isolated ourselves from those we respect and love, by acting egotistically, and some of us may have remained isolated and felt more insecure. However, such moments do not foretell that we are suffering from being an egotist. What it may mean is that covering up our insecurities may be effective in the short term but overall, may not be worth it. Ultimately, this was Doug's struggle in the case study. Was it worth it to practice a charade in order to appear in control and tough? Or, could Doug have been more successful by working with his insecurities, and calling on others at the rehabilitation facility to help make the facility a productive place for clients.

How an Egotism Addiction Works

It should be noted that, not all people who are in control, highly competent, strongly assertive or who seem extremely tough are necessarily classified as being egotistical. Many of the people who show these traits may have worked hard to accomplish such qualities. Furthermore, to inwardly feel insecure while outwardly displaying confidence does not necessarily mean these people practice egotistical behavior. Such behavior may be attributed to personal discipline or a commitment to doing the right thing, even when having doubts about one's feelings.

A different set of feelings and behaviors may be involved when you deceive yourself into believing your insecurity does not exist. We all have our moments of insecurity and who is to judge when we will fall into putting on a perception of strength while inwardly feeling insecure. However, there are those people who seem to make egotism a life style that influences most of their thoughts and behavior (Kirkpatrick, 1989). For these people, the term egotism addiction may apply. Their egotism is not the result of an incident or an insecure period in one's life. There egotism has become a lifestyle that defines who they are, to themselves and to others.

Insecurity and Tolerance—Many of us have insecurities that we cover up by acting differently than how we feel. Covering up our insecurities is one of many methods used to defend ourselves during those difficult and trying moments in our lives (Blackman, 2004). Not showing our true feelings does not have to be considered dysfunctional, or many of us would be considered to be that way. What makes an emotional addiction to egotism different is that it goes beyond our difficult or trying moments. In many respects, someone showing egotistical tendencies, abandons their feelings of insecurity and develops a lifestyle that bases its premise on some form of cover up. For example, in the case study, Doug appeared intensely affected by his father's alcoholism and his mother's lack of intimacy. Instead of facing such insecurities, he abandoned them and acted as though they did not exist. Yet, the problem was not that he did this at a young age. The problem was that, he still tolerated this pattern of behavior, in his present home and employment situations. It was not that Doug acted as a bad guy who wanted to hurt others. Doug's personality was not the main problem. It was the egotistical pattern that had developed, allowing Doug to tolerate behavior that haunted him. In many ways, Doug was not fooling anyone with his cover up. He did not act with confidence when being the administrator at the drug and alcohol facility. Instead, he reacted with an in-genuine sense of confidence that more experienced counselors questioned.

We may ask, "Why would he do this?" It appears that Doug developed a tolerance with his insecurity and paid little attention to it. He chose to believe his cover up rather than his true feelings. He would rather be tough and in control than feel the insecurity taking place in his life. His insecurity did not affect him as long as he kept it buried under the illusion of being in control. In effect, Doug did not work through his insecurity. He learned to tolerate it.

Need to be Right and Dependency—People addicted to egotism are not interested in *wanting to be right*. They *need to be right*. The differentiation between a want and need sends the egotist down a different road than a highly confident person. Wanting to be right, may require a sense of confidence, and a reasonable attitude of compromise to do the right thing for yourself and others. This may also require a person to possibly change one's perspective on closely held issues, in order to make things right. We can see this in strong leaders who show traits of flexibility and compromise (Troester, 1996). They may want to be right but they do not need to be right.

People with an egotism addiction need to be right, and that turns out to be fundamentally different than wanting to be right. Actually, people needing to be right usually lack a sense of confidence or a reasonable attitude. Needing something means that you are depending on it, not just hoping that it will happen. Needing to be right means "being right " will mean more to you than being competent, compassionate, honest and any other characteristic that you may want, but do not believe you necessarily need. Thus we find egotists have a need to be right, and have it at the forefront of solving their problems. For example, how many egotistical people do you know who have been told, "Do not go the direction you are going, because we can prove, it will not be good for you." How many of these people take that road, anyway? In an egotism addiction, a person may act similar to someone with a drug addiction. Needing to be right may be as powerful as needing to take a drug or consume alcohol. Under these circumstances, needing to be right, can form a dependency, which makes admitting that you are wrong a difficult experience to encounter.

Talking Down to Others and Compulsive Behavior—People with an egotism addiction seem prone to having a bad attitude. Between underlying insecurities and needing to be right, it seems less likely that egotistical people are going to be flexible and confident. More likely is the possibility of being overly judgmental. Within this phenomenon, egotists will talk down to others in order to be right. If they only *wanted* to be right, this may not happen, but *needing* to be right may cause them to be defensive and condescending. The good news for people with an egotism addiction is that, it seems highly unlikely their actions are on purpose, all of the time. The bad news is that condescending to others can evolve into a compulsive pattern of behavior that happens whenever they feel insecure. In the case study, Doug condescended to his counselor, Mary, the first time he met her. Again, it seemed unlikely he planned to talk down to her. More likely, he compulsively condescended in defense of his need to be right. The question that may arise for Mary is, "Should I counsel Doug for his bad attitude, or should I begin to counsel him on a possible egotism addiction?" More effective counselors may choose the latter. In many respects, changing someone's addictive patterns of behavior seems less difficult than changing someone's personality.

In the field of addiction, an addict's compulsive behavior triggers most of their drug or alcohol use (Henderson, 2000). The same holds true for an emotional addiction to egotism. The difference being that a drug user compulsively reaches for their drug of choice, where in an egotism addiction the egotist compulsively condescends. This may be why such condescending behavior does not have the same effect on others, as a confident person being critical of them. Criticizing with confidence seems to be something that requires some preparation and forethought. Criticizing with a need to be right appears more as a compulsive reaction rather than an action.

Cut Off from Others and Addictive Thinking—Not many of us enjoy constantly being talked down to, whether it is a boss at work or a psychologically abusive partner at home. Most of us may even form some acutely negative opinions about such people. We may form resentments against them even when we know they are right. Therefore, talking down to others has a higher probability of cutting people off, than in bringing them closer to your way of thinking and acting (Sunderland, 2004). The irony in an egotism addiction is that, in order to be right an egotist condescends, and by condescending an egotist runs the risk of cutting others off from accepting his or her point of view. Furthermore, having people cut off from an egotist does not seem to improve issues with insecurity. It seems to make these issues worse. For example, in the case study, Doug was known for ruling with an "iron hand". Such, behavior made Doug many enemies at the drug and alcohol facility. We may ask, "What was he thinking in his approach to the staff?" It may not be *what* he was thinking but *how* he was thinking that got Doug in trouble.

Doug followed a pattern of addictive thinking similar to the thinking found in drug and alcohol addiction. He did not consider the impact his words would have on others. Instead, he compulsively attacked his staff, focusing more on his own insecurities than on their needs. In many ways, his thinking was counter productive to his role as an administrator. Instead of listening to the problems of the staff and critically analyzing their complaints, he used addictive thinking and compulsively attacked them. His thinking was such that being cut off from others did not matter. Much like an alcoholic, he was influenced by his addictive thinking, and focused primarily on himself.

Defend Position at All Costs and Denial — Much like Doug in the case study, other people with an egotism addiction probably do not realize the tremendous hole they have dug for themselves. Insecurity, needing to be right, condescending behavior and cutting yourself off from others, puts the egotistical person in a vulnerable position to be criticized and resented. Instead, their addictive thinking leads them in the opposite direction. They may resist any form of reconciliation with others, and proceed to defend their positions at all costs. It is almost as if they are in denial that any problem exists. It is the denial of any underlying problem that gives egotists the rationale for their behavior. In the case study, Doug tells his counselor that he has no problems. Everyone else has the problems. Here is a person who has been, suspended from his job, has been criticized by the most senior staff at the facility where he works, and has compulsively attacked those who are responsible for his employment. Like an addict who denies he or she has a problem with their drug use, and that they can control it, here is Doug, acting accordingly, not admitting to any problems, and believing everyone else has the problems.

Many of us have defended our positions at all cost, only to wake up the next day feeling ridiculous and stupid. Or, we have had discussions where we knew the other person was correct, but we just could not bring ourselves to admit it. Most of us walk away from these experiences feeling that what we said or what we did was a mistake. People with an egotism addiction are too much in denial to see these types of mistakes. They firmly believe they are right and, many times, will blame the other party for creating such problems.

Isolation and Withdrawal—In many ways, people with an egotism addiction have painted themselves into a corner. They cut themselves off from others and are defending their positions at all costs. Unfortunately, it appears the cost is high for those with this addiction. How many people want to be around someone like this? There may be those people who may find themselves in the clutches of some charismatic egotist who has collected a flock of followers, and has gotten these people to accept their need to be right, as right. Yet, such groups of people have other issues not covered in an egotism addiction such as issues with, celebrity or greed. For many of us, it may not be a pleasant experience being with egotists, and many of us may opt out of trying. One of the problems facing people with egotistical behavior is the possibility for loneliness and isolation based on their behavior.

However, this may not be the biggest problem with people practicing an egotism addiction. It seems to be an even bigger problem when someone with this addiction tries to re-connect with people. Reaching out and being with others may cause withdrawal symptoms of anxiety and, of course, more insecurity. This may be why some egotists have few friends or have difficulty connecting with others. They may experience emotional symptoms of withdrawal when trying to change their behavior. Much like alcoholics have withdrawal symptoms when they try to stop drinking, people with an egotism addiction may have symptoms of anxiety and insecurity in their attempts at stopping egotistical behavior.

Emotional Connections

An egotism addiction seems to connect well with several physical addictions such as a cocaine addiction or amphetamine addiction. When you combine these drugs with someone purporting an egotism addiction, it seems to heighten ones addiction problems. For example, both cocaine and egotism seem to fit our fast moving society where success, and being on top have become major contemporary themes (Wall & Werkle, 2002).

Yet an egotism addiction may not only make connections in the areas of drug and alcohol addiction. Understanding certain personality disorders such as, narcissism seems to fit closely with egotism, where a person has a need to be right and practices self-centered and self-serving behavior. An egotism addiction is a state of mind that finds connections with anyone who feels insecure, and is looking for methods for covering it up.

An Egotism Addiction and Narcissism—Not all egotists are narcissists and not all narcissists are egotists, but somewhere in the latter stages of both, they seem to combine in interesting ways. Some people might perceive narcissists as cordial egotists, and what initially differs may be their presentation to the outside world. Many egotists have gained the reputation for being obnoxious, patronizing or rude, hardly the reputation given to narcissists. Furthermore, many narcissists have gained the reputation for being charming, witty or seductive, definitely not the reputation given to egotists. However, both seem extremely needy at times, and both seem to put on a false front to cover up their insecurity. Some have commented that mild narcissism does not show signs of insecurity but those of self-absorption and self adoration (Champion, 2002). However, in severe narcissism, the mask of confidence seems to fade, and signs of underlying insecurity, begins to appear.

Narcissists and egotists put much of their energy into trying to impress others, narcissists with their charm and egotists with their strength and both seem to make a game out of their connections with others. Sometimes, we find narcissists combine their behavior with egotistical behavior in attempts at being right and in charge. Not only do they think, for example, they are beautiful but they will condescend until others admit to their beauty. In many ways, narcissism is a seductive way of defending your position at all costs. Unfortunately, both can be overbearing when these people are isolated and alone.

Example—Carol was an extremely forceful person who used her, so called, beauty to get what she wanted. It seemed her whole life was about getting certain men to pay attention to her. When she was not thinking about

herself, she was thinking about how to control several of the men she dated
and kept watch over. It seemed that all of these men fit a certain profile.
They all were needy themselves, and they all appeared weak around Carol's
seductive influences. Carol liked her men a certain way. She had a need to be
right about how they should treat her. She was the "most special person in
the universe," and they all better treat her that way. However, when people
criticized her being in love with herself, she became infuriated, and argued
how she never thought of herself that way. She was someone who cared
about others and in return they cared about her.

Unfortunately for Carol, not everyone saw her the same way. Her track
record for holding on to men was abysmal. Sooner or later men became sick
of her self-centered life style and they would leave, only to be replaced with
a new batch of admirers. All the attention she received and all of the seductive mannerisms she displayed did not seem to make her happy. In fact, she
was suffering from bouts of loneliness and depression.

It was under these circumstances that she went for counseling. Mark, her
counselor, thought that her self admiration and her insecurity were a complicated blend of narcissism and an egotism addiction. However, trying to get
Carol to admit she was narcissistic seemed a feudal enterprise. Even when
Carol tried to seduce Mark, she would not admit that she needed everyone to
love her. Finally Mark changed his approach by showing Carol how she may
be addicted to egotism. He pointed out how all these losses in relationships
would make anyone insecure, and that maybe she needed to develop a lifestyle where; she did not have to be right all of the time, and she did not have
to defend he beauty or her charm, and how such defenses were cutting her
off from those she cared about.

In the end, Carol thought that counseling was a waste of time, and did
not believe that an egotism problem existed. She did not believe she was
self-centered, and she did not believe that people got tired of being around
her. She concluded that if only she could find the right man, then her charm
and talent could be used accordingly. Until that moment, she would have to
spend her time alone.

Summary—At first, it may appear that Carol's narcissism was much
stronger than any pattern of egotism. She seemed to be in love with herself
and practiced seductive behavior to that end. Through Carol's insecurity, she
had a need to get people to love her and to stay with her, neither of which
people wanted to do. Her ego became too large for any of them to endure. In
spite of her seductive mannerisms, she condescended to others by talking
about herself and eventually cutting them off from her. Yet, she felt their de-
partures had something to do with them, not her. Subsequently, she defended
her position at all costs and ended up alone. Even her counseling sessions
seemed to be more about egotism than narcissism. When she tried to seduce
her counselor, Mark, it seemed to be an effort to prove that she was right,

and that people did like her. Mark's comments about her egotism outraged her sensibilities and she quit counseling. It appeared that her need to be right was stronger than her need to get help. Mark was hitting too close to the insecurity controlling her life.

Carol's need to be loved combined with her need to be right showed a personality disorder fueled by an emotion addiction. Carol had withdrawal symptoms when Mark even mentioned her ego. To Carol, she was a loving, sincere person who did not try to fool anyone. However, what we see in Carol was not what was expected. Underneath her seductive, cordial demeanor was an insecure egotist who needed to be right.

An Egotism Addiction and Cocaine—Cocaine can be used for many different reasons. Sometimes it is used because others are using it. Other times, it is used for the hallucinogenic characteristics of the drug. On occasions, it is taken for the rush of stimulant through one's body. However, there are times when people use cocaine to help them feel stronger and more grandiose. Under these circumstances, cocaine is used to obtain a specific goal. For example, some addicted people in business may use cocaine as a crutch to face the needs of their jobs, or to take on the competition connected to rivals at work, or even when not working. For these people, cocaine can be more than a hallucinogenic experience. It may be a means to an end. It may make you a less inhibited; employer, employee, friend, lover or any other experience where looking confident seems important. Under these conditions, cocaine becomes a crutch that can form into an addiction, where the confidence gained from the experience turns out to be false confidence that only hides an underlying insecurity.

In treatment for cocaine addiction, it may make sense to consider the addictive characteristics of an egotism addiction, especially when clients are using cocaine to enhance abilities. Both cocaine use and an egotism addiction have a tendency to exaggerate one's natural abilities. In a sense, cocaine can be seen as one more cover up for the underlying characteristics of insecurity, where egotism becomes a part of such characteristics.

Example—Mike had battled his cocaine addiction for many years. Early in his career, he found himself competing with other business executives for the top spot at his company's headquarters. Unfortunately, for him there were some ultra-aggressive competitors who wanted the same position as he did. Undeterred, Mike had turned to cocaine as a way of bolstering his confidence when faced with company competition for advancement, and for Mike, it worked. The more he used cocaine, the higher he was elevated on the corporate ladder, until he was head of management at company headquarters. However, getting to the top and staying there became two separate matters. In this case, the more he used cocaine, the more incompetent he became. Drug use was bringing him down and he knew that something had to be done.

When he entered the office of Gloria, an addiction's counselor at a local rehabilitation center, Mike was clear about his cocaine addiction, and what he needed to do in order to get back on top. He told Gloria that cocaine had wrecked his professional life, and that he needed to control it so that he could regain his stature as a highly successful executive. The rehabilitation center was set up for helping people like Mike with similar addictions, so it was easy for Gloria to assure him that she would like the same for him.

As the weeks went by, Mike followed the guidelines for detoxification from cocaine and saw Gloria for counseling, and after a number of weeks it was clear that he was drawing away from the withdrawal symptoms of his addiction. Gloria found that, emotionally, Mike seemed to have another problem. His body was moving away from cocaine use but his attitude seemed to be getting closer to someone who was still using. Finally, Gloria asked Mike whether he believed that another form of addiction accompanied his cocaine addiction. She pointed out that before he was victimized by cocaine, he had developed a pattern of constantly needing to be right, and stubbornly defending his positions at all costs, even when he knew his position was wrong. He finally admitted that getting ahead and needing to be right became more important than being fair or being accurate. He had developed a position where, no matter how insecure he was feeling, Mike would show everyone around him that, he was going to be right, whether anyone cared or not. What Gloria had uncovered in Mike's addictive pattern of feelings and behavior was someone who could qualify for an egotism addiction, where admitting you were not always right, could bring on a whole new set of withdrawal symptoms.

Summary—In order for Gloria to treat Mike's cocaine addiction, she needed to treat his emotional addiction to egotism. Without breaking his pattern of needing to be right and defending his position at all costs, Mike ran a higher risk of going back to cocaine use. The addictive characteristics of cocaine, made his battle with the drug risky, solely from a physiological level. Combine this risk with an emotional addiction that had characteristics such as, underlying insecurity, needing to be right and defense of one's position at all costs, and you had a perfect set of variables for returning to cocaine. Many addiction's counselors will tell you that cocaine users, heroin users, and other addicts who act as if they know more than their counselors, may have to eventually face battles with their own egos. It is one thing to believe that a physical addiction is all that needs to be considered in rehabilitation from drugs. It is another thing to consider that one's beliefs, emotions and behaviors may be having a dramatic influence on one's rehabilitation efforts.

In the use of cocaine, one possible reason for taking it is to enhance a person's perceptions of strength, within oneself, and in the eyes of others. The emotional addiction of egotism seems to be a pattern that can reinforce the characteristics found in cocaine. As a stimulant, it may physically enhance peoples' false beliefs of superiority and confidence. Combine this with the phenomenon of egotism that, for the most part, is trying to accomplish a similar goal, and you have doubled your addiction problem. For most addiction's counselors, discussing feelings in cocaine addiction probably becomes an active part of counseling. It may be important to go beyond just treating feelings and consider the possibility that cocaine addicts also may be addicted to egotism.

Potential Counseling Solutions

- It may be important to avoid arguments with egotistical clients. Their need to be right and possible condescending behavior may put them in a position of challenging the counseling process. It may take skills from conflict resolution to help *soften the blow* of their possible attacks. (Williams, 1998). Sometimes the skill of active listening also may help in this process.

- A counselor probably should avoid high levels of emotion with egotistical clients. Usually, these clients win arguments by trying to get the other party emotional, so they can win. Remaining objective seems a safer approach to helping these clients.

- Cognitive behavioral therapy (Laidlaw, Thompson, Dick-Siskin, Gallagher-Thompson, 2003) can be effective when trying to describe how cutting one's self off from others can polarize people and cause the client more insecurity. For example, needing to be right is an addictive way of thinking about a problem. It makes the assumption that there is only one way to solve any crisis that might arise. It may be important to help the client develop other ways of solving the same problem.

- It may be important to actively listen when egotistical people start making justifications for their loneliness. In the course of becoming egotistical, it can be devastating to find yourself alone and lonely. In such cases, helping the egotist with understanding the importance of intimacy may help open up avenues to others.

- Be careful not to take away an egotist's cover story too soon in the counseling sessions. When someone is exposed to their true feelings, it may be important that something else is put in the place of their initial story such as, making it comfortable for the client to be vulnerable.

- Condescending to others can be a compulsive act. Help clients discover when they are compulsively condescending to others. Sometimes having a map of such behavior can be a useful tool in helping these people (Lee, 2003).

Egotism Addiction Short List

- Remember that most egotists base their behavior on insecurity.

- Needing to be right may be more important than needing to recover from an egotism addiction.

- Do not take an egotist's condescending behavior personally. It is their way of hiding their own insecurity.

- Isolating yourself from egotists reinforces their need to talk down to you.

- Describe your position to an egotist. Do not try to explain yourself. It is hard to convince an egotist that their behavior is destructive.

- Remember that egotistical people have an investment in not being a part of a group.

- Defending your position at all costs is a sign of addictive thinking.

- Insecurity may come from an egotist's childhood, and may have justifiable reasons based on someone creating insecurity in his or her life.

- Remember that narcissistic behavior and egotistical behavior can be related. Consider this when treating someone for narcissism.

- Egotism and cocaine addiction can find similar roots, and can reinforce each other under certain circumstances.

- Remember that being obnoxious does not necessarily mean a person is an egotist. Sometimes, we simply have a bad day.

Format for Other Emotional Connections

This is an opportunity to develop a connection between an egotism addiction and some other real life experience. This could mean making a connection between an egotism addiction and some form of physical addiction, or a connection with another process oriented addiction. Also, this could be a connection between an egotism addiction and a mental health disorder. Finally, this could be a connection between an egotism addiction and an everyday life experience where an egotism addiction makes an impact on this experience:

Briefly describe the connection between an egotism addiction and your chosen phenomenon:

Write an example of how an egotism addiction is connected to your chosen phenomenon:

Summarize your thinking on this connection:

Chapter 5: Envy Addiction

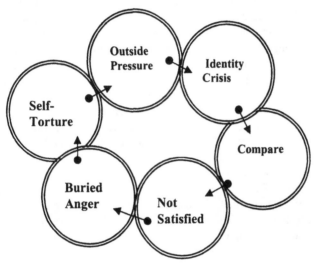

Figure 5

Background

We may be living in an age of envy where the media and pressure from those who evaluate us are gaining momentum in determining who we should, must or ought to be (Clendinning, 2006). Somewhere in our search for personal identity, we may become bombarded by those who think their choices for who we should be as people must be considered over our own. For example, the communication media flood the airways with images of the perfect model, the perfect student, the perfect partner and the perfect success (Matt, 2002). Under such pressure, we may struggle to find ourselves in a sea of others' opinions.

In the field of counseling, we are faced with the casualties of this phenomenon, as we try to help clients in accepting themselves. In counseling, we work closely with clients in finding out what values they would like to practice, and how they can be strong advocates for themselves. For example, anorexic teenagers make comparisons with the latest models, in the hope of losing more weight while, at the same time, gaining more acceptance. Or, families compare themselves to the neighbors by wanting what they have, yet hating them for having it. Envy is an emotional experience that draws us away from who we are or what we want to be. It makes us feel dissatisfied unless we achieve certain outside goals. Envy seems to be prevalent in our age where wanting something and owning something has the approval of those trying to give us direction through advertising, lecturing or social pressure (Nirenberg, 1998).

Yet, envy is not something new. There are countless myths and stories from our past depicting envy from, the Old Testament to Shakespeare (Timmer, 1989; Tiffany, 2002). Usually, envy is about comparing ourselves with peers, not some unreachable iconic figure. Envy is the everyday experience of wanting to be someone or have something within reachable limits. For example, a person has less of a chance in being envious of the President of the United States than the president of the local school board. We are envious of those life experiences we believe are achievable.

In this regard, all of us may have experienced times in our lives where we were envious. Actually, there is one developmental period in our lives where our envious behavior is viewed as a natural developmental stage. Adolescence seems to be a period in development where we tend to emulate others such as, rock stars, athletic heroes, celebrities and so on (Crawford, Cohen, Johnson, Sneed & Brook, 2004). Within our emulation is the emotion of envy. Not so much for those we emulate, but for others around us who seem to have their characteristics such as, friends, colleagues and lovers. These are the people where our comparisons take hold of us, and at times, we may become envious of their, success, beauty or local celebrity. For most of us, adolescence is a period in life filled with experimentation and rebellion and such comparisons seem a part of our development, with the hope of finding our personal identities as we move toward adulthood.

However, there are people who somewhere along life's developmental journey have lost sight of their identities, and have made a firm commitment to invest in the identities of others. These are people who have abandoned their intrinsic values, and have focused outside themselves toward a picture made up by others. We may call such people obsessed, or we may perceive them as groupies, fanatics or "want to be's". Beyond whatever label we give them is an experience filled with comparisons, buried anger and dissatisfaction. We may describe these people as having an envy addiction where their obsession with other peoples' identities leaves them misunderstood.

Case Study

Joe was a tortured individual. At twenty three years of age, he was about to be released from the local jail in his community for burglary charges and auto theft. The past five years were a blur of wrecking cars, breaking into buildings, and getting the people around him in trouble. Ironically, Joe blamed others around him for his problems. He lived in a town where people seemed to take each other at face value. Crime was low, and who you were and what you did was left up to each individual. However, Joe felt inferior in front of his peers. He saw them as richer, smarter and more connected, and Joe's goal in life was to be exactly like them. Fortunately or unfortunately for him, he was a fast talker who could influence his peers with a collection of wild stories about his past that were filled with lies and deceptions about his true identity. Actually, Joe was a fairly handsome, intelligent person who came from modest roots, but was in no way indigent or lacking for everyday comforts.

In his town, Joe did not see himself as socially acceptable. For example, he did not focus on being himself. He focused on being someone else. One person who he seemed to have a particular obsession with was Rick, a handsome, upper middle class acquaintance, who was accepting of many people even Joe. In fact, Rick befriended Joe and tried to help him in relationships with women and other peers. He sometimes gave Joe money to help him, and protected his reputation from those who believed Joe was trouble waiting to happen.

You would think that in return for Rick's generosity, Joe would appreciate Rick, and be thankful for having such a good friend. This could have been farther from the truth. On the outside, it looked as if Joe was Rick. He dressed like him. He talked like him, and he acted like him. Inside of Joe's constant comparisons with Rick was a dissatisfied and angry person. Joe was not Rick and he knew it. Deep inside of him lurked the emotion of envy, an emotion that guided most of his behavior. For example, one night Rick and Joe visited a local friend, and Joe excused himself from the visit. Later that evening, Rick found out that Joe had stolen his car, and rolled it down a hill with three other people in it. Fortunately, no one was hurt, and Joe did not get in trouble. Another time, Rick was moving his car, in order to get a better parking spot. Both had been drinking, yet were not intoxicated. Rick passed a law enforcement officer going a reasonable speed, but Joe yelled out the window. Rick ended up with a DUI and again, Joe ended up with no charges. Another incident had Joe calling Rick on his cell phone for a ride, only for Rick to find out that Joe had burglarized a local store. Rick had no idea what Joe was doing, yet received charges for helping him. Finally, Rick figured out that the two of them had little in common, and did his best to stay away from Joe. This turned out to be a worthwhile decision because Joe continued to steal more money from other people, and wrecked the cars of his new friends, forcing the local community to place him in jail.

All of this activity landed Joe in jail for four months, but now he was leaving. He was free except for one problem. Part of his release was based on getting counseling from a mental health counselor in the community. When Joe arrived at Frank's office, a mental health counselor, he was polite and charming. At first, it seemed that Joe was a person down on his luck that needed empathy and support in order to get his life in order. This ended quickly when a local colleague informed Frank that Joe was counseling people based on the advice he credited to him. Joe had become Frank, and was hurting his friends by being a pseudo-counselor. Frank confronted Joe by saying, "You have told me stories of how you wanted to be like your former friend, Rick, and now you want to be like me. How about you wanting to be like, yourself?" This started counseling that lasted over a year where Joe was faced with searching for his true identity, while Frank tried to counsel him for what he was calling an addiction to envy.

The Experience of Envy

The experience of envy begins with some form of outside pressure influencing how we perceive ourselves (Figure 5) (Jenkins, 2004). It could be pressure that started early in life such as, parental pressure to look or act a certain way, or it could be more recent forms of pressure found in a society that puts pressure on individuals to meet specific ideals based on personal image, social or economic success, and socially acceptable behavior. It is those outside voices telling us how we should, must or ought to be. For example, in the case study, Joe was listening to these voices. Whether it came from his family of origin or from his relationship with his peers, Joe felt some form of pressure to be someone other than himself. In our human development, we all seem to have a need to fit in, but Joe went too far. He lost himself by trying to be someone else. He fell victim to outside pressure, and he made up a replica of who, he should be, not who he was inside. Joe's biggest problem was his inability to find himself. Outside pressure had him looking in the wrong places. In his development, he abandoned personal identity, and followed an identity based on what he perceived as the ideal personality. Rick was the person who he wanted to be, yet his envy was fueled by the fact that he would never be him

In counseling, we see people who have lost their identities to some outside pressure, and we must be careful not to judge whether they have made the right or wrong decision. Sometimes we learn who we are by the influences of others, and sometimes we accept these outside influences as valuable. For example, we may rebel against our parents only to find that eventually in our development some of their outside influences we now accept as our own. The problem with envy is that we do not necessarily know the difference between our values, and those obtained through social pressure from outside sources.

Not accepting and understanding one's identity can cause a crisis in how we believe, think, feel and behave (Figure 5). Envy is based on a crisis of identity for the following reasons:

- Believing in being authentic people requires an understanding of our personal identities. Envy draws us away from understanding these identities.
- Being authentic people requires us to think as ourselves. Envy keeps our attention on the thoughts of others.
- Feeling good about being authentic people requires knowing our personal identities. Envy makes it difficult to feel good about ourselves because we have trouble accepting ourselves.
- Behaving in authentic ways can become difficult. Envy keeps our focus on the behavior of others.

All of the above issues come together to form a crisis of identity. In our development, there may have been periods in our lives where we met all of the criteria for an identity crisis, and we may have fallen victim to the emotion of envy. We may have had experiences where we felt lost, and looked

outside ourselves for our identities. For example, people going through highly emotional divorces may question their identities in marriages that have
rejected them, or people who have invested their identities in certain roles
such as, being the boss at work, may experience envy when no longer
holding that title. The combination of outside pressure and a crisis of identity
can create moments in our lives where our identities are questioned, and this
may bring envy to the surface of our emotions.

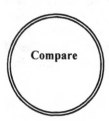

What happens when outside pressure combined with a crisis of identity
enters our lexicon of problems? What do we do under these conditions? In
the experience of envy, most of us have compared ourselves with others, and
these comparisons may have been lessons to remember (Figure 5). However,
what happens when we have lost our personal compass to find our way, and
we turn to others to see how we measure up? We may begin comparing ourselves to those who, we believe, know their way and have the answers. We
may continue to move farther away from ourselves under the strength of outside pressures, and a loss of personal identity. We may find ourselves trying
to understand who we are by comparisons with those we would like to be.
For example, in the case study, Joe is obsessed in his comparisons between
himself and his friend Rick. He compared the way they looked, the way they
thought, and the way they behaved. In all of these comparisons, Joe invested
his energy in, "Who is Rick?" rather than "Who is Joe?" Unfortunately for
Joe and others who are caught within the experience of being envious, such
comparisons do not work. In the end, even if you copy exactly someone's
image, thoughts, feelings and behaviors, you still are not them. At best, you
remain an inauthentic reproduction of them.

In counseling, such comparing distracts envious people from issues surrounding identity. It may be the role of the counselor to help clients return to
an understanding of personal identity; rather than, an identity based on comparisons with others. In some counseling sessions, such comparisons seem a
part of human development, especially with adolescents trying to figure out
who they are or what they want to be (Thompson, 2003). Other times, the
comparisons go deeper where clients have become obsessed with comparing

themselves to others as in, anorexia nervosa or bulimia. We all make comparisons in our lives, but comparisons that affect our personal identities have a tendency in drawing us away from ourselves.

What is the end result when we embrace; outside pressure, cause ourselves a crisis of identity, and look for solutions in comparisons with others? The experience of envy is filled with attempts at finding one's identity by copying others, a practice that fails regardless of the effort. The end result in such attempts is found in the dissatisfaction envious people experience in trying to be someone other than one's self (Honess & Yardley, 1987). Dissatisfaction is almost built in at some psychological and emotional level for those who are envious of others. For example, in the case study, Joe tried to be an exact image of Rick, but found himself dissatisfied even when driving Rick's car, spending Rick's money and sharing in Rick's life. Actually, instead of Joe being thankful for Rick's generosity, he envied him, making Joe increasingly more dissatisfied.

Sometimes in counseling, we see clients where it is hard to imagine why they are dissatisfied. On the surface, they seem to have great lives that are admired by the eyes of others. Yet, within their worlds something is missing. All of their success, wealth or beauty has not made them satisfied with themselves. Counselors may discover these clients have little understanding of their personal identities. They may have spent so much time listening to outside pressure, and finding their identity in others, and comparing themselves to others, that regardless of their success in life, they are dissatisfied with themselves. Here is another way of looking at this, "Their envy has left them an 'empty' shell of dissatisfaction where obtaining success is not connected to people who can accept this success."

What do envious people do with their dissatisfaction? In an experience of envy, one strong possibility is that it will be buried in the unconscious, where it can turn into a subtle form of anger against oneself and others (Feindler, 2006) (Figure 5). Outside pressure combined with a loss of identity where constant comparing leads to an overwhelming sense of dissatisfaction, can lead envious people to feel angry about their lives and their futures. In the case study, we might ask ourselves, "Why would Joe have hostility toward those who accepted him and helped him?" Wrecking his friend's car and getting Rick in trouble with law enforcement seemed like acts of aggression or buried anger; rather than, simply coincidence. Joe wanted to be Rick and also his counselor, yet he tried to hurt both of them. It seemed that even though he emulated these two people, there was some form of buried hostility toward them. Joe seemed a reasonable friend and a reasonable client until his buried anger surfaced to show his true feelings towards the people he envied.

In counseling, we hear of circumstance where people can spend most of their lives concealing their buried anger from those they may envy. For example, take a younger brother who envies an older brother, and holds a life long feeling of buried anger when one or both parents give the older brother more acceptance or attention, or someone at work who accomplishes great success, only for that person to feel the buried anger by those who envy that success. Also, the experience of envy can create buried anger even in those who want others to be successful. For example, a father who wants his daughter to thrive and be successful feels anger when comparing her success to his own.

In the end, what happens to envious people who accept the outside pressure of others to form their identities, and compare themselves to others only to be dissatisfied, and eventually feel hidden anger for these people? What kind of life do these people have to look forward to if they do not eventually find themselves and accept themselves? One possibility is, they may live a tortured life of never really knowing who they are for themselves (Turp, 2003) (Figure 5). They may know who they appear to be for others, or they may know who they would like to be, but being comfortable within their own skin may have eluded them. It seems one of the most subtle yet overwhelming tortured experiences in one's life may be an inability to know one's self. Plato may have words of wisdom for us when he said, "Know thy self" (Gerson, 2004). In an experience of envy, not knowing one's self may end in a tortuous experience. For example, we have talked about anorexia nervosa previously in this chapter. One way to look at it may be in the torture these clients feel when seeking out something that is unachievable, and the torture that may accompany such a journey. Envious people regardless of their efforts seem to come up short of the real thing, of being themselves. Their journey to find themselves is a flawed journey from the start. They are seeking an identity that cannot completely be found outside of their personal identity.

In counseling, the experience of envy can become an existential problem where focusing only on changing behavior falls short of what is needed to understand one's identity. Envy seems to be an experience that goes to the heart of one's existential being. Emulating others is acceptable behavior, yet may not be enough to understand who we are in relation to others, or how we fit in a world where our identity becomes a crucial factor for satisfaction and self-acceptance.

How an Envy Addiction Works

We seem to be a society where celebrity and instant icons draw us to emulating those in the public domain, and we find that some of us copy our heroes in public ways, without any inhibitions or regrets (Sabin, 1999). Sometimes such role models can give us direction and purpose, and eventually help us find ourselves. Yet, for such a public display of acceptance and a need for heroes, some of us torture ourselves privately within our own dissatisfaction and comparisons with others. For those who are engaged in a private war within, we find the possibility of developing an envy addiction where we may torture ourselves for wanting to be someone else. Such an experience, at some point, can be overwhelming and dangerous to lives looking for fulfillment. An envy addiction is an experience filled with loss of identity, comparisons, dissatisfaction, and self-torture. The following are some of the aspects that make up an envy addiction:

Outside Pressure and Dependency—Many of us are subjected to outside pressure from families, peers, and society to follow specific guidelines for how to live our lives. Many of these guidelines we adopt through experience, choice, or habit. Our identities are made up of many influences, and there are few areas where a completely original identity seems possible. In spite of this, each human being can be considered unique, and can have a personal identity (Gerhardt, 2000). When we have this identity, it appears that our personal knowledge of self can be comforting and sustain us through difficult times. Acceptance of self, allows us the flexibility and the courage to accept others. It is something we can depend on when all else is lost.

However, constantly depending on others for our identity can create a serious misdirection of our energy. With time, we grow used to others telling us "who we are" to the point where we depend on them for our identity. In today's world, outside pressure can become too seductive to ignore. Some of us may depend on it to tell us who we are, and who we need to be.

In counseling, depending on outside pressures to form our clients' identities can be manifested in control issues where clients' perceptions of self are controlled by, for example, what a significant other says, or what a group of people does. In effect, our client's depend on these outside forces for their identity. In an envy addiction, a dependency can be formed on these outside pressures to guide our opinions of ourselves. In the case study, Joe began to copy the behavior of his counselor, Frank. He depended on Frank for his identity, and actually acted as though he was Frank.

Identity Crisis and Addictive Thinking—In an envy addiction, we find people thinking in addictive ways similar to a drug addiction. One characteristic that earmarks addictive thinking is the simplicity used in making decisions without any critical analysis of the facts (Donovan & Marlatt, 2005). For example, a cocaine user may think, "If I only use cocaine then I will be successful in my highly competitive working environment." In this thinking, the cocaine user is not taking into consideration that other variables might also be important such as, competence, responsibility and fairness. He or she is using the simplicity found in addictive thinking to narrow one's solutions as to what will work in order to be a success. We have countless cases of cocaine users and others who made such unchecked assumptions, and over simplified conclusions that led them to some form of physical addiction.

In an envy addiction, the same form of addictive thinking seems to prevail. For example, someone with an envy addiction may be thinking along these lines. "If I copy what is important to others then I will form my true identity." Such simplistic thinking may lead people addicted to envy, into a crisis of identity. It may disallow critical thinking in favor of addictive thinking where facts become irrelevant, and where simple formulas are used to solve complicated problems. For example, someone with bulimia may be involved with a crisis of identity surrounding body image. They addictively think that if they purge themselves after every big meal then they will obtain a body shape and the identity they desire. In counseling, we help such clients when their addictive thinking breaks down, and their body image and personal identity are achieved by this method.

Comparisons and Compulsive Behavior—In an emotional addiction to envy, outside pressure and confusion over personal identity, forces people to compare themselves with others. In everyday living, many of us have had moments when outside pressure, and forgetting who we are forced us to compare ourselves to other people. Making comparisons to others is not *the* criteria that determines, whether envy has formed an addiction in our lives. In the course of living, most of us do make such comparisons. In many cases, we realize that our comparisons did not work, and we would be better getting back to our own identities. The difference between this type of experience with everyday envy and an envy addiction is that comparisons in an envy addiction are not necessarily thought through. In an envy addiction, people may compulsively make comparisons without making any attempts at critical thinking. For example, in the case study, Joe did not critically compare himself with his friend Rick or his counselor, Frank, and form conclusions about his identity. Joe compulsively became the people he was around, and acted as if he were those people.

Sometimes in counseling, we find clients who compulsively compare themselves to others (Watkin & Campbell, 2000). When asked how they feel about any given topic, it may be answered based on how someone else would answer it. Other times, clients will find themselves burning inside with envy by simply mentioning another's name, while they compulsively compare themselves to that person. In both of these examples, clients are using compulsive behavior to compare themselves to others. Much in the manner that alcoholics compulsively need to drink, those with an envy addiction compulsively need to compare.

Dissatisfaction and Tolerance—People with an envy addiction are able to tolerate high levels of dissatisfaction. Many of us probably have felt dissatisfaction with ourselves, and have expressed it during the course of our lives, and hopefully, there are times when we also feel satisfied with who we are and what we are doing. In an envy addiction, this does not seem to be the case. These people seem dissatisfied with themselves and their lives most of the time. One might say that dissatisfaction has become a way of life. Regardless of the circumstances, an envy addiction creates an atmosphere where life is not good enough, and they are not good enough. For example, in the case study, Joe was searching for his identity, yet when he emulated his friend, Rick or Frank, his counselor, he still was left with wanting more. In this case, Joe not being satisfied with his personal identity lead him to not being satisfied with his life. However, Joe did not make any effort to feel satisfaction. He learned to tolerate dissatisfaction so he could seek out his identity in the personalities of others.

In counseling, it may be important to realize that clients suffering an addiction to envy have a difficult time being satisfied with their lives or themselves (Cook-Cottone & Phelps, 2004). Trying to find those areas that may give satisfaction can be difficult because these clients have learned to tolerate dissatisfaction. Even when locating areas of satisfaction in their lives, it does not seem to be enough. Personal success, body image, relationships and so on, consistently seem to be based on someone else. Since these clients cannot achieve being someone else, they remain dissatisfied. Their tolerance for dissatisfaction creates an atmosphere where true happiness seems unachievable, thus leading them into the next stage of an envy addiction where they may begin to feel buried anger.

Buried Anger and Withdrawal—Buried anger is a phenomenon seldom seen in an emotional addiction to envy. This is because it becomes the hidden energy that drives envious people to invest in the identities of others. It is the unfulfilled desire to be someone else while knowing at some unconscious level that such a desire is impossible. It is the constant feeling of dissatisfaction that begs for an emotional response. However, in an envy addiction the response seems buried, and out of reach for making any emotional changes to one's identity. For example, in the case study, what was the motivation for Joe to wreck his best friend's car, or to get him in trouble with law enforcement? Why did Joe show similar behavior with his counselor by trying to wreck his reputation with the public? The answer may lie in the buried anger Joe felt for a life filled with other people's identities.

In counseling, facing an envious client's buried anger can be a difficult enterprise. Fundamentally, counselors are asking clients to let go of their buried anger and explore the possibility of understanding their own identities. For most of us, if we had lost our identity for whatever reasons, such a request may be a relief. For example in counseling, consider the younger brother who developed buried anger over the years because his older brother was designated as the family favorite. He could react to getting rid of this anger in a number of ways. He could get in touch with his identity, and feel relief that finally outside pressure from his family did not matter, and the constant comparing of the two brothers had finally ended. Or, he could experience withdrawal symptoms anytime the counselor got close to discussing the buried anger. In the first example, the counselor has successfully helped the client let go of anger that was affecting his life. In the second example, the counselor must face the withdrawal symptoms that are blocking letting go of this anger. Much like an alcoholic has withdrawal symptoms when trying to stop drinking, clients with an envy addiction may experience withdrawal symptoms when someone attempts to remove their buried anger.

Self-Torture and Denial—An envy addiction seems inevitable when certain characteristics are in place. People with an envy addiction find themselves; succumbing to outside pressure for one's identity, having a crisis of identity, making comparisons that do not work, feeling dissatisfaction with one's life, and silently seething with buried anger. These people seem to torture themselves for wanting to be someone that is hopelessly out of reach.

However, their focus is more on trying harder to be someone else than on getting rid of the self-torture. In a sense, they are in denial of the effects that self-torture is causing with their identity. For example, clients with anorexia nervosa are in denial of how much they are torturing themselves both physically and psychologically. Most clients with this disorder do not state, "I have to stop torturing myself and begin to eat." Conversely, no matter how many experts explain what is happening to them, they still cannot eat. They are holding on to an image of themselves that most likely was formed through outside pressure. Their personal experience of self-torture seems secondary to an overwhelming desire to be someone else (Eliot, 2004).

In the case study, Joe remained a tortured person, primarily of his own design. His motivation was not directed toward himself. He was focused on others, no matter how much self-torture he inflicted on himself. He denied his tortured existence and pursued the identity of others. He relied on outside pressure to tell him what to do, thus having the vicious cycle of an envy addiction repeat itself.

Emotional Connections

An emotional addiction to envy can create huge existential problems for those seeking counseling. Anytime one's identity is in jeopardy, an understanding of people's behavior or their feelings is not enough (Miars, 2002). In counseling, we find this apparent in numerous areas where personal dysfunction is based on problems with identity. This section will consider the connection between a mental health disorder, and a social problem, and their relationship with an emotional addiction to envy. First, we will discuss the connection between an envy addiction and anorexia nervosa. This topic has been mentioned previously in this chapter, and seems to be an area where counseling for envy may be a part of the treatment for this disorder. Secondly, the confusion over personal identity may create a connection between an envy addiction and people's relationship with modern day society.

An Envy Addiction and Anorexia Nervosa—For counselors who have worked with clients suffering from anorexia nervosa, the question of identity becomes a paramount issue. Keeping this in mind, trying to model one's self after an image of an acceptable body type can be grounds for an envy addiction. The constant endeavor to be thinner does not come from someone who has a healthy perspective on their identity. On the contrary, clients with this disorder are looking for outside sources to designate what is an acceptable way to look in this world (Lucas, 2004). Furthermore, it can be hypothesized that anorexia nervosa is a disorder that has its foundation in an identity crisis, much in the manner as someone with an envy addiction. For example regarding behavior, both anorexics and people with envy addictions spend a great deal of their time comparing themselves to others. Regarding feelings, both of these groups seem dissatisfied even when others believe they have reached their goal, whether it is body image or success. Finally, both seem tortured by their inability to find answers to their underlying questions. In the case of someone with an envy addiction, "How can I be the person who I admire?" In the case of someone with anorexia nervosa, "How can I achieve the body that I admire?"

Considering these possibilities, anorexia nervosa could be viewed as an addiction, and not exclusively as a disorder. For counselors, this may open other views on this highly personal phenomenon. Sometimes, trying to change a pattern in human experience, as found in an emotional addiction to envy, may be more productive than focusing solely on the person with the problem. It may be that clients have less difficulty changing their patterns than changing themselves. This seems true of those with anorexia nervosa. The amount of attention given to body image and physical health may be putting pressure on these clients to make a personal change. By focusing on a pattern of addiction such as found in an envy addiction, it may allow these clients "breathing room" to focus on something beyond an obsession with body image.

Example—Florence had been struggling with anorexia nervosa since she was twelve years old. Between her peers and her parents, her body weight was of concern. The comments from her peers affected her immensely, and even though her parents stated that, "We want the best for you and we will help you lose weight," their comments were devastating. The image of being thin was something that crowded her mind each day as she prepared to face the world. It was an image that caused her great pain as she looked through countless magazines where she could not find a picture that reflected an acceptable example of her self-image. Dieting and fasting became a way of life, as she lost pound after pound only to look in the mirror and feel fat and ugly. Added to her problems with self-image was the constant comparing she did with anyone she felt was thinner and more beautiful. It was a life filled with dissatisfaction and self-torture.

When she reached the door of Janice, an addiction counselor, Florence had already been diagnosed with anorexia nervosa. She had not been hospitalized but numerous medical doctors, psychologists and nutritionists had tried to help her feel good about herself, and to gain weight. In her discussions with Janice, Florence made it clear that she was appreciative of all that had been done for her. She praised the professionals who tried to help her gain weight and accept her body type. She thanked her parents for spending such a great amount of time on her disorder. However, one problem seemed to develop from all of this attention. She told Janice that all the attention she was getting caused her enormous amounts of anxiety and fear. She wanted the spotlight off of her, and in fact, she wanted to be left alone.

Janice listened to these words with empathy and clarity. She perceived Florence differently than her colleagues. She felt that Florence was suffering from an addiction to envy, and that constantly focusing on Florence may make it worse. What she proposed to Florence was this:

> Let us take the emphasis off you, and all of the responsibility that seems to cause you anxiety and fear. I believe you are suffering from an addiction to envy where who you are and what you want to be has been lost. Much like in a physical addiction, we must look at this emotional addiction not as something that is a part of you, but as something that controls you. Let us stop focusing on you, and start focusing on this addiction. Maybe then you can get the breathing room you need to get through this ordeal.

From that moment on the focus was not on Florence; it was on her addiction. Janice did not say that the help from other professionals should be ignored. She encouraged Florence to seek their help. However, she worked with Florence on the addictive characteristics that may be associated with both envy and anorexia nervosa. Janice did her best in making Florence feel comfortable with herself.

Summary—Treating anorexia nervosa from the perspective of an envy addiction should not negate the facts associated with research with those suffering from this disorder (Ronen & Ayet, 2001). It should not replace this research, but it may be possible to augment traditional knowledge of anorexia nervosa with the human experience found in an envy addiction. What becomes evident with this disorder is its tremendous damage on a client's self-image. In an addiction to envy, similar damage seems evident, and for similar reasons. The connection between anorexia nervosa and an envy addiction gives us one possibility in our efforts to help the clients we serve.

In the above example, Florence was getting proper care for her disorder. However, her care was part of the problem. She already spent most of her life believing that people were looking at her, and concluding that she was too fat. Now she was faced with a similar dilemma. She had a team of professionals, including her parents looking at her, and concluding that she was too thin. What she seemed to need was someone who could help her without constantly looking at her. Janice took the focus off of Florence, and put it on an envy addiction. When Florence considered what happened to her through this pattern of addiction, it may have given her an understanding of her past human experience regarding weight loss and weight gain. Regardless of its effects, at least it took the focus off of something being wrong with her identity. Now she could see the envy addiction as the cause of her problems, and not she as being the sole cause of her tortured life. In other words, she could attack a problem instead of herself.

An Envy Addiction and An Emotional Climate of Envy—

Sometimes the connection between emotional addictions expands beyond the borders of other addictions and disorders. This seems to be the case found in an envy addiction. We may be living in an emotional climate of envy where being someone else becomes a life long pursuit. Through media and other forms of communication, we have a society that has become highly opinionated as to what we should, must or ought to be (Glazer, 2000). This seems especially true in First World societies where educated people have designated themselves as experts on any number of topics. Children growing up in today's modern society have more than parents influencing their identities. In an achievement based society, human development and personal identity may seem less important than what modern day society deems important. Success in psychological, social and financial areas may partially make up our new identities, and in modern thinking, may be considered more important than personal identity. If this hypothesis is correct, it may herald the advent of more cases of envy, and more envy addictions being brought to mental health and addictions counselors. Focusing on outside pressures for one's identity may find people comparing more than they believe should be important, or feeling more dissatisfied than they would expect, and torturing themselves more than they would like. For example in counseling, work dealing with family systems, counselors learn early in their training that, "The emotional climate is bigger than the people in it." This rule may also apply to how we perceive an envy addiction. In a world where outside pressure may dictate identity, it may become problematic when we find ourselves envious of the people around us. It may be a byproduct of an emotional climate that compares one person against another, based on rules for body image, success, and happiness. Take this argument to its limits, and we might consider the possibility that the emotional climate in our society as a whole encourages envy as an acceptable behavior, and part of a process that generates comparisons, and dissatisfaction as a mechanism for societal growth.

Example—Jesse always did what he was told. He followed the blueprint that his parents had prepared for him, and he combined that blue print with the wishes of the schools he attended, and now was in a high powered job where he continued to do what he was told. Jesse worked from the assumption that satisfaction comes by following all of the rules given to you, and this assumption seemed to have paid off. He was highly successful, well liked among his peers, and a pillar of his community. It was hard to believe that he had developed such an addiction to drugs and alcohol. What possibly could be wrong? On the outside, people admired him and emulated his behavior, yet on the inside something was missing.

This is how Jesse presented himself to Linda, an addictions counselor who decided to take him on as a client. At first, Linda had difficulty understanding why Jesse had turned to drugs and alcohol. He did not present a story filled with pain, heartache or failure. His story seemed to be based on a textbook version of happiness and success. It was only after Linda moved away from talking about Jesse's accomplishments did she begin to see a clearer picture. In spite of his success, Jesse still compared himself to others. He did not seem satisfied with success, and believed that others may be more successful and, "Why wasn't he more successful?" Linda kept silent, and did not give him the question that was being analyzed her mind, namely, "Why not be happy with what you have? You have more than most people." Instead, she listened closely to his words. Actually, Jesse had become a tortured individual. Even though, all his life he did what he was told, he had no idea as to what he wanted out of life. His comparisons with others actually made this worse. Most of these were in comparing himself with others less fortunate, yet he harbored subtle anger for their happiness, and tortured himself as to why he was not happy.

In the end, Linda approached Jesse's problem from the perspective of having an envy addiction where he seemed to have all of his desires except the desire to understand who he was as a person. He felt like an empty shell filled only with other's expectations. The concept of having a personal self was alien to him. He saw himself as a product of his society, and envied those who had escaped such an ordeal. Jesse was lost and addicted to envying others who were not lost. Linda told him that over the years his envy had turned into an addiction, an addiction that most people would not acknowledge or believe. She told him that finding himself and accepting himself may be the pathway back to his personal happiness; however, this was a decision that he would personally have to make.

Summary—In mental health and addictions counseling, we normally focus on clients, not the emotional climate in which they are living. However, in considering an emotional addiction to envy, our society may have as big an influence as other more personal experiences. In the example, Jesse seemed to have as big a problem with his interpretation of society as he did with his interpretation of himself. Linda, his counselor, could not effectively help him without including society's impact on his identity. In many respects, Jesse lost a sense of balance between personal desires, and the desires he believed came from the emotional climate found in modern day society.

In counseling, losing one's identity by an overemphasis on society's needs versus personal need's can be seen in school counseling, family counseling, career counseling and addictions and mental health counseling. The emotional climate within which people have everyday experiences can have a profound effect on one's identity (Ladd, 2005). In an emotional addiction to envy, we may find this to be the effective focal point of the counseling experience. In Jesse's counseling this became the case. His personal identity was not co-created between himself and society. He was a product of the emotional climate created by society, and he envied others who were not creations of society. Linda's counseling effort helped Jesse balance society's desires with his own. She started by having him face his emotional addiction to envy, along with facing the emotional climate in which he experienced it. Much as a client faces a physical addiction, Jesse needed to face an emotional addiction, and in an emotional climate that may or may not have been one where Jesse had a clear choice.

Potential Counseling Solutions

- It may be important to map out potential pressures from the outside that could cause a client to feel envious. An example may be the pressures parents put on their children to look a certain way, and succeed in certain ways. Any behavioral techniques that can help in dealing with outside pressures can be helpful (Arieti, Freedman & Dyrud, 1975).

- It may be important to point out how a crisis with identity can generate an envy addiction. Some form of cognitive behavioral therapy may help in sorting out the addictive thinking that seems to take place during an envy addiction. Especially, the thinking that states, "If I only see myself as others want me to be, then I will be happy."

- Values clarification can be important when helping someone with an envy addiction. It may be important to know the difference between personal values, and those given by outside forces. Envious clients need to get back to their intrinsic values, and decide whether they are practicing their values, or have they inherited the values of others.

- The compulsive act of comparing oneself to others is a common characteristic of an envy addiction. Breaking out of this compulsive act may require some form of behavioral therapy to overcome compulsive, learned behavior. The ability to stop comparing can be a successful behavioral adjustment for overcoming an envy addiction.

- Active listening can be an effective skill, used in counseling that can help clients realize their buried anger. Sometimes it requires a client to peel away layers of superficial emotions to get to deep seated emotional experiences. Active listening can allow clients to realize how their buried anger can add to a problem with envy.

- Self-induced tortured feelings can be the consequence of an envy addiction. An example of this, are clients who may suffer from anorexia nervosa. Some anorexic clients may need some form of cognitive behavioral therapy to stop the torture. Thinking differently about personal identity can lead to feeling differently about it.

Envy Addiction Short List

- Accepting an identity from outside pressures can be the beginning stage in an envy addiction.

- Envious people usually have a crisis of identity. Help them stay away from quick solutions to their identity problems.

- Comparing yourself to others can be one of the characteristics of an envy addiction.

- Remember that the dissatisfaction that comes from envy is found in wanting to be like someone else but knowing it is an unachievable goal.

- Help clients with an envy addiction to share their buried anger. Getting anger out in the open will help relieve feelings of dissatisfaction.

- Desiring someone or something you cannot have can be a torturous experience. Help client adjust their desires to more achievable goals.

- Remember that clients with anorexia nervosa may have a connection to an envy addiction.

- Watch out for clients that emulate your identity. They may have an envy addiction.

- Sometimes people who say they are your friends may have problems with envy, and desire to be like you while feeling buried anger towards you.

- Envy can lead to self- hatred and possibly hatred of others.

- Remember that people having envy problems, may copy your self-image and your behavior.

- Remember that people who compare themselves with you may end up resenting you.

Format for Other Emotional Connections

This is an opportunity to develop a connection between an envy addiction and some other real life experience. This could mean making a connection between an envy addiction and some form of physical addiction, or a connection with another process oriented addiction. Also, this could be a connection between an envy addiction and a mental health disorder. Finally, this could be a connection between an envy addiction and an everyday life experience where an envy addiction makes an impact on this experience:

Briefly describe the connection between an envy addiction and your chosen phenomenon:

Write an example of how an envy addiction is connected to your chosen phenomenon:

Summarize your thinking on this connection:

Chapter 6: Guilt Addiction

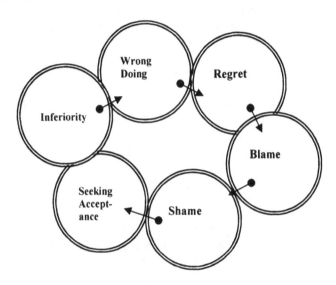

Wrong
Doing

Regret

Inferiority

Blame

Seeking
Accept-
ance

Shame

Figure 6

Background
The phenomenon of guilt dates back to the beginning of religion and myth in many ancient cultures (Kubany & Watson, 1992). People of antiquity used guilt to create a sense of wrong doing in members of their tribal communities. However, in the early days of civilization it was the entire village that was held responsible when a wrong doing was committed by a tribal member (Grinberg & Trollope,1992). It was not until religion became more formalized that individual guilt emerged as a part of a person's everyday reality (Kubany & Manke, 1995). This phenomenon developed when religions became more mono-theistic, where believing in one god dominated the world's psychological landscape for everyday people.

To understand guilt we need to go beyond the perceptions found in the ancient history of religion. Historically, there have been numerous studies that associate guilt within the context of traumatically stressful life events (Roseman, Weist & Shwartz, 1994) such as an unexpected death of a loved one, or one's experience with sexual abuse. Within these and other traumas, unsuspecting individuals may find themselves trying to justify their behavior through guilt, in order to make sense of these personal traumatic events. Thus, people blame themselves for what has happened when trauma arises. Sigmund Freud in the early Twentieth Century understood how society tied guilt to social responsibility, especially when traumatic events occurred (Plunka, 2000) and trauma and guilt have been closely connected to social pressure in a world filled with traumas such as, bigotry, violence and war.

Guilt, beyond trauma or history, may be best understood in the context of everyday living where it has not escaped our personal experience. Trauma is not a necessary condition for one to feel guilty. In a society that has become increasingly self-reflective, guilt may fall under the category of social pressure, keeping wrong-doing just under the surface of our behavior (Ladd, 2005). In many ways, we have gone beyond the ancient civilizations in our use of guilt. Today, guilt may mean more than breaking the dogmas of a religion or social rules of behavior, and it may go beyond experiences depicting personal trauma.

In our contemporary world, guilt can be found in the behavior of individuals who use it for personal and strategic gain (Freedman, 1998). In this regard, guilt becomes more than a reaction to something else. It may be a method for justifying one's personal behavior where it is used as a part of a personal style of living. Carried to its extreme, this lifestyle can develop addictive characteristics where a person depends on the use of guilt, and may experience symptoms of withdrawal when guilt is no longer used as an everyday pattern of behavior. Under these conditions, an individual may treat guilt as an addiction, but may be in denial of its existence.

Case Study

During many counseling sessions, Harry was more than willing to admit to all his wrong doing over the years, but when the counselor pointed out his accomplishments, he found ways of sabotaging each one of them. Harry perceived himself as; a poor father, a failure at connecting with others, a burden to his wife and a social outcast. However, this was in drastic contrast to those who knew him. His son rarely made any mention of Harry's poor performance as a father. The opposite seemed to be more the case. Harry's son constantly sought his father's approval, only to have Harry refocus father/son interactions onto Harry. Also, he seemed to have numerous friends attending to his every need, and his wife waited on him in the most extraordinary ways. Yet, Harry found methods for finding the negative side of all of these experiences. To his counselor, he seemed to depend on the attention he received when others came in contact with his constant complaining and regret. He frequently looked for some form of acceptance from others; even though, it did not appear to change his negative self image.

During counseling, it became apparent, that in the course of his daily living, Harry made a point to openly blame himself for imperfections in his life. For example, if a problem developed affecting family members, he would blame himself for these problems. This would force other family members into the position of convincing Harry that it was not his fault. In fact, many family problems went unresolved because fixing Harry remained the center of attention during family conflict. Harry's counselor came to the conclusion that he compulsively blamed himself regardless of the problems that came up in his life. Life seemed to be his fault, regardless of the facts, or the conclusions of others.

Some might say that, "Harry was a good guy who was too hard on himself." While others may have commented that, "He seemed to indulge in an abundant amount of whining." However to Harry's counselor, either point of view appeared to reinforce his low self–esteem, yet in no way change his behavior. It could be argued that Harry had developed a tolerance to such comments, and it seemed that he had an investment in his own worthlessness and shame. When Harry's counselor tried to point out his numerous positive attributes, he would shrug them off as inconsequential and inaccurate. Harry seemed to have little tolerance for positive statements, but tolerated the negative comments of others as an affirmation of his personal self loathing.

Harry's counselor also observed that when positive progress was made in counseling, Harry would experience physical and emotional symptoms of withdrawal. He would get extremely agitated when his counselor pointed out how his thinking caused low self–esteem, and he would even, at times, become physically ill when progress was being made. Harry would sometimes call ahead after a highly positive and productive session and inform his counselor that he was too ill to attend the next session. It was only after the momentum of their counseling sessions were lost that Harry would return to counseling, spouting a similar pattern of blame and shame, yet denying that any growth had taken place.

His counselor concluded that Harry's guilt was more than a reaction to his life. He seemed to compulsively use it, depend on it, and have symptoms of withdrawal when asked to give it up. Yet, Harry resisted these conclusions. Guilt had become a part of his everyday thinking, and his acceptance of guilt seemed to trap him into an emotionally addictive lifestyle.

The Experience of Guilt

The phenomenon of guilt has key elements that need clarification. First, it may be important to talk about the subtly guilt holds as an everyday emotion. Unlike anger, jealousy or revenge, guilt begins with a subtle feeling that a person is doing something wrong (Figure 6). This may be brought on by the judgments of others who find wrong-doing in a person's behavior, or it may be self-inflicted judgments by guessing what others may want or need, and feelings of wrong-doing that subtly form, when a person cannot meet these wants and needs. Whatever the case, guilt seems to be a phenomenon that enters into a person's life in subtle ways, and it may start subtle changes in peoples' thinking about themselves and others. For example, highly judgmental parents may create a climate where their children sense something is wrong even when no family rules have been broken. This may cause these children to feel a subtle sense of wrongdoing even during the most positive occasions.

In experiencing guilt, people at some point, may go beyond subtle feelings of wrong doing. In a sense, a climate of wrongdoing sets the stage for people to openly question their feelings and behavior. During this stage, guilt can enter into one's consciousness as the experience of regret (Figure 6). Regretting is a more conscious experience than having subtle feelings of doing something wrong. With regret, a person begins to clarify the wrong doing in his or her mind, and joins these thoughts with his or her emotions. A person may justify this by concluding, "I did something wrong and I clearly regret it." Whether people speak to themselves about their regret or share it with others, the effect seems to be the same. Now, people have an image in their mind of openly doing something wrong without any subtleties getting in the way.

All of us may reach a stage in our emotions where we regret our behavior. At this stage, guilt does not seem to be fully formed and regretting simply becomes a response to thoughts of doing something differently, the next time. In such circumstances, a person has the opportunity to specifically pinpoint what they regret and to develop a plan to change it. Successfully changing our regrets can lead to highly productive behavior (Shores & Scott, 2007). However, talking about regret with little change can set the stage for more acute stages of guilt.

People who regret yet do not specifically face these feelings, can put themselves in a position to experience blame for their wrongdoings. The blame stage seems to be critical in having a full understanding of the experience of guilt. Simply put, it takes guilty people out of the realm of feelings and into the realm of judgments, where people begin to judge themselves, rather than their behavior (Figure 6). For example, in the case study, Harry blames himself for his behavior with others; even though, others comment that his behavior is perfectly acceptable. In this way, Harry can ignore his problems and talk about himself.

Also, the shift from regret to blame can lead guilty people away from solving some of their most pressing problems. Blame has a way of generalizing one's thoughts and feelings (Konstan, Chernoff & Deveney, 2001). When people start blaming themselves, it can become generalized into regretting more than one particular incident. It can trigger negative perceptions of being incompetent, unreliable or inept. Blame can detach itself from any given situation and put the focus more on the guilty person; rather than, regrets for doing something wrong. In this way, blaming detracts from solving problems, it focuses more on making judgments about self-worth.

Guilty people practicing self blaming behavior or who have accepte
blame placed on them by others are now in a position to experience shan
(Figure 6). Shame goes beyond personal judgments of blame and becomes a
issue of identity (Williams, 1993). Unlike the regret stage of guilt where pe
ple feel guilty about a specific incident, or in the blame stage of guilt whe
people begin to generalize their behavior; with shame, guilty people come
the conclusion that, they are no good. The experience of shame fundamental
draws the conclusion that guilty people are bad regardless of their behavic
and must accept this belief as a fact of life. Furthermore, the experience o
shame may dictate to guilty people a sense of inferiority that impacts their pe
sonal beliefs. At this stage, people's beliefs about being ashamed can have a
enormous impact on their future actions. For example, a person who fee
ashamed may be asked to take a risk, possibly in a relationship or in the pe
formance of a job. However, shame may cause this person to think somethir
like this, "Don't ask me to risk. I am not worthy." thus limiting opportuniti
in either of these endeavors.

Feeling ashamed takes us beyond regret for any specific wrong doing,
for blaming ourselves in general for how life experiences have unfolded. Wi
shame, we declare ourselves as worthless. We accept a conclusion that can i
fluence both positive and negative moments in our lives. Shame runs the ri
of freezing peoples' identities as inferior, and with time, shameful people ma
be forced to seek some form of acceptance from others.

One of the realities in an experience of shame is when we seem mo
ashamed of ourselves. It may be at that point where we desire the most accep
tance. Many of us would like acceptance by others, but the experience o
shame seems to make that desire far more important. Seeking acceptance fro
others may be so important that we give over control of ourselves, in order
get their approval (Gaylin, 2003) (Figure 6). For example, two brothers mee
at the breakfast table and for one month the older brother says to his younge
sibling, "You are a great guy." One day he says, "You are a jerk." If th
younger brother feels good about himself during that month, the commen
about being a jerk may hurt but they probably will not change his view of hin
self. However, if the younger brother is living with shame, he may rely on h
older brother to accept him, and be devastated when his brother sees him in

negative light. Such a need for acceptance in the younger brother may slowly erode self-confidence while in his pursuit of acceptance from others. Over time, seeking outside confirmation may lead to feelings of inferiority, increasing his need for acceptance. Here we find the younger brother's *need* for acceptance seems stronger than *wanting* acceptance. Under these conditions, seeking acceptance may not be a strategy for improving social relationships, but an attempt to counteract the shame experienced in one's life.

The final stage in an experience of guilt can lead guilty people full circle; a subtle feeling of doing something wrong can lead to regret, regret can lead to blame, blame can lead to shame, shame can lead to seeking acceptance, seeking acceptance can lead to inferiority, and inferiority can lead back to subtle feelings of doing something wrong (Figure 6).

We may find it difficult to believe that people seeking acceptance for their shame, are not more positive about their lives when they get acceptance. In the case study, Harry sought acceptance, yet needed a constant barrage of people confirming him, in order to function from day to day. And, even when he was confirmed, Harry found others' opinions unacceptable based on his inferior belief about himself.

Yet, Harry had other problems. Since he did not allow outsiders to build up his self-esteem, he was left to his own judgments about personal identity. And, since he had judged himself as inferior, Harry was more open and susceptible to feelings of wrong doing. Under these conditions, Harry might find that he was experiencing another round of subtle feelings of doing things wrong, not based on his behavior, but on his inferior perception of himself.

How a Guilt Addiction Works

If you look at the pattern found in Figure 6 in this chapter, it may become apparent that we may experience any number of the stages relating to guilt. Even the experience of feeling ashamed and looking for acceptance can be found at our moments of personal judgments and decision making. To feel we have done something wrong, to regret our actions and even to feel ashamed for some of these actions, seems a human yet vulnerable life experience that may, in the long run, add to our wisdom about making mistakes in an imperfect world.

However, there may be people who go beyond experiencing guilt as one more of life's experiences. These people may treat guilt much like an addict treats addiction. They may not possess guilt, but rather guilt possesses them. For these people, many of the warning signs of physical and social addictions may appear in their lives as an emotional addiction. The following are guidelines for identifying the emotional addiction of guilt:

Subtle Wrong Doing and Denial—The issue of guilt and denial may be the beginning point in developing a guilt addiction. Constant denial of one's productive moments can create a sense that no matter how positive a person performs in life little recognition can be given for success. For example, in the case study, Harry had successfully blocked any mention of success. He consistently used his relationship with his wife and son as a testament of his personal failure. Regarding his connections with others, he couched himself as a social outcast. Harry was in a state of denial. He held an inflexible point of view, even with help from his counselor. Much like an alcoholic denies a problem with alcohol by continuing drinking, Harry's denial of any success, allowed him to continue practicing negative thoughts and feelings.

This subtle form of giving into wrong doing, and denial of any form of success, may set the stage for a person to develop a guilt addiction. Now, subtle feelings of wrong doing are expected and accepted as a way of life. In the case study, Harry may have thought, "I sincerely do not want to feel bad about myself or my family and friends." but his constant denial of his successes helped him mimic the denial found in other forms of addiction. In a way, people addicted to guilt may find justification in their negative life styles and the subtle wrong doing they accept as a way of life, may force them to openly deny success in many of life's experiences.

Regret and Dependency—A person addicted to guilt seems to go beyond what most of us encounter when we regret. Most people recognize wrong doing in circumstances where a mistake has taken place, and we openly regret our actions (Freedman, 1998). However, people with a guilt addiction seem to regret even in circumstances where no visible wrong doing has taken place. They seem to find the negative portion of any given set of behaviors and regret their actions. Actually, they may depend on regretting, in order to justify their guilt. For example, in the case study, Harry received attention when he openly regretted his behavior to his family and friends. His wife waited on him and his friends told him he was a good person. As long as, Harry can regret his life successfully, others came to his aid.

Considering Harry's circumstances in the case study, common sense may lead us to believe that Harry depended on "feeling sorry for himself" in order to have others meet his needs. Instead of having his needs met through personal empowerment, Harry developed a dependency on others to tell him that he was acceptable. Ironically, he had to develop a dependency on being unacceptable in order to maintain his acceptance with himself. The case study shows how a person can develop a dependency on their regrets to gain acceptance. Much like the experience found in a physical addiction, a guilt addiction also can form dependencies, as in the case study, where Harry forms a dependency around personal regrets, or a co-dependency where he must feel sorry for himself in order to receive his "emotional fix" from his friends and family.

Blame and Compulsive Behavior—Most of us experience feelings of wrongdoing, and regret our behavior, and have blamed ourselves for some incident that, next time, we would act differently. Upon reflection, we may have reconsidered our judgments either positively or negatively and have tried to put such an incident into perspective. Such forms of blame may end in statements like, "I have learned my lesson." or "I won't do that again." Like these statements, blaming ourselves becomes a process where we may have started out too hard on ourselves, but eventually discovered a logical explanation for our behavior.

However, such a process seems to be overlooked in a guilt addiction. For example, in the case study, Harry, compulsively practiced self blame for many of life's imperfections. This was not blame connected to a specific problem, but an compulsive act that he used when conflict arose around him. The case study demonstrates how Harry compulsively turned problems facing his family into personal self blame. Ironically, Harry's compulsive behavior of blaming himself almost guaranteed that actual family problems were not addressed. The case study points out that fixing Harry had become the main problem.

We see similar compulsive behavior in physical addictions where the use of drugs may help the addict seek out, for example, money for drugs instead of using the same money for food or clothing (Esterly & Neely, 1997). In a guilt addiction, compulsively blaming one's self may have a similar effect. In the case study, Harry compulsively practiced self blame for the problems in the family, and in doing so, manipulated family members to give him attention. Instead of being a part of solving family problems, Harry spent his time feeling self pity, and over time compulsively used self blame to justify his problems, much in the manner as any physically addicted person uses drugs to justify their problems.

Shame and Tolerance—It may be surprising to realize how quickly some people experiencing shame will develop an identity focusing on feelings of worthlessness, and it may be just as surprising how quickly these people get used to this identity. In a sense, shameful people may develop a tolerance against, compliments, praise or positive feedback. They may learn to tolerate feelings of shame, and may tolerate increased judgments of shame from others. For example, in the case study, Harry seemed used to his shame. He almost defended it. When his counselor tried to compliment him or look for positive growth, Harry found ways of sabotaging his actions. One might say that Harry had become tolerant of his shame, and would rather experience worthlessness than taking the risk of feeling complimented or accepted. Harry had developed a tolerance for his shame which seemed more of a viable option than reducing it.

Peoples' tolerance for shame seems to have similar characteristics to tolerance found in physical addictions. Many addiction's counselors recognize tolerance as one of the reasons for addicts to take increasing amounts of any given substance (Henderson, 2000). Addicts may need to take increasing amounts of a substance in order to maintain the same "high." In a similar manner, persons addicted to shame may need to increase their shame in order to maintain the same level of worthlessness in their lives. They may need to develop a tolerance to their shameful identity, in order to have justifications for their beliefs and behavior.

Seeking Acceptance and Addictive Thinking—It may seem a logical response for people addicted to guilt to seek acceptance through others. However, there may be an irony in seeking acceptance only to ultimately reject it. All of us have, at times, sought acceptance from others and when given it, we may have been comforted or motivated to feel better about ourselves. Yet, this does not appear to be the case when experiencing a guilt addiction. Many people addicted to guilt do not accept such compliments for fear of having to risk improvement in their lives. For example, in the case study, Harry was complimented by his wife, son, neighbors and his counselor. All of these people attempted to accept him. Yet, Harry did not listen to any of them. The question may be "Why not?"

One possibility is that an emotional addiction to guilt was controlling his thinking. Instead of responding positively to what was being said, Harry was only listening to those words that would help him stay addicted to guilt. Such addictive thinking had little investment in being accurate. Harry could have thought, "It is really touching how many people care for me. I cannot let them down." Instead Harry's addictive thinking may have sounded more like this, "Why are all of these people caring about me. Don't they know that I am a loser?" Harry's ability to think negative thoughts in spite of positive support demonstrated how his thinking was more controlled by his addiction than by what was being said by others.

Inferiority and Withdrawal—As stated in the last section, "Instead of Harry seeking acceptance and being comfortable with it when achieved, Harry was drawn to thoughts and feelings of shame, and he fought to uphold this inferior perspective about his identity." Again, why would anyone who was seeking acceptance reject it when obtained? The answer may lie in the withdrawal that Harry might experience if he embraced the positive views of others. In a sense, his addiction to guilt may be stronger than his ability to accept positive growth and change. Actually, the opposite may be more accurate. Harry seemed to be in a better position to see the world as if he was doing something wrong, thus keeping the vicious cycle of guilt ongoing. He may eventually depend on guilt as a way of avoiding the withdrawal experienced when trying to give it up.

In many respects, peoples' addiction to guilt may have similar consequences regarding withdrawal, as found in physical addictions. We know that withdrawal from a physical addiction creates imbalances in peoples' bodies that generate physical and psychological symptoms (Hood, 2005). In a similar manner, withdrawal from a guilt addiction may create a similar disruption with an emphasis more on the social rather than the physical. In Harry's case, he seemed to be experiencing anxiety at the thought of counseling gaining momentum towards personal growth. Harry seemed to sabotage the counseling sessions in order to avoid withdrawal, so he could continue to feel that he was wrong.

Emotional Connections

Occasionally, guilt addictions will connect with other physical or process oriented addictions where connections are established between these patterns, making it more difficult for people to separate physical and emotional addictions. They may, in fact, have to face both in order to achieve a level of recovery in their lives. The following are two examples of connections between physical and emotional addictions where solving other addictions may also require facing an emotional addiction to guilt:

Guilt Addiction and Alcohol Addiction—Have you ever had a recovering alcoholic in counseling, possibly he or she has not had a drink for many years, yet appears to be what some might call, a "Dry Drunk?" (Davis & Jansen, 1998). Sometimes the connection between alcohol and guilt can be a difficult phenomenon to understand. There seems to be no doubt that some recovering alcoholics have shared their regrets, blame and shame either in a counseling setting or at some form of Alcoholics Anonymous meeting. This can have a healing effect on someone who may have come to the conclusion that their abuse of alcohol has hurt them, their families and others who sustained their abuse of alcohol. However as addiction's counselors, we may have a client who has intentions that seem different than healing or gaining support. This may be a client who has traded in an alcohol addiction for a guilt addiction. The following example may shed some light on this phenomenon:

Example—George judiciously attended Alcoholics Anonymous meeting almost every night of the week for ten years. He seemed to thrive on the meetings, especially when he was able to be the center of attention. Georg was an excellent story teller, and he would share many stories of the horrib behavior he practiced while drinking. He also would make statements such a "I am going to devote the rest of my life to helping others with drinking prol lems, so they do not end up like me." However, the time George spent helpi others was limited. That does not mean he did not make attempts. Unfortu nately, for those George attempted to help, it was only a matter of time befo he refocused his help back on himself. It almost seemed that George use helping as a disguise so that he could talk about himself and fortunately f George, most people felt sorry for such a "nice guy" that they would def their problems to hearing about George's former life.

When his addiction's counselor pointed out to him that possibly he wa using guilt as a way of avoiding growth and change, George became offende "How can you say that my relating to others can be a problem? I try to hel others who hopefully will not end up like me." However, George did not see to have such a bad life. As long as he whined about his life, it seemed rich an full. Yet, George's shame seemed like an addictive trap to his counselor wh observed that George had no intention of giving up his shame. He seemed t have developed a tolerance for it, and blaming himself only made his storie more rich and interesting. His counselor believed that as long as George fe guilty he would receive a steady stream of attention, unfortunately at the ex pense of others, who could have benefited from his help.

Summary—This example should not be confused with all of those recove ing alcoholics who do help people by telling their stories and listening to oth ers. However, in the case of George, his tendencies seemed more along th lines of someone who had traded in one addiction for another. He seemed t have the need to feel guilt, and share it with others, more in the manner o needing a drink or one drink not being enough, and developing a tolerance fo more. In some respects, George may have become just as intoxicated with h guilt as he was with his alcohol.

For addiction's counselors, George's behavior may be something to loo for when working with clients who have difficulty letting go of guilt. Wit guilt, ultimately the question that becomes most important is, "What are yo going to do about it?" If a client decides to face guilt and work through it, the the results can be a client that wants to move on, and change his or her lif However, if an addiction's counselor has strong difficulty helping a client l go of guilt, then the guidelines for understanding an addiction to guilt may b appropriate.

Guilt Addiction and Bulimia—At times, people can have a combination of problems where not treating them together may create a different outcome (Skinstad & Swain). This can be seen in the case of people suffering from bulimia. Ironically, people who purge may feel guilty if they purge and may feel equally as guilty if they do not. Somewhere in the feelings of a bulimic person there may be a sense of guilt that is just as difficult to encounter as bulimia.

It may be important for counselors to consider facing the emotions of a bulimic from an addictions point of view, and especially when considering guilt. For a bulimic person, the danger of feeling guilty and having it reinforce the bulimia may be substantial. It may be that in some cases, guilt and bulimia feed off of each other, causing guilt to increase one's need to purge, and one's need to purge creating more feelings of guilt. The following example may be something to consider when treating a client for bulimia:

Example—Recently, Nancy spent a significant amount of time purging in the bathroom of her apartment. She was a 28 year old single woman who held down a high powered job, which seemed to require quick meals filled with thousands of calories. Needless to say, Nancy understood food. In her case, if you ate too much of it, then you became fat, a physical state she dreaded under any circumstances. Purging allowed her to eat the food then quickly get rid of it before there were added numbers to her apartment scale. Though she knew this behavior was unhealthy, she justified it by saying to herself, "I need to look thin to be successful at my job." And, who could argue with this thought. At her place of employment, social pressure remained high, and one's weight seemed fully absorbed in that pressure.

One evening, Nancy was looking in her bathroom mirror, and noticed that her teeth seemed to be turning an ashen color of gray. She knew what this meant. Stomach acid had damaged them from constant purging, and she needed to do something about it. However, instead of directly facing the problem, she purchased "white strips" from the local drug store in an attempt to cover up the damage. The strips seemed to work, yet she could not stop blaming herself for being so foolish for the damage to her teeth.

Unfortunately for Nancy, the purging continued. Actually, it seemed to get worse. Anytime she was out in public and people were laughing, Nancy would cover her mouth; even though, her teeth seemed reasonably normal. Yet, her shame for purging, whitening and covering up her mouth were having their toll on her self esteem. Instead of being content with her methods for justifying her subversive behavior, Nancy felt inferior and seemed to believe that getting acceptance from others would help. Even though her popularity did not change, Nancy was no less insecure. She was ashamed of her purging, yet her purging was increasing because of her shame. Nancy had as big a problem with guilt as she did with bulimia.

Summary—Nancy's response to her bulimia did not seem to solve the problem. In some respects, her solutions created a bigger and more complex set of circumstances for her to face. Nancy found herself in a reciprocal conflict where her bulimia was feeding into her guilt, and her guilt was feeding back into her bulimia (Ladd, 2007). She had a certain compulsion to purge, yet she also had a compulsion to blame herself for this action. Also, she depended on the way she looked to maintain a certain self-image; however, her purging and the whitening of her teeth caused her to feel ashamed of the self image she had created.

For addiction's counselors or mental health counselors, an understanding of the reciprocal relationship between bulimia and guilt, may have an impact concerning a counselor's thinking about both of these problems. For example, it may be important to work closely on themes such as, regret, blame, shame and inferiority when treating clients for bulimia. The possible reciprocal relationship between bulimia and guilt seems too enmeshed to overlook, and it may be that a client's guilt addiction may reinforce a bulimic disorder, and a bulimic disorder may lead to a guilt addiction. In either case, the emotions of the client with bulimia need to be addressed, and the possibility of these emotions developing into an addiction need to be considered, if this and other eating disorders are to be perceived correctly by a competent counselor.

Potential Counseling Solutions

- The more direct addiction's counselors can be with clients, the more difficult it may become for clients to subtly act as if something is wrong (Jeffery & White, 2005). Subtle wrong doing seems to flourish in the vague language expressed by clients upholding a guilt addiction. The more assertively the client expresses his or her feelings and behavior, the more difficult for clients to uphold that they are doing something wrong.

- Sometimes, an inexperienced counselor may fall into the trap of actively listening to a litany of regrets without helping the client become more specific with these experiences. Any form of sincere listening by the counselor, without helping the client to become specific and clear on what exactly they regret, seems less effective in discussing guilt in an addiction's counseling setting (Lemanski, 2000).

- The blaming stage in a pattern of guilt can blur peoples' problems through the use of generalizations (Marlatt & Gordon, 1995). It may require an addiction's counselor to focus on generalizations with guilty clients. For example, if clients says, "I never do anything right." an addiction's counselor may say, "So everything you have done today was wrong. You got out of the wrong side of the bed. You ate the wrong food and did everything wrong at work." The ability of the counselor to help guilty clients not to generalize may determine whether the stages of guilt are allowed to continue, or are redirected to solving specific problems.

- It seems far easier to help clients with their regrets or even with their generalizations of self-blame. In both of these settings, the counselor can rely on some form of cognitive or behavioral therapy, or both, to demonstrate ways of pinpointing guilt (Longabaugh & Morgenstern, 2004). However, with a client experiencing shame, the counselor has the added responsibility of exploring their clients' conclusions regarding their identity.

- Counseling clients with a guilt addiction probably will include some form of seeking acceptance. Sometimes it is seeking acceptance from others outside the counseling session, while other times, it may be the act of seeking acceptance from the counselor (Weiss, 2001). In either of these scenarios, it may be that seeking acceptance is an attempt to cover up one's feelings of shame.

Guilt Addiction Short List

- A subtle sense of wrong doing can be the beginning stage of guilt.

- Be specific when dealing with a client's regret.

- A client who practices self blame needs to focus on personal behavior and not on personal identity.

- Shame when experiencing guilt, is more an identity crisis.

- Shameful clients may seek acceptance from others, or possibly the counselor.

- Guilty clients may create more feelings of doing something wrong.

- Being direct and specific works well with guilty clients.

- Have clients experiencing guilt become descriptive, not judgmental.

- Guilty clients may develop a high tolerance for shame.

- Try to redirect the locus of control away from others and back to the guilty client.

- Guilty clients may fall into a "safe rut" and experience withdrawal symptoms when trying to get out of it.

- Compulsive blaming may be a sign of a guilt addiction.

- Wanting acceptance and needing acceptance are different phenomena when counseling guilty clients.

- Clients who feel ashamed may have developed a tolerance to their shame.

- Occasionally, an addiction to alcohol can be replaced by an addiction to guilt.

- Bulimia and feeling guilty can create a guilt addiction.

Format for Other Emotional Connections

This is an opportunity to develop a connection between a guilt addiction and some other real life experience. This could mean making a connection between guilt addiction and some form of physical addiction, or a connection with another process oriented addiction. Also, this could be a connection between a guilt addiction and a mental health disorder. Finally, this could be a connection between a guilt addiction and an everyday life experience where a guilt addiction makes an impact on this experience:

Briefly describe the connection between a guilt addiction and your chosen phenomenon:

Write an example of how a guilt addiction is connected to your chosen phenomenon:

Summarize your thinking on this connection:

Chapter 7: Jealousy Addiction

Figure 7

Background

Some researchers believe that jealousy is an essential part of our human nature and the phenomenon of jealousy exists in many different ways all over the world (Kristtianson & Griffiths, 2002). It appears that all cultures manifest some form of jealousy, especially between the sexes, and it becomes difficult to imagine jealousy not being an innate part of gender differences, and the conflicts that may arise from these differences (Durell, Brady, Monair & Congdon, 2007). Furthermore, we find a rich history of literary writings discussing the jealous differences between men and women, and these writings solidly confirm the common experience held by jealousy in relationships (Lloyd, 1995).

Yet, the differences between men and women or the innate jealous characteristics found in all of us, may lead to conclusions that are stereotypical, at best. Statements such as, "There will always be jealousy between the sexes because men and women are different" or "There is little that can be done about human jealousy because it is an innate characteristic of human nature." are statements that do not inform us of the everyday reality of experiencing jealousy.

First of all, jealousy can go beyond sexual connotations between men and women, such as found in professional jealousy (Beyan, 2004). Here the jealous behavior seems more concerned with "professional turf" rather than sex. Or, in instances of "sibling rivalry" where brothers and sisters find they are experiencing jealousy where positions in the family seem in jeopardy of being lost to someone who might change them or take them away (Lamb & Sutton-Smith, 1992).

Yet, even these examples do not describe an understanding of jealousy that will help us define it in more general terms. If you study the everyday interactions of jealousy, the following definition may come closer to the essence of most jealous experiences. Simply put, "Jealousy is the fear of losing something to someone else" (Ladd, 2005). Whether it is sexual, professional or based on rivalry among peers, jealousy is the act of having something and being afraid someone will take it away.

Within this definition of jealousy, most of us can remember times when we were afraid someone or some event would take away what we called our own, and we probably acted defensively to make sure whatever we were protecting did not get out of our grasp. Such experiences of jealousy seem common in a world where holding on to someone or something helps us feel secure, at least theoretically.

However, there are people who seem to go beyond our common understanding of jealous behavior. These are people who seem to let the theme of jealousy dominate their everyday actions with others (Bevan, 2004). These are jealous people who may go, to what some of us would consider "unusual extremes" to possess, horde or dominate another person or thing. Within this category of jealous behavior, we may find people addicted to a fear of losing something, so extreme that they are willing to use whatever means necessary to protect what they believe are their possessions. Such people run the risk of becoming addicted to a phenomenon that may chronically possess them; rather than, having feelings of jealousy *only when* there is fear that something may be lost. Such people may develop a dependency on jealousy to the point where being jealous causes them major symptoms of withdrawal both physically and emotionally. These people may have addictive tendencies yet justify their actions as acceptable, even when they have become highly unacceptable to the people around them.

Case Study

Frank appeared to everyone who knew him as a very jealous man. This was especially evident to his wife, Donna. It seemed that Frank had an obsession with keeping her behavior under control. This was ludicrous to the people who knew them since Donna would not even think of making a move without Frank's approval. However, this became the basis of why Frank was now mandated by the Courts to seek professional counseling.

Reluctantly, Frank participated in counseling by telling a story of violence and abuse. He prided himself as a man who women seemed to love, yet in his marriage, Frank hardly reflected love. For example, if Donna wanted to talk to her friends, Frank would control the amount of time she spent with them. Or, if she tried to meet the needs of their two children, Frank would tell her to pay attention to him, not them. However, it was his use of violence that forced him into counseling. He had a pattern of warning his wife about almost anything that he disapproved of, and his constant claiming of her time made the relationship threatening and dangerous. When he hit her, there were always justifications by him for his actions. He would say statements such as, "Well, I warned her!" Or, "The way she acts shows me that she had it coming." These and other pronouncements made Frank a difficult client. He did not believe that any wrongdoing had taken place.

Actually, Frank called his behavior "love". He truly believed that by possessing his mate, and controlling her behavior, he was acting as a loving partner. Yet, something seemed critically wrong to his counselor with this argument. It appeared that Frank practiced similar behavior at work where he protected his "turf" so new employees would not possess his position at the office. Or, when he participated in sports, he seemed to get upset when someone from his own team performed well. He desired getting all of the credit for most areas of his life, and found it difficult to share success with others.

In counseling, Frank resisted any notion that his behavior was unacceptable, even when the Courts accused him of domestic violence. His thinking was more about protecting his property, even when part of that property seemed to be another human being. Actually, Frank showed numerous odd patterns of behavior while in counseling. For example, he would interrupt each session by checking in with someone on his cell phone, and when the counselor would point out this pattern of behavior, he would retort that, "Can't you see that I care about people and want to look after them." In response to such statements, the counselor confronted him with the possibility that maybe it was not care, but being constantly jealous of other people having their own time. During such confrontations, Frank became extremely angry and began to argue how counseling was a complete waste of time, and hitting his wife was an isolated incident, a mistake that would not happen again. In spite of these statements, the counselor held his ground and stopped him from calling.

Yet, Frank could not live up to the declaration of "no cell phones" during

the counseling session. He frantically wanted to know what others were doin
It seemed that claiming and controlling others was something he depended (
and his counselor witnessed symptoms of withdrawal when he could not be
control of making these inappropriate phone calls. Furthermore, the level (
violence he was able to justify and tolerate in his marriage, without any sig)
of personal blame, left his counselor believing that Frank had a high toleran(
for violence and abuse. Frank's counselor concluded that he had an addictic
where jealousy controlled him. Much like an addict takes a drink or inhales a
addictive substance, Frank needed similar fixes on a daily basis. The thoug'
of having symptoms associated with jealousy seemed out of the question f(
him. Yet, Frank was in denial. He saw his behavior as filled with concern f(
others. If only people would listen to what he was saying, then life would pr(
ceed in an orderly and productive manner.

The Experience of Jealousy

Jealousy seems to be an escalating emotion that develops when peop
lack confidence and security, and become afraid of losing some "one" or son
"thing". Under this premise, jealous people make attempts at getting life bac
the way it used to be before they were provoked by some outside thre;
(Bevam & Samter, 2004). Unlike envy, where people feel they desire som(
thing and seek their desires, jealousy is the act of protecting what people fe(
they already have obtained (Figure 7). However, jealousy has some traits sim
lar to the emotion of greed — not so much in obtaining goals at all costs, b(
in the hoarding behavior where both jealousy and greed eventually make a
tempts at holding on to what was obtained, and protecting it from others wh
may want these acquired possessions.

Usually, jealousy begins in dramatic ways. There seems to be little my;
tery surrounding the behavior of jealous people when they are afraid of losin
something. For example, it does not take members of a family long to reco;
nize when someone in the family has become jealous. They may send very d
rect signals to others stating, "Do not try and take away my possessions or m
personal control." In this manner, jealous people create numerous warnin
signals where others need to back off or back down, until the fear of losin
something has passed.

Sometimes, simply to understand that jealous people are afraid of losing something alters their behavior, where outsiders will not disturb the boundaries or the "turf" established by jealous people (Figure 7). Yet, being aware and backing away from the boundaries of jealousy may not always be possible. Occasionally, these boundaries are crossed regardless of another's awareness, and this causes warning signals to be sent out, fundamentally with the message, "You are stepping over the line. Get back!" Sometimes these signals are disguised as a look or a gesture indicating that the person or persons are crossing the line. Other times, they may come in the form of distractions where the violators must "mind read" exactly what is meant by these warning signals, and sometimes our guesses are inaccurate.

Yet, many of us have had the experience of feeling protective of our possessions or of significant others that we know and love, and sometimes the people we know and love can be threatening to us. Within our fear of losing something, warning signals may be sent; even though, we run the risk of objectifying others as though they were someone or something to possess. Yet, we send these warning signals in order to counteract the fear that seems associated with jealousy. Many of us fall into the category of being afraid of losing something or someone, and it is not that uncommon for us to send out subtle warning signals when we fear losing time, control, love or "turf".

However, sending out warning signals may not be enough. Jealousy seems to be an escalating emotion where more action may be required if the warning signals in jealousy do not work. At this juncture, there is a tendency to "up-the-anti" by putting in a claim as a response to the ignored warnings (Figure7). Claiming is an overt way of drawing attention to the jealous situation that goes beyond any indirect warning signal. In many ways, claiming in jealousy tries to restore a sense of security and confidence that, what is in fear of being lost will not be lost. Unfortunately, restoring security is not always the case. Sometimes claiming someone or some thing in jealousy can lead to counter-claiming where another party is just as threatened with losing something. An example of this can be seen in single parent family situations where a new significant other enters the picture, and one of the children of the single parent puts in a jealous claim, in fear of the new boyfriend or girlfriend claiming the parent for his or her own. Numerous conflicts can develop when two different people are claiming another person for themselves.

However, this phenomenon is not exclusively reserved for single parent families. Any number of situations can occur where a claim is made only to have someone else make a counter claim. The important point to remember is that the claiming behavior of jealous people seems to escalate the experience of jealousy. Sometimes to the point that such escalations can lead to the use of force.

One of the dangers in the escalating tendency of the experience of jealousy is that jealous warning signals can lead to claims and claims can lead to the use of force (Figure 7). For example, in the case study, Frank entered counseling as a consequence for a domestic violence charge where, in his mind, the use of force seemed justified. If we look more closely at this reaction, it may become more understandable. In his thinking, he believed that sufficient warning signals were sent and appropriate claims were made; therefore, he now had a justification for using force. We might even hear Frank obstinately saying to his counselor, "Well! I warned her!"

It is the use of force that can make jealousy a dangerous, unjustifiable response to a fear of losing something. However, other consequences can appear beyond making justifications for one's behavior. Force has a way of putting the jealous experience beyond simple warning signals or embarrassing claims. It seems much more difficult to treat jealousy after someone has used force; rather than, after one has used warning signals or claims. Furthermore, using force as an expression of jealousy has contributed to the cultural phenomenon of domestic violence which has become an escalating problem in our society.

Unfortunately, understanding the use of force and its association to jealousy may not change the thinking of persons with jealous feelings. In fact, it may have the opposite effect. Some jealous people may defend their behavior by stating that such actions are not jealousy at all but a form of *possessive love* (Figure 7). The argument may be that if you love someone or some thing, then you protect and defend that love. Within such thinking, defending one's mate, one's honor or one's "turf" can be an act of passion rather than an act of force. Such defensive statements have been heard by many counselors who have tried to re-direct jealousy away from force toward more constructive feelings and behaviors.

However, practicing possessive love as a reason for using force may not help jealous people lessen their fear of losing something. Possessive love may have the opposite effect. It may create a climate of jealousy where those around jealous people also feel that force is acceptable, thus creating more reasons to use force (Ladd, 2005). In the case study, Frank defended his behavior to his counselor and seemed more convinced that domestic violence in his family situation was justified. However, his defense of possessive love seemed to make him more defensive.

Ironically, people's fear of losing something may cause them to end up losing the very possession they are protecting (Figure 7). Jealousy can fall into a self-fulfilling prophecy where the more jealous people defend losing something, the more they become afraid of losing something (Lloyd, 1995). Thus the cycle has an opportunity to begin again. In other words, fear of losing something increases jealous peoples' chances of losing something.

In the case study, Frank ran the risk of losing his relationship with his wife. He may have believed that his jealousy was an expression of possessive love; however, that may not be the way his wife saw it. She may have seen his behavior as an expression of uncontrolled violence. Furthermore, even if he believed that controlling his violence would lead to controlling his partner, there still was no guarantee that his diluted jealous behavior would work. What he may not have understood was that, the act of forgoing force may not, in any way, stop his fear of losing something. Frank still must contend with possessing and controlling those people that he claimed to love.

How a Jealousy Addiction Works

If you look at the pattern found in Figure 7 in this chapter, it may become apparent that we may experience any number of the stages relating to jealousy. Even the experience of sending out warning signals or putting in claims, may be found in our personal judgments and decision making. To feel afraid of losing something, to desire claiming what we feel are our possessions, seems to be a common phenomenon in everyday living. Some of us have obtained certain goals, and the thought of losing them can lead to fear and insecurity.

However, there may be people who go beyond experiencing jealousy as one more of life's experiences. These people may treat jealousy much like an addict treats addiction. They may not possess jealousy; but rather, jealousy possesses them. The following are guidelines for identifying an emotional addiction to jealousy:

Fear of Losing Something and Dependency—Most of us have experienced a fear of losing something but with time, such fears pass and we hopefully return to more safe and secure circumstances. This does not appear to be the case in a jealousy addiction. These people seem to keep a constant vigilance on remaining safe and secure where a fear of losing something can become a dependency. For example, in the case study, Frank went far beyond *wanting* to control his wife. He *needed* to control her, in order to avoid being threatened. In many ways, Frank had developed a dependency around his wife remaining a certain way. Any changes in her behavior were seen as unacceptable, and possibly threatening. Under these circumstances, even talking to a friend could be seen as a threat. In order to control Frank's fears, his wife had to be consistent, according to the roadmap for living he demanded within their relationship.

In the case study, Frank had developed a dependency on life remaining predictable, and any changes in behavior around him appeared as a threat (Kristiansson, 2002). For example, he depended on others as a crutch to cope with his fears, yet he may have alienated those he needed by attacking them. Paradoxically, he needed others yet may have treated them with disdain. We see similar paradoxes in the realm of physical addictions. For example, alcoholics may depend on alcohol as a crutch for dealing with their problems, but depending on alcohol may block them from solutions to these problems. Parenthetically, people addicted to jealousy that depend on force to resolve issues of insecurity, are much like people depending on gasoline to put out a fire. The saying, "We hurt the people we love most." may have validity for those with a jealousy addiction.

Warning Signals and Compulsive Behavior—People addicted to jealousy may require constant vigilance regarding their dependency on others (Marlatt & Donovan, 2005) and compensating for such a dependency may require reminders to others that, "I am depending on you to stay in line and not make waves." However, in an imperfect world, depending on others may not satisfy the dependency needs of people with a jealousy addiction. Furthermore, jealousy addiction does not appear to engender large amounts of trust in others. In response to the lack of trust, people with this form of addiction may begin to send out warning signals when they feel others are not living up to their imposed codes of behavior. For example, in the case study, Frank had an odd habit of checking in on people by cell phone even during counseling sessions. One may believe Frank's argument that checking in with others, was an act of well intentioned concern. However, another motive may be in action. If Frank had become addicted to jealousy, his checking in may be a compulsive act of distrust in others. He may have needed to remind others of their *duties* to him. From this perspective, Frank may have fallen into a form of compulsive warning signals based on distrust

We can see similar behavior in physical addictions where people's compulsive behavior stems from a dependency on drugs. In this area of addiction, physical dependency may cause compulsive acts of distrust to be sent to others. This also can be seen in a jealousy addiction. For example, in the case study, Donna, Frank's wife, did not know when Frank's compulsion to check in on her would take place. She had little warning as to when these warning signals would disrupt her everyday living, or when she must keep up her guard as a defense against these signals. Frank's compulsive warning signals may have caused Donna to suffer from emotional exhaustion, making Donna more cautious and Frank more insecure. Its seems the compulsive behavior found in a jealousy addiction is characterized by the jealous person posing the threat of constant warning signals, while others ward off the threat of emotional exhaustion and distrust.

Claims and Withdrawal—In some cases of jealousy, sending warning signals is effective, at least to people addicted to jealousy. If others comply with the warning signals, then the receivers of these signals have complied, and find themselves waiting for the next round of signals to be sent. However, what happens if they do not comply or they ignore these warning signals? For example, in the case study, Frank's counselor did not comply with his need to use the cell phone. He confronted Frank and set off a conflict between them. The discussion that followed created a chain of emotions in Frank, when he was asked not to call others. However, Frank had a dramatic response to his counselor's request. One could argue that Frank had withdrawal symptoms of anxiety and anger when he was forced to stop calling people during counseling. It appeared that Frank *must* call them not that he would *like* to call them, and had symptoms of withdrawal when he could not call them.

Under these conditions, it may make sense that Frank went beyond simply sending warning signals to others. If warning signals do not work, people addicted to jealousy, may increase pressure on others by putting in a claim. Claiming is an overt way of applying pressure on others beyond any

indirect warning signals. In the case study, Frank put in his claim to control t
counseling session while his counselor was forced to counter-claim in order
continue with counseling.

The question that may need an answer is, "Why would Frank need to ca
people during a counseling session and why would he argue about it with h
counselor?" "Why not call after the session?" The answer may fall into th
category of being addicted to jealousy, and having withdrawal sympton
when unable to call. In physical addictions, we see a similar pattern whei
people have withdrawal symptoms, and need to get a "fix" regardless of ho
inappropriate such behavior appears to others (Bell, 2002). In the case stud
Frank exhibits withdrawal symptoms, and needed his "fix" by trying to clai
control over the counseling session.

Force and Tolerance—In the case study, Frank used force on his wif
Donna but appeared to have ample justifications such as, "It was a one tin
event." or "She knows I love her." The question that may need to be answere
is, "How did Frank get to the point where he showed little remorse but amp
justifications for his behavior? The answer may be found in the phenomeno
ogy of a jealousy addiction. Within this phenomenon, we are characterizin
people who have a fear of losing something, try to keep others in line by wan
ing them, put in claims when they do not heed these warnings, and may fin
force to be the next logical step in their thinking. Under these circumstances,
may make sense why people addicted to jealousy are constantly building a
emotional tolerance for their behavior from one stage of jealousy to anothe
Much in the manner that alcoholics drink more alcohol because their toleranc
level for alcohol increases with continued drinking; people addicted to jea
ousy do not develop a physical tolerance, yet show signs of an emotional to
erance for their increased aberrant behavior.

It may be that people addicted to jealousy have developed a level of to
erance where their behavior appears justifiable, even in the use of some for
of force. This seemed to be the perception held in the case study where Fran
treated hitting his wife as an isolated incident that he could tolerate. Possibl
through a series of warning signals and constant claims made against Donna
behavior, Frank may have said to others that using force was wrong; howeve
emotionally he may have developed a tolerance where he personally exper
enced little shock or disgust for his behavior. In seems that any number of vi
lent acts happen because of this thinking where force is tolerated as the logic:
next step in a jealousy addiction (Shipway, 2004).

Defensive Behavior and Addictive Thinking—It may seem a b
absurd that anyone would vehemently defend a position that justifies a jealou
use of force. Yet, such defensive behavior may contribute to the thinkin
found in any number of addictions where, defending one's thinking can be
come more important than logically solving a problem (Twerski, 1990). In th
case of jealousy addiction, this may be especially true. By others showing n

compliance to warning signals or giving into claims, or tolerating the use of force, jealousy addicts may seriously believe that they are the victims of unco-operative behavior caused by others. Their defensive behavior may be a state-ment that justifiable action must be taken when the fear of losing something "rears its ugly head." Within such addictive thinking, being defensive and be-having in threatening ways may be acceptable behavior, and force becomes one more behavior to make such a position valid. For example, in the case study, Frank thinks more like an addict than a logical person. He saw life in black and white terms. He had a compulsive desire to get his needs met and his inflexible point of view made it difficult to grasp the perspective of others. Frank suffered from addictive thinking that made him stubborn, unresponsive and dangerous. He seemed more determined to manipulate the circumstances in his life then to face those circumstances that haunted his fear of losing something.

Losing Something and Denial—So people addicted to jealousy have come full circle; their fear of losing something forces them to compulsively send out warning signals, and their unanswered compulsive warning signals throws them into withdrawal where they begin to claim, yet their unsuccessful claiming helps them accept and tolerate the use of force. However, using force does not make them any less defensive about their feelings or their behavior. Under these conditions, people addicted to jealousy ironically may lose some-thing, yet may be in denial that anything was lost.

This lack of understanding that the process of jealousy may cause a sense of losing the very thing you are afraid of losing, creates an absurd sense of de-nial that can have a forceful impact on jealous people. They may circle back for another round of warning signals, claims and force. Whether it is fear of losing a loved one to another or other fears such as; loss of face, loss of con-trol, loss of power or a loss of personal possessions, a jealous person's sense of denial can override an understanding of these losses, allowing people addicted to jealousy to start the process again.

In the case study, what real lesson did Frank learn from his jealous behav-ior? Did he truly believe counseling would help him, or was he in a state of denial where he would rather go to jail than face an addiction that threatened the way he interacted with others?

Emotional Connections

Occasionally, jealousy addictions will connect with other physical or process oriented addictions where connections are established between these patterns, making it more difficult for people to separate physical and emotional addic-tions. They may, in fact, have to face both, in order to achieve a level of re-covery in their lives. The following are two examples of connections between physical and emotional addictions where solving the physical addiction may require also facing an emotional addiction to jealousy:

Jealousy Addiction and Sexual Addiction—Some of the behaviors marking a sexual addiction are; multiple affairs, compulsive masturbation, consistent use of pornography, exhibitionism, voyeurism, sexual harassment and molestation or rape. Within these and other symptoms, one specific theme seems to resonate. Sexual addiction is just as much about lack of attachment and intimacy as it is about sex (Griffith-Shelley, 1997). It is in this regard, that an emotional connection appears to exist between a jealousy addiction and a sexual addiction.

It may be important for counselors to consider both, when treating clients with sexual addictions. First of all, a lack of intimacy and acceptance can be found in both addictions, and both seem to overact in compensation for this phenomenon. Sexual addiction having aberrant expressions of sex and sex related activities, makes up for an addict's failure at attachment and intimacy. In jealousy addiction, overreacting to a fear of losing something is an attempt to make up for lack of perceived acceptance by others, and the problems with intimacy that may follow. Furthermore, both addictions fail to understand acceptance or intimacy as fundamental ingredients in the resolution of their problems. When a sex addict finally can accept intimacy, then pornography, exhibitionism or a compulsive need for sex can be minimized. In a similar fashion, when a jealousy addict finally can accept the intimacy that comes from mutual cooperation with others, then warning signals, claims and the use of force also can be minimized. The following example may be important to consider when treating a client for a sexual addiction:

Example—Mike had a habit of collecting women much like some people collect stamps. He had come to counseling with his girlfriend, in order to get her help with insecurity. However, he did not ask for counseling for himself but commented that he "wanted the best for her". The first few sessions seemed to focus on Mary, Mike's girlfriend, but as sessions continued, it was obvious to the counselor that other dynamics were at work. Mary told the counselor of a sorted lifestyle where Mike was never home, and of the pornography and the bizarre sexual behavior that he demonstrated in and out of bed. Through Mary, the counselor discovered that Mike had several girlfriends that he would frequently see, until they made intimate remarks that put Mike on the road to the next lover. He seemed to have a fear of intimacy, yet bragged about his overactive performance in bed.

Since Mike would not agree to couples counseling, Mary's counselor focused on her co-dependency and her self esteem. After a series of sessions, Mary announced that next week would be her last because she planned to return home, a place located several States away. However, when Mike heard of Mary's plans, he beat her, and told her that she could not give up their love for each other. The next session, Mary entered counseling with a black eye and a bruised lip. She told her counselor that Mike had done this, but it was no surprise, because he beat all the women in his circle of friends. After a serious discussion, Mary's counselor convinced her to go to the police.

What the police found at Mike's house was an assortment of sadistic sexual implements, and a sophisticated collection of pornography. It appeared that Mike's sexual addiction caught up with him. Between the jealousy and the sex, Mike had developed a distorted perspective on relationships, one that would require more than law enforcement to resolve.

Ironically, part of Mike's sentence was to seek counseling and for some reason, Mary's counselor was his choice. As the sessions passed, it became obvious that Mike's fear of losing something was as strong as his fear of intimacy. Mike's counselor decided to combine counseling for a sexual addiction with counseling for an emotional addiction to jealousy.

Summary—In the example of Mike, it seemed difficult to treat his sexual addiction without considering treatment for his addiction to jealousy. Actually, it seemed that Mike had a pattern of substituting his jealousy addiction into his relationships, when his sexual addiction became too violent and abusive. Yet, the opposite also seemed true. Mike would respond to his jealousy addiction by becoming more sexually active, whether it was through behavior with other partners, or by entering a world of pornographic perversion.

For the counselor, it seemed difficult to treat Mike's sexual addiction without treating his jealousy addiction. Both seemed connected to Mike's inability to be intimate with others. In Mike's case, sexual performance might have been one more example of putting in a claim or using force found in people addicted to jealousy. The counselor had an opportunity to explore Mike's fear of intimacy through the guidelines of two addictions that seemed to work concurrently. It may be that Mike's resolution of his sexual addiction may have resolved his addiction to jealousy. It seemed a reasonable argument to treat both with the hope that one will negate the other.

Mike's emotions and his behavior seemed intricately connected. His sexual behavior seemed connected to his use of the emotion, jealousy, and jealousy seemed to be his emotion of choice when control over others by sexual violence did not work.

Jealousy Addiction and Borderline Personality Disorder—Some of the diagnostic features of borderline personality disorder are; frantic effort to avoid real or imagined abandonment, having unstable and intense interpersonal relationships, impulsivity and self-damaging behavior in such areas as sex and substance abuse and affective instability due to marked reactivity of mood (Martens, 2005; DSM IV, 2005). Here is where perceiving a personality disorder from an addictions point of view may add to the ability of a counselor to help clients with certain identity and abandonment issues. Counselors who treat borderline personality disorder have found clients to be difficult, especially in controlling their behavior. One possibility is to focus on borderline abandonment issues and visualize their connection to people addicted to jealousy, and their fear of losing something. In many ways, these phenomena are similar. Borderline personality disorder seems to focus on abandonment issues and a jealousy addiction focuses on fears of losing something. In many respects, both phenomena are originating from the same source. Abandonment may be as much connected to jealousy as it is to personality disorders. The difference being, that personality disorder's main focus is on causes and symptoms, while emotional addictions focus more on patterns. Combine these two together and it may create a more comprehensive understanding of when our clients feel abandoned. The following example may be an experience to consider when treating a client for borderline personality disorder:

Example—No one ever seemed to satisfy Linda. She had a whole book filled with people who she had some form of relationship, yet she had a difficult time keeping any of them, unless her friends got time off for good behavior. Even Linda's counselor had a difficult time when she asked for her undivided attention. Linda would do almost anything to have someone take away her insecurity, yet her ability to calm down and enjoy the company of others without a major crisis, seemed impossible. When she was around people, her behavior made them feel so uncomfortable that they would show extreme caution when she showed up. However, it seemed to be worse when she was alone. She would contact them by any means possible to make sure they were not being with others. Linda depended on others to calm her down, yet her behavior seemed to agitate others. Sometimes she would compulsively call them and make sure they were all right. Other times, she would make statements of possible suicide, in order to get their undivided attention.

This especially was true regarding her counselor. She was jealous of anyone who took up her counselor's time, and she would become disruptive, even in the waiting room. Linda was living on the borderline of life and found it difficult to hold onto love, or even be loved. Her extreme obsession with Jane, her counselor, became noticeable to anyone who knew and loved Jane. The reality was that Linda had become a stalker, and put in her claim every time she saw her for counseling. Jane knew that treating her for borderline personality disorder would be difficult. It always seemed to be difficult. However, Jane decided to take a different route. Instead of treating her for a mental disorder, Jane treated her for an emotional addiction to jealousy. She believed that if she could get Linda's jealousy under control, then it may be less problematic when counseling her borderline personality disorder. She believed that if she could reduce her fear of losing something, then Linda would stop claiming others for safety and security reasons.

Summary—In the example of Linda, it seems difficult to treat her borderline personality disorder without at least considering treatment for a jealousy addiction. Actually, it seemed like Linda used jealousy as a method for dealing with her abandonment issues, and justified her erratic behavior as forms of jealous claims that sought out feelings of love and security. Yet, both methods seemed to create less love or security; but instead, created a climate of chaos where Linda panicked or fell into constant crisis, while she pursued the comfort and security of others.

However, counselors may be of assistance to clients like Linda by having their borderline personality disorder combined with their jealousy addiction. However, this last statement may raise the question, "Why combine these two phenomena?" To answer this, we may want to consider with caution the treating of any personality disorder before treating peoples' addictions. This is certainly true with addictions to cocaine, methamphetamines or any other stimulants that mimic the symptoms found in personality disorders. In these cases, counseling professionals want to rule out a drug addiction before labeling a client with a personality disorder. This may be the case in counseling for an emotional addiction to jealousy. If a jealousy addiction is treated successfully, there may be no reason to diagnose or treat borderline personality disorder.

Potential Counseling Solutions

- A behavioral approach (Matlatt & Donovan, 2006) may be neede that systematically charts out when and where jealous people sen warning signals. Instead of compulsively trying to control insecuritie and fears, it may be more significant to understand when warnin signals are used. We see similar counseling methods used in helpin abusers understand their patterns of abuse (Morrison, Erooga & Beckett, 1994). Understanding jealous warning signals may benef from a similar approach.

- It may be important to point out to jealous clients the limitations of having inflexible boundaries in their lives, and how these boundarie can create more insecurity and fear. Ironically, rigid boundaries wi require an increased need to put in jealous claims, yet jealous claim may reinforce rigid boundaries, creating more possibilities for feelin threatened.

- Common ground is used in numerous conflict resolution problem but seems applicable to counseling for a jealousy addiction (Lade 2005). When a counselor can find common ground, then the need fe putting in a claim is neutralized. Common ground can make claimin unnecessary.

- One of the more effective counseling techniques when confrontin people with a jealousy addiction may be found in using some form o cognitive behavioral therapy (Neenan & Dryden, 2002). Part of coun seling for a jealousy addiction, seems to be working through the justi fications made by these clients regarding how they perceive their fea of losing something. If their view takes into account the feelings o others, then force may seem an unacceptable option.

- Many jealousy addicts have objectified people into mere possessions no matter how much they purport to care. This objectification, lead them to justifications which, in turn, leads to the use of force. Some where in this vicious cycle, an effective counselor may be able to dis rupt their objectifying behavior and thinking.

- It may be important for jealous clients to learn patterns of action, no reaction (Engel, 2002). When clients are afraid of losing something, i may be more effective in helping them with skills that assertivel confront this problem; rather than, aggressively causing more prob lems.

Jealousy Addiction Short List

- Fear of losing something can be the beginning stage in jealousy.

- Check to determine whether unresolved grief has created these fears.

- Map out a jealous person's warning signals when treating for jealousy.

- Claims in jealousy can be resolved by finding common ground.

- Make sure that jealous claims are not followed by counter claims.

- Watch for clients justifying force in jealousy experiences.

- Help jealous clients be assertive, not aggressive when afraid of losing something.

- Have clients understand that defensive behavior helps in clients losing something.

- Jealous clients may develop withdrawal symptoms when warning signals do not work.

- Try to understand a jealous client's high tolerance for using force.

- Compulsively sending warning signals can cause emotional exhaustion in others.

- Remember that jealousy is not only about being afraid of losing another person. It can be fear of losing "turf", time, power, face and control.

- Consider the connection between jealousy addiction and sexual addiction.

- In some cases, treat for an emotional addiction to jealousy before considering a diagnosis of borderline personality disorder.

- Counseling for emotional addiction may be the first step before treating a personality disorder.

Format for Other Emotional Connections

This is an opportunity to develop a connection between a jealousy addiction and some other real life experience. This could mean making a connection between a jealousy addiction and some form of physical addiction, or a connection with another process oriented addiction. Also, this could be a connection between a jealousy addiction and a mental health disorder. Finally, this could be a connection between a jealousy addiction and an everyday life experience where a jealousy addiction makes an impact on this experience:

Briefly describe the connection between a jealousy addiction and your chosen phenomenon:

Write an example of how a jealousy addiction is connected to your chosen phenomenon:

Summarize your thinking on this connection:

Chapter 8: Resentment Addiction

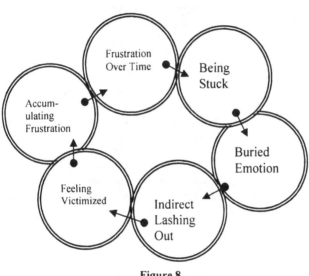

Frustration
Over Time

Being
Stuck

Accum-
ulating
Frustration

Buried
Emotion

Feeling
Victimized

Indirect
Lashing
Out

Figure 8

Background

Two words that ring loudly when discussing resentment in today's world, and throughout our history are freedom and oppression. Resentment is a common feeling we experience when freedom is denied (Peterson, 2002). Whether at the societal level under some form of dictatorship, or more close to home as in an abusive marriage or a dead end employment experience, resentment is the emotion that exemplifies the loss of freedom. And, with the loss of freedom may develop that frustrating occurrence of feeling stuck and victimized that we call oppression.

For example, history shows the United States of America harbored a culture where African Americans were formally without certain freedoms until the Civil Rights Amendment of 1964, and within this denial of freedom, was buried the seeds of oppression for millions of hard working Americans (Holloway, 1969). Of course, we can make examples of thousands of experiences throughout history where people lost their freedom and experienced oppression, yet do we fully understand the emotion of resentment that developed among these people?

Resentment seems to be an emotion that has conjured many labels. (Mainly, from those who have denied others their freedom.) Sometimes, resentment has been confused with laziness, where millions of people have had to bear the inaccuracies of such a label. Other times, it has been described as bitterness for a marriage filled with abuse, or the label of malcontent for a job that offers little advancement or promise.

One person who understood the emotion of resentment was the existential scholar, Max Scheler in his book, *Resentiment* (Scheler, 1961) where he skillfully depicts the impact of oppression on those who were promised freedom, yet wallowed away their lives in meaningless activity. On the political front, Martin Luther King, Jr. took on an entire political system that had racial detractors who saw his people as lazy, unmotivated and possibly, inferior (Pyatt, 1986). He understood the difference between laziness and resentment, and exemplified hope in his ground breaking speech, "I Have a Dream" (Bush, 2003).

From an emotional point of view, most of us who believe in freedom and find it lacking in our lives, may have experienced some form of resentment. Psychology most closely associates resentment with buried anger (Retzinger & Scheff, 2001) while sociologists may describe it as civilized anger (Scrull & Wyer, 1993) and the premise that it is buried or civilized does not make it any less abundant. In fact, in civilized countries, resentment is far more acceptable than anger, and we find it in the gossip and innuendo of our neighbors, our friends and even ourselves. It seems most probable that all of us have had resentments, or still have resentments toward situations that we find oppressive.

However, most of us do not harbor resentment, all of the time. It usually is connected to some circumstance where feeling stuck seems to be the prevailing emotion. Yet, there are people who feel resentment, no matter what circumstances arise. These are people where resentment muddies the problem, and actually causes a loss of freedom, and an establishment of oppression. These are people where resentment seems to be a chosen life style. We might say these people are emotionally addicted to resentment, and it permeates most of what they do.

This phenomenon can be seen in countless cases where freedom is restored, yet the words of oppression still are heard. With freedom comes responsibility (Schlipp, 1997), yet people who appear addicted to resentment may have withdrawal symptoms when asked to be responsible. They may depend on their resentment to continue an addictive way of life, and they may combine this emotional addiction with irresponsible forms of drug and alcohol addiction in order to justify their behavior, at least to themselves. The emotional addiction of resentment seems to be a common companion for some drug and alcohol abusers because it may give them the emotional state of mind to continue using. A resentment addiction also may allow our schools to label our children with numerous antisocial disorders where treatment for addiction is overlooked in preference for some type of psychotropic drug. In this chapter, we will explore the emotion of resentment, and try to understand its influence on addiction and mental health problems.

Case Study

Nicolas roamed the streets of New York City in a heroin daze, sarcastically lashing out at passers by who he viewed as targets of his personal frustration. Once a successful stock broker, he had fallen on hard times, and the mellow sensation of heroin was his downfall. Now he was homeless, both literally and figuratively. Not only did he live on the streets of New York, but found himself at odds with his country, his home for the past 42 years.

It was hard to remember when he first felt trapped in his work, but trapped he was, both emotionally and physically. At first, he coped with what he called his oppressive working conditions by hanging around the water cooler while criticizing those in authority. Yet, Nicholas was not only critical of his work environment. He had negative feelings toward his wife of ten years, and talked about her with a gang of similar malcontents from the neighborhood.

Somewhere, near the end of his marriage, he had bouts of anger that launched a series of referrals to psychiatrists. He found himself staying afloat through anti-anxiety and anti-depressant drugs. However, Nicholas had a better solution. Heroin entered his life through a girlfriend who he met in a popular night spot. At first, his friends commented on how satisfied he appeared, then his satisfaction quickly diminished with the frequency of heroin use, and this eventually led him to homelessness and addiction.

For many years, Nicholas roamed the New York streets, trying to justify his life to anyone who would listen, while indirectly keeping in touch with friends and relatives who did not completely abandon him. Finally, after much coaxing, Nicholas went to a methadone clinic where he slowly began to confront his addiction. Most of his treatment followed a detoxification schedule that eventually stopped his heroin use. At that point, those close to him truly believed he would recover, and continue a life of successful entrepreneurship on the New York Stock Exchange. Yet, something still was missing. His fight to become drug free seemed only part of his problem. He still seemed frustrated with the world around him, and he continued to make his life miserable along with those who he called friends.

Time went on and Nicholas continued his dissatisfaction, and unfortunately, with time he was beginning to revert back to old patterns and habits.

His friends finally convinced him to see a counselor, as a pro-active attempt at stopping his re-use of heroin. His first visit with Brad, the counselor who was recommended to him, became a much different experience than what he encountered when using heroin. Instead of focusing on Nicholas's addiction possibilities, Brad asked questions about his frustration and the sarcasm that seemed connected to it. He wanted to know why Nicholas seemed so stuck in such an unmotivated state, and why going back to being a stock broker seemed such an unreasonable request.

Brad understood that beyond an addiction problem, Nicholas was having emotional problems; however, they did not seem to fit any specific mental health disorder. Yet, he realized that being a former user of heroin did not guarantee that his client was not still addicted in some way. The conclusion that Brad eventually made was that his client had an addiction to resentment; and even though, he was not presently showing any symptoms of a physical addiction, Nicholas's condition still showed an addictive pattern.

During the next several months, Brad and Nicholas focused on an emotional addiction to resentment. With time, Nicholas began to realize that his loss of freedom and his obsession with oppression were phenomena of his own design. He began to understand the fallout in motivation and risk taking that seemed to accompany this addiction. Much like in his heroin use, Nicholas's addiction to resentment was slowly moving him back into a world of oppression and a personal loss of freedom.

The Experience of Resentment

Resentment is a subtle emotion that accumulates over time. It usually begins when we become frustrated with any given situation where freedom is taken away from us (Ladd, 1976) (Figure 8). In a civilized world, all of us have been in situations where we feel there is little we can do to change things. For example, frustrated with a dead end job, marriage, or lifestyle can bring anyone to feel resentment; however, resentment does not happen immediately whenever we feel stuck. It is the accumulation of resentment that sets it apart from other feelings such as, anger or revenge. Resentment is much too subtle to illicit an immediate response. For example, in the case study, Nicholas spent ten years accumulating his resentment toward his wife and his job. He did not immediately take on his problems with a pro-active stance. In fact, he did the opposite. He accumulated his frustration until heroin allowed him to un-stick himself from it.

In some respects, the accumulation of resentment over time may not be solely the fault of Nicholas's inability to face his problems. In First World countries, we live in an environment where resentment is far more acceptable than anger, (Fien, 1993) and where accumulating frustration seems less dangerous. Schools, marriages, workplace environments, will tolerate resentment in the fear of people becoming openly aggressive. Frustration over time seems more tolerable and acceptable when we realize the consequences of loosing a job, or leaving a marriage, or disrupting a school. Frustration over time seems to be one of our ways of coping with problems that appear too overwhelming to resolve.

Being Stuck

However, at some point, our subtle accumulation of our frustration may bring us to the realization that we are stuck with certain problems. This is a crucial stage in resentment because, up till this point, we probably have been accumulating our frustration unconsciously and unknowingly. At the point where we realize our accumulated frustration means, "I am stuck" is the point where we decide to give in to our problems, with the conclusion that no apparent solution seems possible (Figure 8). For example, in the case study, Nicholas concluded that life was a series of dead end propositions until he was introduced to heroin. He came to the conclusion that being in a bad marriage and a dead end job meant his life was filled with oppression, and he saw no way out.

Many of us have had the experience where we believed our plans held great promise for the future, and we invested time and effort into them, only to find at a future date, that we were now frustrated with these plans, and had to endure our past decisions, until better opportunities presented themselves. Therefore, the realization of being stuck in life is not unfamiliar to any of us who have risked and failed. Yet, staying stuck and realizing it, can change the direction our frustration will take. If we un-stick ourselves from situations that appear to have little freedom for change, then freedom is regained, and we are independent to pursue other adventures in life. If we do not, we may have to find a place for storing our frustration.

Stuck in untenable circumstances, resentful people bury their frustrations, and attempt to get on with their lives (Figure 8). With most of us, there seems to be some balance between those situations where we are stuck, and those that offer some form of freedom. In effect, most of us are not stuck all of the time. Some of us may be stuck at work, but find relief in our family and friends. Others may have physical exercise as a balance between a life style where inactivity takes up most of our schedules.

And, we may have other ways of bearing with feelings of being stuck. Some of us practice an "illusion of harmony" that makes our contrived happiness a bit more bearable. We may "put on a happy face" while we bury the frustrations of work, school or family life. Actually, buried emotions connected to resentment may be a choice to *implode* rather than *explode*. It appears that our Western Culture finds explosions far more dangerous than civilized implosions of frustration, (Scrull & Wyer, 1993) and our culture may actually reward us for burying our frustrations and not "making waves."

However, the realization of being stuck and burying our emotions may have its consequences. The constant brewing of buried frustration may lead us to anxiety, ulcers and other maladies that have a connection to buried feelings with no relief or release. For example, in the case study, it appears that Nicholas had many years where his buried emotions ate away at his optimism and self-confidence. Instead of facing his feelings of oppression, Nicholas buried these feelings until the remedy of heroin seemed a plausible solution. This is not to say that all heroin addicts are motivated by the possibility of heroin un-sticking them from a life of oppression. However, it does give, at least, one explanation why seemingly successful people become addicted. Eventually, buried feelings may find a way to express themselves, with heroin being one possible option.

Fortunately, most of us do not un-stick our buried frustrations by using heroin. However, the possibility of buried frustration eventually coming to the surface seems a probable event (Figure 8). Most of us have more socially acceptable ways of indirectly lashing out and relieving buried feelings. Sarcasm, joking, gossiping, the "silent treatment," are ways we indirectly get out the frustrations that have been cooking in our unconscious minds. To a certain extent, we find ways of dealing indirectly with those circumstances in life that take away our freedom and make us feel oppressed. For example, teachers who feel the brunt of an oppressive school climate may go to the "teacher's room" and gossip about other teachers, administrators and students. They may find such a room an ideal place to express their buried frustrations. By indirectly lashing out, they to a certain extent, relieve the symptoms of their frustrations. Much in the manner of an alcoholic having a drink in order to take the edge off his or her problems; resentful people may indirectly lash out in order to take off a similar edge.

Indirect lashing out may be one of the most common problems found in institutions, where the social climate is filled with frustration (Ladd, 2005). This phenomenon can be seen in the establishment of an institutional "grape vine" or gossip networks where people find comfort in others, suffering their same oppressive lifestyle. This may be where the saying, "Misery loves company" found its roots? Yet, many of us vent our frustrations with others and usually, we talk about something specific that helps us to express our buried feelings. However, venting our feelings in a direct way seems different than the indirect lashing out found in resentment. Instead of working through these feelings, resentful people seem to indirectly create a climate of more frustration where others begin to indirectly talk about each other.

Lashing out indirectly may relieve our frustrations, yet one reality seems to be missed. Usually, lashing out indirectly does not resolve the underlying problem (Figure 8). For example, gossiping to a friend about how your wife has oppressed you in your marriage may relieve built up frustrations, but may do little in changing the underlying marital conflict. Mocking your boss at the water cooler may relieve the frustrations of the moment, but may do little in changing the behavior of your boss. Unfortunately, constant indirect lashing out may reinforce one's views that he or she is stuck and oppressed. Much like an alcoholic takes a drink to take the edge off problems;

resentful people will lash out indirectly for the same reason. However, in both cases, problems usually are not resolved but only buffered, and eventually the stark reality of these problems reappear.

Over time, feeling like a victim may motivate people to let go of oppression and feel free. For example, Martin Luther King, Jr. had a political message in the 1960's to "let my people go!" (Kirk, 2006). He demonstrated the power of letting go of oppression and achieving freedom through nonviolence. Yet, it could be said that his message from a psychological standpoint, was a direct attack against the emotion of resentment, and the hold it had on some people. This is not to say that all cases of resentment leave people feeling victimized. However, feeling like a victim can slowly develop in the hearts and minds of anyone who feels oppressed. With time, this subtle emotion can accumulate without one knowing it or doing much about it.

Accumu-
lating
Frustration

Time is the factor that must be reckoned with when discussing the experience of resentment. With time, resentful people may begin an accumulation of frustration that can reinforce their resentful feelings (Figure 8). In the case study, Nicholas spent years accumulating frustration and was superficially set free by a heroin addiction. Yet, when he went for treatment, his physical addiction was the focus. His emotional problems surrounding resentment were hardly touched, and over time, he began to accumulate more layers of frustration, leaving him vulnerable for further drug abuse.

Some of us accumulate frustration over time until we have had enough, and for example, quit a job, get a divorce or enroll in a different school. Others may find they are not fortunate enough to do any of these things, and try to work from an illusion of harmony, with the belief that we live in an imperfect world, and should try to make the best of it. While others such as Nicholas, accumulate frustration to the point that resentment becomes a way of life, and a possible addiction, where being resentful shows similar characteristics to other addictions.

How a Resentment Addiction Works

Not all people who are oppressed suffer from a resentment addiction. Throughout history we read about oppressive events that victimized millions of people, yet in most of these cases, people found creative ways to combat it. Through music, art, humor and other means of surviving their plight of being stuck human beings, they weathered the climate of resentment that engulfed them. That is not to say, they did not have the experience of resentment; it seems to be fairly common when people lose their freedom (Stack, 1993). Historically, we can site thousands of examples. However, these people recognized it, and found creative outlets to compensate for its victimizing tendencies.

The following section talks about a different group of people. In some cases, they do not recognize resentment as a problem; however, they have withdrawal symptoms when someone un-sticks them from their oppression. This section talks about a group of people who have gained a tolerance for being frustrated and stuck, by depending on it in giving direction to their lives:

Frustration Over Time and Tolerance — In our human development, frustration is perceived as a normal behavior that most of us experience, sometimes quite frequently. However, when someone becomes addicted to resentment this frustration can become highly tolerable, and this tolerance can affect risk taking and personal confidence. One of the apparent problems in recovery from many addictions may be the inability of clients to regain personal confidence or to take risks. Sometimes we can contribute this inability to fear of the unknown, as found in different forms of anxiety. Yet, anxiety may not exclusively hold the market on an addict's personal confidence or willingness to risk.

Frustration over time, without any attempt to overcome this frustration, may make it highly tolerable, especially to people who already have addictive tendencies. For example, people involved in abusive relationships may develop a tolerance for their circumstances and not notice how stuck their lives have become. They may accept their frustration as a way of life that must be tolerated. They may believe that life is about oppression, and the thought of being free is just a passing dream, and they may be seriously tempted to use drugs or alcohol as methods for further toleration of such oppressive conditions (Kusner, 2003). In many respects, people with a resentment addiction learn to tolerate resentment, much as they learn to tolerate other forms of physical addictions, and with time, their tolerance levels may increase in a similar manner. For example, in the case study, Nicholas learned to tolerate his frustration to the point that he became a homeless person. The values of being successful that he once possessed were overshadowed by his tolerance of homelessness. It could be argued that not only heroin became more tolerable, but also his resentment.

Being Stuck and Addictive Thinking—Frustration over time, may force people with a resentment addiction to take account of their lives. It is highly probable that, at some point, they may come to the conclusion that they are stuck. However, with resentment addiction it appears one's understanding of being stuck may be different than people who are resentful, yet not addicted. Most of us have come to the conclusion, at some point in our lives, that a certain circumstance has been frustrating and we conclude that we are stuck in it. Yet, there may be numerous other circumstances where we find freedom, hope and understanding. This does not appear to be the case with people addicted to resentment. In their conclusions, they seem to apply addictive thinking where they over-generalize their circumstances. They may be working from the unchecked assumption that there are only two realities open for them. You are either stuck, or you are unstuck, with neither of these realities completely representing the imperfections that we all experience in the course of our lives. People addicted to resentment, act as if life is; black or white, right or wrong, good or evil. Their addictive thinking forms the conclusion that, "If your stuck in life then, that's it! Stuck is stuck and there is nothing you can do about it."

We see a similar phenomenon in physical addictions (Twerski, 1990) where drug addicts sabotage their positive growth with thinking that does not allow them to be specific or productive. "Black or white thinking" allows many addicts an opportunity to justify their behavior, and conclude that not much can be done about their conditions. This also seems to be the case with resentment addiction. Being stuck is accepted as the way life must be, and there is nothing that can be done except tolerate it.

Buried Feelings and Denial—In counseling, working with clients who are experiencing resentment may require challenging these clients to talk about their buried feelings. Frustration over time, realizations of being stuck, and the continual "cooking" of these buried emotions, may call for counseling that helps people explode instead of implode. Another way of saying this is, "Try to get clients to talk about their buried frustration." Usually when they do, some form of anger surrounding lost freedom emerges as a significant talking point. For counselors, having clients acknowledge their frustration seems productive; even though, this frustration may emerge as anger. Such anger can be therapeutic, especially for people who have accumulated frustration over time. (Unfortunately, in non-therapeutic situations, people seem encouraged to keep frustration buried for fear of angry outbursts.)

However, in counseling clients with a resentment addiction, getting them to openly express their frustration and become angry can be a daunting task. There seems to be too much riding on openly expressing buried frustration. Tolerance of frustration combined with addictive thinking may force these clients to protect and deny they have any anger or frustration. Instead, they may deny such emotions exist, and try to avoid any discussion of emotions, let alone frustration. We see this happening with adolescent youth who may avoid their buried feelings by using sarcasm, silence or kidding (Schaeffer, 1988). In an addiction to resentment, denial of deep-rooted feelings becomes one of the major obstacles to successful counseling. For some counselors, seeing their clients finally show some form of anger, can become a breath of fresh air that may be used for their eventual recovery. A resentment addiction relies, in part, on keeping emotions buried; even though, they rarely remain that way.

Indirect Lashing Out and Compulsive Behavior—Many of us have experienced moments in our lives where our frustrations led us to sarcasm, gossiping, and other forms of indirectly lashing out. In a civilized world, it seems to be encouraged when we become frustrated, and is especially preferred over anger. We may even join gossip networks at work or in our neighborhoods, to vent our frustrations about almost anything. Yet, usually when we do this, something in particular is on our minds. It may be the unreasonable directives of the boss, who has fallen in love with power, or those neighbors who never seem to go along with everyone else, while the rest of us talk about them. In these and other examples, we complain because in some way we feel stuck, and it seems better to talk about it than to bury it. Needless to say, many people feel that forms of indirect lashing out can be therapeutic, at least in venting of one's feelings.

This does not seem to be the case in those suffering from a resentment addiction. For these people, any situation can be grounds for indirect lashing out. This may lead us to believe that such forms of lashing out are not meant to solve problems or to vent feelings. For people addicted to resentment, indirectly lashing out may be a compulsive act of buried frustration about life in general. Through addictive thinking and a tolerance for accumulated frustration, people with a resentment addiction may compulsively attack anything, regardless of whether it is a problem. For example, in the case study, Nicholas roamed the streets of New York, attacking anyone in his path. He indirectly lashed out in what most of us would consider inappropriate behavior. Yet, lashing out had become a major portion of his lifestyle, to the point that he did it compulsively. For some counselors, the difference between someone compulsively lashing out and others merely venting, seems clear. Much as an alcoholic compulsively takes a drink, people addicted to resentment may compulsively and indirectly lash out.

One final point should be made on this subject, regarding the indirect nature found in a resentment addiction. If someone directly lashes out, at least their anger and frustration are focused on a specific problem. However, the indirectness found in this form of lashing out, allows resentful people an opportunity to deny that actual problems exist.

Feeling Victimized and Dependency—As stated previously, people addicted to resentment do not need a frustrating situation to feel victimized. They depend on their identities as victims, but a dependency on this role may eventually cause more frustration. People needing to be victims, seems very different than people victimized by an oppressive outside force. In a resentment addiction, it appears that people need to market themselves as victims, in order to reinforce their identities. Unlike those who have been oppressed, yet seek freedom, (Neuman, 1992) people addicted to resentment seem to accept their victim status. They seem to need it, in order to justify their behavior.

In counseling for a resentment addiction, it may become clear to the counselor, how important being a victim can be for someone who depends on victimization, in order to have an identity. Sometimes, clients will combine a resentment addiction with guilt, in order to create an identity based on being a victim while continuously blaming themselves for their behavior. The combination of feeling resentful, only to feel guilty about one's resentment, can create an identity that victims can depend on.

At this point, it may be important to discuss how complicated and fragile the role of victim has become in our society. In some respects, we all are victims at some point in our lives, and relating to, "being a victim" may not be that unfamiliar to us. However, most people see themselves as more than victims even when victimized. In an addiction to resentment, being a victim seems to hold a stronger place in one's identity. It may be *the* role that is depended on to continue a life of frustration over time.

Accumulating Frustration and Withdrawal—It appears that within resentment addiction, accumulating more frustration is an ongoing activity that goes uninterrupted over time. The question may be, "Why would someone accumulate an emotion that initially caused them the problem?" The answer may be found in the withdrawal symptoms people with a resentment addiction, may experience when they attempt to confront their frustrations. Ironically, even though resentment starts with frustration over time, withdrawal symptoms of fear or anxiety may be experienced when attempts are made to confront these frustrations. For example, in the case study, Nicholas eventually confronted his heroin addiction however he experienced withdrawal symptoms when friends and neighbors, in effect, asked him to give up his resentment. Actually, it may be his accumulated resentment that brought him back to considering the use of heroin. Changing one's addictive habits and changing one's identity are two different considerations. Nicholas stopped using heroin but it is questionable whether he no longer identified with his resentment.

For counselors, it may be important to recognize the amount of investment any addict puts into their identity, especially when they strongly identify themselves as, "victims". In most physical addictions, accepting the term of addict can be one of the first steps to recovery. However, in the emotional addiction of resentment, identifying too closely with being an emotional addict may cause withdrawal symptoms to occur, especially when presented with the negative impact their accumulating frustration is having on their recovery.

Emotional Connections

Resentment addiction has subtle characteristics that might hide it from connections with other physical addictions, or connections with contemporary problems facing our society. For example, the social problem of bullying that takes place in numerous public schools may be understood by knowing the characteristics of a resentment addiction. Both bullying and a resentment addiction have similar themes such as, buried frustration and forms of lashing out. Also, a resentment addiction indirectly can be connected to the use of the drug, ecstasy where adolescents may find their freedom through Raves, where frustration can discover avenues to overcome so-called oppression. The following are two examples where solving present day social problems may require facing the emotional addiction of resentment:

Resentment Addiction and Ecstasy—MDMA, also referred to as ecstasy, is a stimulant form of methamphetamine that also has the effects of a 'psychedelic drug' where communication is enhanced and defenses become eliminated (Hodgson & Kizior, 1998). It falls into the category of 'designer drugs' where well know substances have been redesigned in order to create specific effects on their users. In the case of ecstasy, we see an adolescent sub-culture rallying to its use by the development of "Raves"— gatherings where ecstasy creates open expressions of heightened feelings and behavior (Ross & Rose, 1994).

The connection between ecstasy and a resentment addiction may be difficult to see under the above description. One seems to be an open expression of freedom of emotions and the other appears to be a frustrating accumulation of them. Furthermore, it is not assumed that everyone who uses ecstasy is resentful. Yet, the developmental process found in adolescence helps us connect the two phenomena. For example, both are heavily involved in the phenomenon of freedom, with resentment as a response to losing it, and the drug ecstasy, in some cases, in getting it back. Their connection, again in some cases, can be seen in the use of ecstasy, as a way of coping with the rebellion so closely connected with adolescent years (Hier, 2002). Even though, most counselors could make claims for other drugs being used as a remedy to one's feelings of oppression, ecstasy seems a perfect fit for adolescents who are coming to terms with not being a child, yet faced with the responsibilities of being an adult.

Example—Tom had a mixed childhood where his parents showed him affection, yet their personal problems constantly sabotaged any intimacy they would gather as a family. By the time Tom reached sixteen, he felt stuck in the middle of a messy divorce, and with personal problems surrounding his inability to make friends. For the most part, he felt abandoned in a world that seemed to offer little happiness, and his response was to protect himself against his shy nature.

All of that changed the first time he went to a Rave. Here he found the flow of the drug, ecstasy to be everywhere. The first time he took it, a liberating feeling came over him. No longer did his parent's problems bother him. No longer did he feel shy in the presence of others. He was free from the challenges of being sixteen. All of his old resentments seemed to vanish and all of his future problems were consumed within this little pill, at least for awhile. Around Tom's seventeenth birthday, he was faced with a large dilemma. The use of ecstasy and other stimulants, had taken him away from those dreams and goals that others expected from him. Ecstasy was not truly making him free but began appearing as an escape from the responsibilities of becoming an adult, and old resentments were returning in spite of drug use. As it turned out, going to Raves and taking ecstasy gave him moments of freedom, but returning to the world of responsibility, Tom began to feel even more frustrated. It was as if, going to a Rave would create unrealistic highs but the rest of the time, he experienced frustrating emotional lows. Tom had gotten into the habit of solving his frustration, not by working through them but by substituting ecstasy in order to avoid them.

Tom eventually went to an addictions counselor, recommended to him by his parents. Their concern was his use of ecstasy and going to Raves. However, Fred, his counselor saw a connection between using Ecstasy and his overall resentful attitude. Underneath Tom's drug use, Fred saw a person addicted to resentment that even ecstasy could not overcome. Fred decided to work on Tom's use of drugs in combination with treating him for a resentment addiction.

Summary—Sometimes, it becomes difficult treating an addiction without considering treatment for a larger social problem. This may be the case when treating some adolescents for drug abuse. Being aware that a larger social phenomenon may be taking place actually may help in the treatment of drug abuse. The larger social problem being referred to includes oppression, pursuit of freedom and successful transitions (Ladd, 2007). This phenomenon could be called, "The Right of Passage" that takes place between being a child and being an adult. It is a phenomenon that places adolescents in an uncomfortable position, directly in the middle between childhood and adulthood. It is a social problem where they may feel frustrated, stuck and oppressed, and it may give rise to countless questions about their behavior.

One of these questions may be, "Why do adolescents, sometimes, appear so oppressed, when they seem to be given everything they desire?" For the most part, the answer falls somewhere in their attempts at seeking freedom without a thorough understanding of what it means to be free. Adolescents may fight against the guidelines of their parents and society, yet may not have achieved those personal guidelines that mark them as adults. In spite of this, society has many hidden social pressures that ask adolescents to make a successful transition into adulthood, and sometimes without much help. Somewhere between the social pressure of the adolescent years and the yet unachieved skills of adulthood, is the experience of resentment.

Under these conditions, it may be understandable why adolescents would find taking a drug, with hallucinogenic tendencies, at a party, to be a popular solution for all of the challenges facing a right of passage into adulthood. Combine this possibility with some of the factors making up a resentment addiction, and we may have a connection where a drug reinforces one's resentments and one's resentment reinforces the drug.

In the example of Tom, ecstasy seemed like a way out of his personal form of oppression. It appeared to work. However, Tom's emotional addiction was too strong even for ecstasy. Eventually, the drug's delivery of new found freedom let him down, and Tom realized that his journey to adulthood only was interrupted by some pleasurable moments along the way. He still felt stuck, shy and less an adult. Fred, his counselor, needed to focus on his right of passage into adulthood by finding other means for him to obtain freedom and responsibility.

Resentment Addiction and Bullying—Bullying has received much attention in recent years but bullies have been around since the beginning of time (Williams, Forgas & von Hippel, 2005), and many of us have our own definitions of a bully. Bullying is the act of intentionally causing harm to others, through harassment, assault, or more subtle methods of coercion such as, manipulation (Einarsen, Hoel, Zapff & Cooper, 2003). Some of us have been targets of bullies, and some of us have found ourselves acting as bullies, whether we intended to act this way or not.

The connection between bullying and resentment has been researched and correlations have been established between one's emotional state and when a person decides to bully (Hazler, Carney, Green, Powell & Jolly, 1997). In this section, we will focus on the connection between emotional addictions and bullying, and some of the bully's motivation originating in a resentment addiction. When we think about these two phenomena, both bullying and a resentment addiction have roots in oppression. One of the intentions of most bullies, is to overpower someone who is weaker, or not in a position to defend his or her self. One of the intentions for developing a resentment addiction is to compensate for the oppression felt by situations that are out of the resentful person's abilities to change.

To a certain degree, bullies and people addicted to resentment compose a perfect storm for violence, such as demonstrated by the Columbine Massacre and other similar events (Peterson & Hoover, 2005). People addicted to resentment have accumulated frustration over time, and have buried this frustration, sometimes to the breaking point of violence. They remain victims with buried anger and frustration waiting to come out. On occasions, bullies are the catalyst for resentful people to explode in violence, (Lafee, 2000) in order to cope with their buried anger and frustration. Other times, people addicted to resentment may become bullies, in order to "un-stick" themselves from accumulated frustration and oppression. In other words, bullies may dominate others to relieve personal resentments, and other people may become bullies as a result of their accumulated resentments.

Example—Tony had a difficult childhood. First of all, he was the focal point of a physically abusive relationship between his parents that usually ended with the abuse eventually falling on him. At twelve years old, Tony had to keep his feelings buried for fear of retaliation from one or both of his parents. At home, he spent most of his time hiding in his room hoping the next round of fighting would not include him. Most friends and relatives may have perceived him as shy or at least quiet, and some worried whether he could stand up for himself. This seemed obvious to those who were aware of his parent's ongoing fights.

However at school, Tony became a different person. Some of the other students probably might describe him as a bully. It seemed that Tony was constantly looking to pick a fight, and this was usually with some unsuspecting shy student who wanted to be left alone. Finally, the eventful day came when Tony physically assaulted one student who he had previously kidded, extorted and embarrassed in front of his friends. The principal of the school was quick in referring him to the school's counselor for some form of rehabilitation, along with punishment for the assault.

Ms. Clark, his school counselor, was prepared to talk to him about bullying and the warning signs that he demonstrated when assaulting another student. She discussed his need to be dominant over others, and the power he gained at the expense of others. She also discussed how his friends put pressure on him to be a bully, and how he did not have to bully people in order to feel important in his life. Yet, all of these discussions seemed to fall short of Ms. Clark's intended goal of helping Tony with his bullying. It was only when she began to understand his home life that progress began to happen. She realized that bullying was an outlet for his deep seated resentment toward his parents, and how years of feeling stuck were emerging in his bullying of others, and how his resentment did not go away even when practicing bullying behavior. For the next several months, Ms. Clark refocused their counseling sessions toward understanding his resentment, and the pursuit of a more acceptable solution, other than bullying.

Summary—For Ms. Clark it became difficult to treat Tony for a problem with bullying, without having him understand the underlying problem he had with resentment. Yet, in numerous cases especially in schools, the connection between resentment and bullying seems to be overlooked (O'Meara, 2001). Schools have a tendency to treat behavior that primarily *affects schools,* especially where bullying has been an ongoing problem. School counselors also may want to consider the impact of certain emotions on the behavior of their students taking place outside of school, as demonstrated in the above example of bullying—especially, when school problems and family problems may be different aspects of a student's real problem.

In our example, Tony had two problems. One originated at home where he demonstrated many of the characteristics of someone who felt oppressed. He demonstrated many of the themes described in this Chapter regarding a resentment addiction. However, at school, Tony became a bully and appeared more as an oppressor than as someone oppressed. Schools and families may need to connect all aspects of student problems, in order to resolve them, and counselors may need to connect family and school problems emotionally, in order to thoroughly understand the problems of their students. In some instances, families, schools and the workforce all seem to be proficient at defining problems for themselves yet may lack a *team effort* in defining these problems to people having the problems. Take Tony and his bullying as an example. He started out in his family with the emotional problem, resentment. He goes to school, and he now is perceived with the behavior problem of bullying. If he graduates and goes into the workforce, Tony may bring both of these problems along with him, and be perceived as being a malcontent with a job performance problem. The family, school and workplace have all defined the problem according to their needs without directly meeting the needs of the individual having the problem. Whether it is family counseling, school counseling or EAP counseling; family, schools and workplaces need to understand the whole problem as opposed to simply redefining it.

Tony seemed to have a direct connection between his resentment and his bullying, and this connection could be a theme that follows him throughout his education and later career. It was a pattern that had momentum yet was only being addressed in part. Ms. Clark, his school counselor, was trying to address the whole problem. Her understanding of the connection between a resentment addiction and bullying may have been as important as her understanding of the important connection between families and schools.

A resentment addiction can be seen from a psychological perspective and also from the perspective of sociology. When treating our clients for such problems as bullying, it may be important to drop our labels and our expertise, and pursue the problem at hand. In the case of bullying, it may be important to look at it as a social phenomenon, a psychological disorder, and as an emotional addiction. In some cases we may need to look at bullying from all three perspectives.

Potential Counseling Solutions

- One phenomenon that seems to accompany a resentment addiction is when clients put on an "illusion of harmony." This may be an attempt to mask underlying frustrations. For inexperienced counselors, such harmony may indicate that the counseling climate has not been established and that a bond has not been made between the counselor and the client. Sometimes in a resentment addiction, it may require confrontation in order to reach underlying frustration (Nicholson, 2001).

- Resentment can breed mediocrity. Any risk that seems positive can help clients with a resentment addiction come out from the mediocrity accompanying many situations where people feel oppressed (Seligman, Olson & Zanna, 1996). Sometimes, the method of values clarification about hope and dreams can help clients beyond seeing a world that appears mundane and boring.

- The more assertive counselors can be with resentful clients, the more difficult it becomes in keeping emotions buried (Sandoval, 2002). Buried frustration can cause denial, unless counselors challenge clients to express themselves. The more assertively the client expresses his or her feelings and behavior, the more difficult to uphold frustration and being stuck.

- Sometimes it is difficult to create a dialogue with resentful clients because of their indirect manner of communication. This tends to have counseling sessions bog down. It may be important to use some form of cognitive behavioral therapy in order to change how clients view their feelings (Longabaugh & Morganstern, 1999).

- Helping clients with a resentment addiction may include some form of survey of one's identity. Being a victim seems to be a large part of this emotional problem, and the more the counselor can empower the client, the easier it will be to change their identity as a victim.

- Empowering clients with a resentment addiction may require some form of challenge where the client lets go of buried emotions, and openly begins to express their feelings. Sometimes, a constructive form of behavior therapy can be used to have clients express their feelings openly (Todd & Morris, 1995).

Resentment Addiction Short List

- Empower clients to develop alternatives to un-stick themselves from frustration.

- Encourage resentful clients to make choices.

- Let resentful clients talk until buried emotions emerge.

- Watch for an "illusion of harmony." It may mean buried feelings are being covered up.

- Realize that ambushing, sarcasm and joking may be forms of indirect lashing out.

- Be assertive with resentful clients. This is one method for counseling buried feelings.

- Watch for signs of inferiority. Sometimes resentful clients may fall into feeling guilty.

- Have clients experiencing resentment, think of alternatives to their problems.

- Do not let resentful clients dwell on feeling like a victim.

- Try to have resentful clients control any compulsive indirect lashing out.

- Recognize that resentment addiction can develop a tolerance for accumulated frustration.

- Compulsive lashing out at others may be a sign of a resentment addiction.

- Those who depend on feeling like a victim for their identity may be suffering from a resentment addiction.

- Become specific with oppressed people who deny they have any buried frustration.

Format for Other Emotional Connections

This is an opportunity to develop a connection between a resentment addiction and some other real life experience. This could mean making a connection between a resentment addiction and some form of physical addiction, or a connection with another process oriented addiction. Also, this could be a connection between a resentment addiction and a mental health disorder. Finally, this could be a connection between a resentment addiction and an everyday life experience where a resentment addiction makes an impact on this experience:

Briefly describe the connection between a resentment addiction and your chosen phenomenon:

Write an example of how a resentment addiction is connected to your chosen phenomenon:

Summarize your thinking on this connection:

Chapter 9: Revenge Addiction

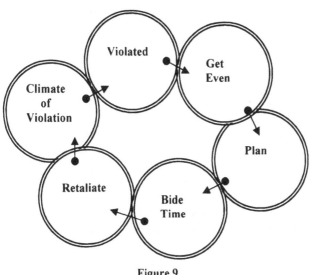

Figure 9

Background

Revenge is found throughout history from the use of vendettas or blood feuds to historical figures professing to balance out feelings of violation through such sayings as, "An eye for an eye" or "Revenge is sweet" (Anonymous). In such quotations, we find people engaged in reactions, not actions. Revenge is based on retaliation for being violated in some way.

Sometimes revenge is confused with justice; however, they have different intentions based on different plans of action (Durham, 2000). Justice is what a society, community or a person seeks when someone breaks the rules or knocks down the boundaries of any given situation, and certain consequences are expected to combat such actions. Revenge is not concerned with clearing up violations based on rules. Revenge focuses on the act of retaliation. Its main purpose is to violate another person, or persons. It responds to one violation by creating another (Konstan, Holmes, & Levine, 2003).

In counseling, revenge can become a chronic problem when the clients seeking revenge remain focused on the past. We find this in personal feuds where clients cannot get over violations made, and bide their time waiting to retaliate. Such clients seem to live in the past, and create counseling problems by not being in sync with the people around them. For example, a divorced man may have felt violated by his wife for leaving him, and has difficulty getting over the trauma caused by the divorce. He may bide his time, waiting to retaliate instead of moving on, and trying to develop new relationships.

All of us may have felt violated at times, and we all may have had moments when the thought of getting even gave us satisfaction or comfort. In a sense, such feelings and behaviors are normal. Being violated by another or others throws us out of balance both emotionally and behaviorally. Emotionally, we may feel loss, anger or shock while behaviorally we may want to get clarification, look for justification, or seek retaliation. We all have our comfort zones and violating them, causes us to feel differently, and to respond differently than before the violations took place.

However, there are people who do not need an outside violation in order to seek retaliation. These are people where life itself has become a violation, where most behavior is in response to chronically feeling violated. Outside incidences have long since been the root of their reasons for retaliation. These are people who look for moments when they can retaliate against others regardless of whether others have violated them. These people seem to base their lives and their personalities on seeking revenge against society, friends, lovers and anyone else who may disagree with their point of view.

From a counseling perspective, such people may be suffering from an addiction to revenge. They may have developed a pattern of feeling violated and wanting retaliation that permeates many facets of their lives. Revenge may be the fundamental theme in their lives that human experience must pass through in order to be understood. In counseling, these clients usually have a plan of action of how they are going to get society back, or a friend or lover back that has violated them. For these people, a revenge addiction has become a lifestyle that allows for pre-mediated acts of retaliation. However, unlike anger where there is some open expression outrage, or like resentment where there is some ongoing expression of frustration, in a revenge addiction, people have developed a pre-mediated plan where they bide their time, waiting for the right moment for retaliation.

Case Study

Earl was a Vietnam veteran who came back from the war confused and angry. He felt that his country had abandoned him, and that his life was ruined by the humiliation he felt when protestors spat upon him while getting off a plane upon his return. Earl had seen combat and the atrocities of war, and he was suffering from post traumatic stress disorder. Beyond the flashbacks and the sleepless nights was his view about the future. He believed that someone should be paid back for how he was treated, and he seemed to retaliate against anyone who got too close to him.

His family was the largest recipient of his outward retaliation. Over the years, he seemed to look forward to incidences when his son made mistakes. He would yell at him and sometimes hit him for his behavior. However, it was not the type of punishment that came out of anger. It seemed to be planned, and his son seemed to know it. As far as his wife was concerned, Earl was a partner who looked for trouble. He found most of her behavior unacceptable, and he waited for those moments with a certain amount of pleasure when he could put her down, and embarrass her.

This was the description of Earl and his family as they sought family counseling; even though, the reason for counseling was supposed to be about his son, who was getting in trouble at school. The family was now seeing, Sallie, a family counselor, who understood how a family system can break down whether it was family communication or family rules. Sallie was an acute observer of family dynamics, and could spot other areas of concern beyond the direct family problems. Actually, the family counseling that they all participated in had been a success. The family had worked on patterns of communication that had broken down, and family rules were updated where all three family members felt that the discussions had been fair and productive.

As the family was making their last visit to family counseling, Sallie took Earl aside, and asked him about his personal issues, and if he wanted to pursue them. Earl became a bit defensive, and asked her what she meant. Sallie told Earl that he seemed to be a person where certain issues were offensive to him, and that his responses seemed calculated and rehearsed. She told him that he seemed to be holding a grudge against something, yet she had no idea what that grudge could be. She felt that whatever was going on inside of him seemed to affect other portions of his life, and color them in a negative light.

Earl was taken aback by these comments. He knew that he was difficult at times but had not realized that others could see it so clearly. He told Sallie that he did not know what she was talking about, but since the family counseling went well, he was willing to try individual counseling. The next week, Earl showed up at Sallie's office and began to share his feelings. He had stated that it was not like him to talk about himself, and that he had been a good provider for his family; even though, he knew his attitude could be difficult. He also knew that others had mentioned that he seemed to have a "chip on his shoulder", and was intolerant of any behavior which he did not agree with.

Finally, he began to talk about Vietnam, and the terrible atrocities he witnessed in battle. He told Sallie that he had received counseling for post-traumatic stress disorder at the Veterans Administration and that his flash-backs and nightmares were gone. However, when Sallie began to delve into his attitude about the war, Earl dramatically changed. He gave a litany of how his country did not appreciate his actions and how they rejected him when he returned. He shared the outrage that he still felt about being used and being made a fool of. He also made a point of listing all of the examples of similar outrages that he experienced since Vietnam. He was outraged by; working conditions, the community in which he lived, the lack of patriotism, young people's behavior, the decay of marriage vows, the lack of loyalty with friends, and the list went on to include many other areas.

Sallie listened attentively to Earl's litany of violations, and also to his re-taliations when given the chance to address these violations. Earl described how he had done this to one person and that to another. As he described his retaliatory behavior, Earl seemed to be uplifted and buoyant in his attitude. Finally, Sallie told Earl, "You seem to have put a lot of preparation into get-ting certain individuals back for their behavior, and you seem excited when talking about it." Earl had never been faced with such a statement. He wanted to set up a similar plan for Sallie but she did not say these words with any sense of judgment or recrimination, so he just listened to her. Sallie con-tinued by saying:

> I believe the Vietnam War did you a grave injustice. Beyond the effects of post traumatic stress disorder, you seem to be suffering from an ongoing bat-tle with revenge. I do not believe that you personally want to be this way. I believe you have acquired an addiction to revenge that can be treated and re-solved.

Earl immediately realized that his assumption about himself was incor-rect. He believed that he was a vengeful person, and that his behavior was a part of his personality, which ironically he saw as one more violation. Now he was being told that it was an emotional addiction that could be treated. Earl's relief was obvious. He worked with Sallie for six months while slowly feeling less hostility and hurt.

The Experience of Revenge

Revenge is an emotion based on violation (Figure 9). It usually begins with an incident where someone feels violated by family, friends, strangers, communities or society (Rushbult, & Van Lange, 2003). It is the feeling of violation that creates conflict within people and it triggers reasons for getting even in some way (Figure 9). For example, in the case study, Earl felt violated by strangers spitting on him as he got off the plane from Vietnam. Something within Earl went out of balance and he did not begin to recover from it until the counseling sessions with his counselor, Sallie. Revenge differs from anger in that the violation is not addressed immediately. It is allowed to linger in one's memories until the time is right for retaliation.

Many of us have felt violated by others where we wait for the right moment to say something or do something. In a civilized world, revenge can be our way of planning what we are going to do or going to say. Usually our plans are based on how we approach the prior violation. If we come up with a plan that clears up the violation then we do not call it revenge. We call it justice. For example, on 9/11 planes flew into the World Trade Center, and from that moment the world was looking for some form of response. Our response was to create a sense of justice not get revenge (Greenberg, 2003). However, other violations are not resolved through just means. For example, at Columbine High School, two students, who felt violated by the school system and the people in it, opened fire on their classmates killing innocent people (Cook, 2004). In this example, the violation was handled by retaliation and had no intention of clearing up a violation.

Get
Even

The "getting even" stage in revenge seems the most misunderstood. Usually, getting even refers to retaliation and payback. However, in a phenomenology of revenge getting even seems a natural response to being violated (Figure 9). For example, if your husband after twenty years of marriage suddenly says, "I am leaving you," and walks out the door, you may feel that you need to get even. However, how you get even is another story. You may accept his statement and start a new life, or you may go after him with a gun. In our society, we judge getting even as retaliation when, in fact, it has little to do with how we behave. When violated, getting even has more to do with our state of mind than our behavior. Before someone violates us, our state of mind usually is in balance where we are conducting ourselves within the boundaries of normal behavior. When violated, we are thrown out of balance sometimes emotionally, psychologically and possibly spiritually. It is a natural experience to want to get back in balance or to get even (Ladd, 2007). In the case study, Earl felt violated by protesters spitting on him. This violation threw him out of balance on many levels. It was *how* Earl got even, not whether he had a natural right to get even that created his revenge addiction. We all have right to get even when we are violated.

In counseling, we see this in clients called "cutters." These are clients who cut themselves for many reasons but one that seems to be common is when feeling violated by others. In a cutter's mind, he or she feels violated by others and has a natural instinct to recover from the violation, or to get even emotionally, psychologically or spiritually. If you say to these clients, "You have no right to get even." Such a statement goes directly against the imbalance they feel. Most effective counselors would authenticate their right to get even, but ask if they could think of a better plan than cutting themselves after such violations. In effect, people do have a right to get even after being violated. The issue becomes, "What is the plan?"

The act of coming up with a plan, separates vengeful people from those who seek justice (Figure 9). If people develop plans that clear up violations, it is perceived as a just plan. For example, if you were a victim of child abuse and in order to get even emotionally and psychologically, you started a home for abused children, that would be a plan based on justice not revenge. However, if you were a victim of child abuse and you got even by becoming a pedophile, you would probably be getting revenge. In the case study, Earl's plan of taking out his bitterness on anyone that disagreed with him was a plan based on revenge. He was not making attempts at clearing up violations. He was more focused on retaliation for what happened to him after the Vietnam War.

In counseling, we have an opportunity to help clients who have decided to get even. Instead of moralizing or judging their need to get even, it makes more sense to accept getting even as a personal right, and then to begin focusing on what type of plan they want to develop. Plans based on justice clear up the original violations. Plans based on revenge are not interested in clearing up violations, but focus more on retaliation.

Many of us have felt violated in our lives in subtle ways, and have wanted to get back in balance by coming up with some type of plan. For example, if someone embarrasses you and puts you down, you may decide that the next time they try it, you will respond assertively. Or, you may decide to bide your time, and embarrass and put that person down at the right moment. In revenge these are two different plans with two different intentions. One tries to balance out something in one's life while the other tries to violate the person in retaliation for their original violation.

Biding time can be one of the most dangerous stages in an experience of revenge (Figure 9). Being violated throws people out of balance but waiting to retaliate, forces them to stay out of balance until a successful retaliation has taken place. In counseling, some of us have worked with victims of rape who have felt violated and wanted to get even. However, they may feel continuous violations each day as they bide their time waiting for retaliation. Sometimes biding their time causes as much violation as the original rape (Cahill, 2001).

One of the problems with biding time is it forces you to freeze yourself in time. Others around you may have moved on, but biding of time keeps you transfixed on the original violation. For example, in the case study, Earl in many respects is living a similar life as when he departed from the plane after the Vietnam War. Even though the years have passed, he still bides his time waiting for anyone to cross his path and disagree with him. Earl finds himself living in the past, at least emotionally, when he retaliates against his family and friends. A portion of Earl's feelings and behavior are affected by a thirty two year commitment to biding time. Because of this, Earl has become a victim of time. He now was making everyday decisions based on something that happened to him in the distant past. Such decisions make a portion of Earl's behavior irrelevant. He seems out of sync and out of touch. This was what his counselor, Sallie, saw in his behavior, and it was why she wanted him to continue with individual counseling.

Vengeful people who have been violated, and decide to get even, and have come up with a plan, and are biding their time, do not find consolation unless they retaliate (Figure 9). People looking for revenge, need to retaliate in order to get balance back into their lives. Retaliation seems justified to those who feel violated. It is the payback that seems needed in order to move on. Without retaliation, revenge falls into an isolated dialogue with one's self as to when retaliation can take place. If you asked people, "Why does revenge seem so satisfying?" The answer may be found in the act of retaliation. People who retaliate do it for some form of gratification and consolation (Wendt & Slonaker, 2002). That is why many people may secretly tell you how sweet it was to finally get that violator back in some way.

In the case study, Earl seemed to be addicted to retaliating against his family, especially his son. He seemed, in some way, to enjoy his son's mistakes so he could retaliate against him. This pattern seemed so pronounced that Sallie, his counselor, pointed it out to him, and wondered if he would like to pursue this pattern in individual counseling. Earl had gotten so used to retaliation that he actually looked for reasons to do it. Over time, the people around him began to accept his retaliations as a part of his personality. Sallie believed that Earl's retaliations were not about him, but about a pattern of retaliation that he had used for many years.

One of the problems with retaliation when practicing revenge is that, what is one person's retaliation becomes another person's violation, and what is one person's violation can lead to another's retaliation. This vicious cycle is how feuds are started. After a while it is hard to remember who violated whom, and who retaliated last. Constant retaliation causing further violation can create a climate of violation where it seems understandable that if you are violated that you need to retaliate and if you retaliate one can expect future violations (Figure 9).

In counseling, we see clients who have gotten into back and forth violations of each other to the point that they create a climate of violation. Even events where there seems to be no violation taking place can be affected by a climate where violations are commonplace. For example, in a family where family members constantly are violating each other, over time, the family may begin believing that it is alright to violate each other. They may have created a climate of violation that has become acceptable, with acceptable rules on violating each other, and acceptable ways to violate each other. Furthermore, in such a climate the status of revenge itself may be raised to acceptable levels of violence such as, in the thinking of suicide bombers or terrorists spouting vengeful ideologies.

How a Revenge Addiction Works

Revenge seems to have addictive characteristics simply because of its pre-meditated nature. When we think about revenge it appears more as a pattern; rather than, a single incident that people act out when they are violated. Getting even, developing a plan, and biding time waiting to retaliate, makes revenge a phenomenon with complicated motives. Yet, some of us may practice revenge, though are plans for it are informal and not fully developed. For example, "I will get my wife back for spending all our money," may be thoughts that influence the violated feelings of a spouse, but there may be no strong commitment to biding time or a need for retaliation. Such an example could merely be perceived as a chance to retaliate, in some way, if the opportunity presented itself.

In an emotional addiction to revenge, a commitment for retaliation seems more acute. People addicted to revenge seem to make revenge a life style, a pattern in life that simply will not go away. For these people, revenge may be experienced as an addiction, with symptoms of denial, tolerance and withdrawal included in understanding this experience. The following may be some of the characteristics making up a revenge addiction:

Violation and Dependency—There is a difference between being violated by outside forces and seeking out violations. Some of us may find ourselves in situations where we feel violated, and the experience was unexpected and possibly a shock. Under these circumstances, revenge may be a considered option that is either used or rejected. In an emotional addiction to revenge, personal violations are not taken so lightly. For example, in the case study, Earl felt violated by the Vietnam War, and took this violation as a serious moment in his life. Actually, he used it as the basis for his retaliatory behavior against his family, especially his son. He seemed to depend on feeling violated to justify his behavior with others. It was his cross to bear, and he depended on it when conflict became a part of his life. Much like an alcoholic depends on alcohol when problems arise, Earl depended on feelings of revenge when confronted with some of life's problems.

In counseling, we see clients who depend on violations in life to justify their behavior. We have already discussed Earl from the case study. If his counselor, Sallie, could read his mind he might be saying, "If people could only know what I went through in Vietnam, they would know why I am constantly feeling violated." Earl seemed to depend on violations to be a part of life. Without Earl constantly feeling violated how could he justify his behavior to himself and others? Under these circumstances, Earl would be more susceptible to creating violations even when they do not exist. For example, Earl's waiting for his son to make a mistake seemed as though he needed his son to make a mistake, so he could feel violated. Sallie realized that many of Earl's violations were self induced. She understood this pattern of behavior based on his need to feel violated.

Getting Even and Compulsive Behavior—When some of us are violated by others, we may retaliate or we may try to deal with the violation through discussion, mediation or some other form of conflict resolution. Our feelings of violation probably throw us out of balance, and we may decide that something has to be done. For example, Adult Children of Alcoholics may have felt violated by their alcoholic parents. They may have spent time feeling emotionally out of balance in this experience. When they decide to get even it may be through education and support, not retaliation (Fitzgerald, Lester & Zuckerman, 2000). However, in an emotional addiction to revenge getting even can become a compulsive act anytime another violates someone practicing this pattern. For example, some people feel violated if they are touched, and they compulsively want to get even (Parshall, 2003). Getting even in this case is not something that is thought through as in the actions of some Adult Children of Alcoholics. It is a compulsive act that happens anytime someone touches them. In the case study, Earl practiced getting even as a compulsive act. That was why his family believed he was so moody. Actually, it had little to do with being moody. He compulsively wanted to get even anytime someone violated him. Since he depended on violations to justify his behavior, Earl had justification for compulsively getting even.

In counseling, we sometimes see this compulsive, wanting to get even, when working with people with anger management problems. If we treat the client only for anger problems, we may not go deep enough. They may have problems with compulsively wanting to get even. We also see this with physical abuse cases in marriages where one partner may feel violated by the other for any trivial behavior, and the other partner compulsively wants to get even (Blanchfield, Blanchfield, & Ladd, 2007). In such cases, treating for a revenge addiction may be as important as anger management.

Vengeful Plans and Addictive Thinking—People with an addiction to revenge do not seem to rely on critical thinking skills to resolve violations in their lives. From a critical thinking point of view, being violated and wanting to get even can affect other people beyond one's personal feelings of violation. In other words, vengeful plans based on retaliating against another person may create problems for more than that person. For example, in the case study, Earl decided after Vietnam to retaliate anytime he felt violated. However, his decision was self-centered and self-serving. He had been embarrassed and humiliated after Vietnam, yet his plan to get back at society also hurt his family and especially his son. Here was an example where someone created a vengeful plan that satisfied only that person's need for retaliation. Drug addicts may use the same form of addictive thinking when deciding to use drugs. They may be aware that a plan to solve problems by taking heroin does not measure up to any form of critical analysis. It is a plan based on addictive thinking where the person taking heroin is concerned about only one person. Those addicted to revenge seem obsessed with the same form of addictive thinking. Their plans seem to benefit themselves over anyone else. They do not seem concerned with the effects their plans might have on others. For example, in the case study, Earl is willing to go for family counseling; even though, he had continuously taken out his revenge on his family. His addictive thinking about dealing with revenge went against his critical thinking about improving his family.

In counseling, clients may want to get even, but may have not thought through the ramifications for such retaliation. Possibly one of the most important practices we can perform for vengeful clients is to help them change their plans from addictive thinking into plans based on critical thinking.

Biding Time and Denial—It may be a surprise to those biding time, waiting to retaliate, as to how much time they are wasting. In counseling, when confronting vengeful clients who are biding time, and discussing how much time they could be putting into more productive activities, these clients invariably want to disagree. Such clients feel that biding time waiting to retaliate is not a waste of time, but time well spent. In effect, they are in denial that life is passing them by, and that others around them are moving on. In the case study, Earl bided his time waiting to retaliate, especially against his son. If you asked Earl, "Why were you biding your time waiting to retaliate against your son?" Earl would probably deny answering the question. However, if you asked Earl's son whether his father was waiting for him to make a mistake, the answer would probably be yes. Earl was in denial of his relationship with his son until Sallie, his counselor, pointed it out.

In counseling, clients with a revenge addiction may be in denial much like an alcoholic with an alcohol addiction will deny they are an alcoholic. However, when you drink too much and it creates problems, you may be an alcoholic. The same may hold true for someone with a revenge addiction. If you bide your time waiting to retaliate, you may be in denial of how this practice may freeze you in time, and you may be in denial of how others are moving ahead in time. Unfortunately, biding time is such a personal practice that it may take some effort before a client will admit to biding time, in order to retaliate.

Retaliation and Withdrawal—People addicted to revenge may experience withdrawal symptoms when asked to give up forms of retaliation against others. This can best be demonstrated in the behavior of fanatics and terrorists who cannot possibly consider giving up their ideology or their terror (Whittaker, 2004). Another example is found in the case study. Earl may have withdrawal symptoms if he tried to give up his retaliation focused against his family. He had terrorized them for many years and to stop without understanding his past behavior, would probably be rejected at some level of his thinking. This characteristic mimics a similar pattern found in physical addictions. For example, people who are trying to get off cocaine my go through withdrawal symptoms that push them back towards using again. In a similar manner, people who have made a life of retaliation may have similar psychological withdrawal symptoms when looking for other avenues to clear up violations in their lives.

In counseling, the withdrawal symptoms experienced in trying to stop retaliation may be as big an issue for the counselors as helping vengeful clients develop a just plan. We see this at a societal level when factions at war agree to stop fighting. Even with an agreement in place, trying to stop the actual fighting may be difficult. Retaliation is a behavior that is planned, and sometimes it becomes difficult to stop regardless of agreed upon plans for peace.

Climate of Violation and Tolerance—Our present day society shows us examples where we have learned to tolerate years of violence. Wars in Afghanistan or Iraq have created climates where people continuously are violated, and have developed a tolerance for these violations (Cordesman, 2003). Closer to home, people do not need a major war to develop a tolerance for a climate of violation. We have countless reports concerning cases of domestic violence where the violator and the person being violated have learned to tolerate conditions that may seem intolerable to most of us. However, for those involved in domestic violence there seems to be a tolerance for being violated, and the retaliation that accompanies it.

In counseling, it may be difficult to convince someone who is the victim of retaliation to leave the situation, and seek proper help. Some of these clients have developed a tolerance for the retaliation inflicted on them from their violators, and some violators have developed a tolerance for retaliation where they have little perspective on how much damage they are doing to the other person.

A climate of violation found in a revenge addiction may make vengeful acts tolerable. It is the experiences that people may have gotten used to. Sometimes we find this phenomenon in the makings of a feud, where horrific acts of retaliation and further violations have become a way of life that people have learned to tolerate. In an emotional addiction of revenge, the emotional climate can be one of the leading factors in making a revenge addiction tolerable.

Emotional Connections

A revenge addiction may play a role in numerous physical addictions where the addict gets revenge on others or society by taking drugs. In recovery, people with this addiction may stop using the substance, but do not necessarily give up the emotional addiction. For example, drug and alcohol users may find themselves practicing domestic violence as their plan for retaliation against another (Scheff, 1997). They may get treatment for their drug and alcohol problems but that does not guarantee they will stop abusing their partners. It may be that domestic violence is influenced by an emotional addiction to revenge where violating another is a compulsive act that is difficult to stop.

Beyond domestic violence are those people who find it impossible to get along with others and seem to have disdain for the people around them. These people may be suffering from antisocial personality disorder where their conscience and ability to be empathic toward others seems low. It may be that some of these people have developed an addiction to revenge where violating others seems a natural part of life.

A Revenge Addiction and Domestic Violence—It is estimated that over a million incidences of domestic violence occur each year, and they are the incidences reported to law enforcement (Bureau of Justice Statistics and Crime Data Brief, 2003). While the public may see domestic violence as an act by people who are out of control, in counseling, we work with clients who have violated their partners or other relatives, and we soon realize that all violent behavior is not spontaneous or irrational (Claiborne, 2005). There are clients who have thought through how they are going to deal with conflict in their relationships, and the plan is to violate the other person. Sometimes this plan is developed with the help of drug and alcohol abuse, and sometimes it develops on its own. For counselors, developing a plan to stop abusing another requires more than anger management skills. The counselor may be dealing with a client who pre-meditatively abuses others, and may have difficulty stopping this behavior. For these clients, it may be important to see their actions from the perspective of an emotional addiction to revenge.

With domestic violence, both drug addiction and emotional addiction may be a part of any recovery. Trying to help clients who violate others may need to consider that violators may have behaviors that are compulsive, and have developed plans of retaliation based on their addictive thinking, or have learned to tolerate violence against their partners. Incarceration of these people does not seem to be an effective deterrent. It seems to be more successful in protecting the abused rather than changing the actions of the abuser (Blanchfield, Blanchfield, & Ladd, 2007). Domestic violence may be one area where looking at the abuser as having an emotional addiction to revenge may help in changing that person's view about how to treat others.

Example—It was obvious that something had to be done. Ralph was constantly beating his wife, and he needed to be stopped. It was a fact that both of them had been cocaine users, and it was true that both of them could become violent. However, Ralph had been violent long before he started using cocaine. He had a history of assaults, and had been put behind bars more than once for these charges. Now he was serving time in a local jail for his previous behavior.

James was a counselor working for the jail where Ralph was being held. This facility had a program where inmates could get help if they requested it. Ralph had a plan. He believed that they may reduce his sentence of six months if he attended counseling. This was the reality as Ralph entered James's office at the facility. He was more concerned about his plan than his recovery, and it did not take James long to figure this out. At first, Ralph wanted to talk about his addiction to cocaine, and how it was cocaine that was the cause of his violent behavior. He promised James that jail had enlightened him about the dangers of drugs, and that he swore off of using them in the future.

The conversation between Ralph and James seemed to be typical of clients who are repentant for their behavior, and are looking for new ways of living a more healthy life. The problem for James was that, he did not believe that Ralph's violence problem would be solved by quitting cocaine. He believed that cocaine added to the problem, and he believed that violence happened while doing cocaine, but there was something completely premeditated about the way Ralph explained his violent behavior. It was as though he planned it. Ralph had all kinds of assumptions about women and how they should be treated, and he talked about them as though they were possessions that must obey him, and listen to his wisdom.

Working from these assumptions, it was hard for James to visualize Ralph leaving jail, and giving up violent behavior. Ralph seemed to have a plan about how he was going to treat others, and it was a plan that included some form of violence. However, when James confronted Ralph concerning his beliefs and assumptions, he vehemently denied such a plan. Ralph believed that James was wrong, yet he did admit that he had been physically abused as a child, and he learned to protect himself. In a similar manner to alcoholics denying a drinking problem, Ralph was denying his problem with violent behavior.

The breakthrough with Ralph came when James approached his problem as though it was an addiction; something that he could have acquired rather than something that was a part of his personality. It appeared that Ralph much rather view his violent behavior as a learned pattern than as a genetic trait. James also believed that inside of Ralph there was not a gene dictating his behavior, and he told Ralph that he could treat his problem as an emotional addiction to getting revenge. He could treat recovery in the same manner as recovery from cocaine. Over the time that Ralph spent in jail, James helped him with his revenge addiction. It was encouraging that a year later James received a letter from Ralph indicating that his addiction was still under control.

Summary—The reality in domestic violence cases is that concern for the victim of violence must be a priority. They are the individuals who are the recipients of retaliation from abusers. Counseling victims of abuse, is a common practice for addictions and mental health counselors. However, the problem, many times, is bigger than the violent behavior of the abuser and the submissive behavior of the victim. Sometimes both parties are suffering from addictions, and sometimes these addictions are not physical in nature. A common combination found in those looking for emotional addictions in clients are, the victim having an emotional addiction to guilt and the abuser having an emotional addiction to revenge, where both parties have obtained this addiction over time.

In the example of Ralph, it may seem clear that he was not going to solve his violent behavior problem either by going to jail or by stopping cocaine use. His problem seemed buried in the emotion of revenge where his beliefs, thinking, feelings and behavior accepted revenge as a solution to solving problems. James, his counselor, believed that Ralph needed to change more than his behavior. He needed to question his beliefs about retaliation, he needed to change his addictive thinking, and he needed new behaviors for his own feelings of being violated. Only then did James believe that Ralph had a chance at recovery.

A Revenge Addiction and Antisocial Personality Disorder

—Antisocial personality disorder is characterized by; a tendency to violate the rights and boundaries of others, aggressive, often violent behavior, lack of remorse and persistent lying and stealing (Psychiatric Association, 1994). These and other symptoms describe a person who does not seem to fit in with the values and beliefs of their social situations. They seem to be in their own world of rules and behaviors. Their self-centered and self-serving attitudes seem directed towards unsuspecting others who have expectations of civility and respect; however, their actions prove otherwise. Somewhere in the minds of people with this disorder is a sense of entitlement that their behavior is acceptable regardless of what others say (Rotgers & Maniacci, 2006).

In an emotional addiction to revenge, a similar phenomenon takes place. Often the plan developed in a revenge addiction is about entitlement that violates the boundaries of others, and under these conditions such plans seem to lack any remorse. In counseling, we may treat people with antisocial personality disorder by discussing their belief systems, and their behavior through some form of cognitive behavioral therapy. We may work on their aberrant behavior by using some form of behavior modification. In spite of our attempts, antisocial personality disorder still seems a difficult problem to deal with in counseling. One possibility for counselors is to look at this personality disorder as though it was a revenge addiction; both are involved in violating others, both have a need to get even, both seem to have a plan or at least a belief system that acts as a plan, and both find little concern for the consequences of retaliation against others.

Example—Felix came from a moderately wealthy family that had fallen on hard times. The financial crisis they were going through required adjustments to be made. Being an only child, Felix was used to getting what he wanted. Instead of being grateful for his good fortune, he took his parents for granted. He did not seem to care that they were struggling to make ends meet. It was unfortunate that he did not want to help because at twenty four and living at home, he had many chances to contribute, and be a part of the family. Felix was not concerned about family problems. He was concerned about himself. This was evident when he was told not to spend money because of the low finances. Felix's answer to this problem was to take his parent's credit cards, and spend money on whatever he wanted. Beyond this, Felix was unemployed. It was not that he refused to work, but no job was good enough for him. What Felix liked to do was hang out with his friends, though the friends he had were much like him, and they had little difficulty stealing from each other.

These were the circumstances when Felix entered counseling with Ruth, a mental health counselor. Felix, at first, seemed deceptively pleasant as though he was this caring individual who understood the problems of his parents, and who was willing to change his behavior. Unfortunately for Felix, it was a superficial act because he had no intentions of listening to anyone even his counselor. He would say one thing and do another. He did not care who he hurt or who suffered from his actions.

Ruth believed that Felix was suffering from antisocial personality disorder as described in the DSMIV manual on mental health disorders. He seemed to meet the criteria, and she began attempts at cognitive behavioral therapy in order to help Felix consider his beliefs, and how they affected his behavior.

After several months, Ruth considered a different approach. She believed the cognitive behavioral therapy had worked to a certain extent, but it did not seem to change the underlying problem driving Felix's behavior. Instead, she began to talk to Felix about the possibility that he may have an addiction to revenge. After explaining to him about a revenge addiction, she asked him for a response. Felix shocked Ruth with this reply, "Yep, that's it, and I have been doing it most of my life." Ruth responded by telling Felix that if it was an addiction, then he could change it, if he wanted to. His antisocial behavior was not something he openly wanted to do. Maybe it was something he needed to do according to his view about life. Under these circumstances, Felix seemed in a much better state of mind to face his problem.

Similar to any other addiction, an emotional addiction to revenge is filled with denial, compulsive behavior, addictive thinking, dependency and withdrawal. Ruth began helping Felix with all of them.

Summary—Being diagnosed with antisocial personality disorder may be a reality according to the DSMIV (Moeller, & Dougherty, 2004); however, owning that label may ward off any possibilities for change. Telling someone they are antisocial does not necessarily make them want to be social. The problem with antisocial personality disorder may be a similar problem to treating clients with anorexia nervosa. Directly treating the disorders as though they were their personalities, may create a bigger problem. Hardly any client shows excitement while in treatment for being too thin or too antisocial. In treating clients with antisocial personality disorder it may be important to take the focus off of who they are, and on what they are doing. The connection between antisocial personality disorder and a revenge addiction give counselors an opportunity to focus more on a pattern than on a person, giving these clients an opportunity to look at what they are doing and not how others have labeled them.

In the example, Ruth tried cognitive behavioral approaches, in order to change the beliefs and behavior of Felix. This certainly was in the direction of treating Felix for his disorder. However, it did not go far enough in letting Felix separate himself from his pattern of behavior, so that he could objectively make changes. When Ruth began to treat him for a revenge addiction, Felix stopped focusing on himself, and began to focus on the addiction. He began changing a pattern that had become addictive, and was hurting those around him. It created the possibility that he was not only an antisocial person that his parents and society would have to tolerate. He was a person with an addiction and could be treated, and given the same consideration as other people who suffer from addictions.

Potential Counseling Solutions

- It may be important to point out how getting even is more about the type of plan being used than about whether you have a right to get even. Plans that clear up violations are based on justice. Those that create more violations are plans based on revenge. Some form of cognitive behavioral therapy may be important in coming up with plans based on justice (Wilson, 1998).

- It may be important to create boundaries for clients who want revenge. Getting even can be important only with acceptable boundaries for the clients and others around the clients. Creating acceptable ways of getting emotionally back in balance can be a productive enterprise.

- Make sure that clients know they have a right to get even, but be clear about what that means. When you are violated your world is thrown out of balance. Clients have a right to get their worlds even again both emotionally and psychologically. This is different than retaliation, where getting back in balance is not a consideration.

- Help clients separate plans based on clearing up violations and those based on retaliation. This may require a systems approach to counseling where clients look at their social systems, and determine whether their plans are based on revenge. Using a systems approach with a revenge addiction can broaden the discussion, and help clients see the whole picture. Revenge has a tendency to be personal. A systems approach helps to include others (Conyne, 2004).

- Help clients act out constructive plans to ward of feeling of retaliation. Watch for clients who live in the past, biding time. The sooner they act out their plans, the higher chance for personal growth. Biding time can leave clients with a revenge addiction, where they are living in the past and isolated from others who have moved on. It becomes important to help these clients live in the present, and make decisions based on information from the present.

- Discuss with clients what their major violations in life are, as they perceive them? Help these clients understand how they feel about being violated in these areas. Follow up with plans to be back in balance without having to retaliate against those who caused the violation. Sometimes, clients with a revenge addiction want to compulsively get even when they feel violated. Having these clients practice critical thinking as opposed to addictive thinking may help them develop plans based on some form of justice.

Revenge Addiction Short List

- If clients are looking for revenge, isolate issues based on personal rules, family rules, and rules of society.

- Let your clients know that you understand when others violate them. Try to find the line of demarcation as to when other peoples' actions become a violation.

- Develop a plan, for people addicted to revenge that is balanced and is not only for the benefit of vengeful clients.

- Let clients know they have a right to get even, but in terms of getting back in balance not in violating someone else.

- Explain to clients that emotional addictions counseling is a positive alternative to plans based on retaliation.

- Look for clients' unspoken plans when talking about their behavior. Revenge is different than anger or resentment. Neither of them requires a plan.

- Help clients develop constructive plans that help people other than themselves.

- In counseling for a revenge addiction, the counseling should reflect the violations that took place causing the revenge.

- Help clients with this addiction to act out constructive plans, and encourage them to restore balance in their lives.

- Remember that revenge can be a stepping stone to hatred of others. An addiction to revenge can be found in fanatics, racists and terrorists.

- Discuss with clients what happens when they bide their time, waiting to retaliate. Show how such actions make these people victims of time.

Format for Other Emotional Connections

This is an opportunity to develop a connection between a revenge addiction and some other real life experience. This could mean making a connection between a revenge addiction and some form of physical addiction, or a connection with another process oriented addiction. Also, this could be a connection between a revenge addiction and a mental health disorder. Finally, this could be a connection between a revenge addiction and an everyday life experience where a revenge addiction makes an impact on this experience:

Briefly describe the connection between a revenge addiction and your chosen phenomenon:

Write an example of how a revenge addiction is connected to your chosen phenomenon:

Summarize your thinking on this connection:

Chapter 10: Self-Hatred Addiction

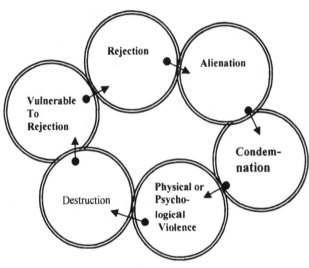

Figure 10

Background

The word hatred usually has the connotation of some extreme emotion where some form of violence is involved, and acceptance of others is undermined by an overwhelming sense of rejection. We see this in a contemporary world where fanatics from many walks of life have decided to condemn other people. Examples of hatred permeate our modern world through terrorism, fanaticism, and forms of oppression (Ronczkowski, 2004), and it appears that hatred is not declining any time soon (Bergesen & Yi, 2005). Much of the focus in studying hatred seems directed towards social problems and the increase in conflict has made it a common theme among those commenting on our present day society.

There is another form of hatred that does not seem to receive as much attention; even though, it is connected to many forms of addictions and mental health disorders. This is the phenomenon of self-hatred. Though not formally listed as a disorder or an addiction, the emotional impact of hating yourself makes both disorders and addiction a bigger problem. Self-hatred associates most closely with many of the causes for addictions and psychological disorders. For example, alcoholics who drink for many years may find that at some point in their childhood someone rejected them, which planted the seed of self-hatred, and this seed grew by acting out some form of self-inflicted violence physical or psychological.

In addictions and mental health counseling, self-hatred takes on many forms. It may be as simple as a client constantly being complimented but unable to accept these compliments (Owens, 1995). Sometimes self-hatred may be perceived as inferiority, and that individuals do not believe they are worthy enough or good enough among other people (Fichman, Koestner & Zuroff 1996). Other times, self-hatred may surface as self loathing for some act or some inherited trauma from the past where people believe they deserve to be hated for whatever has come to pass (Edwards, 2000). In all of these examples we find elements of rejection, alienation and possibly destructive behavior Yet, many of us have had these symptoms at low moments in our lives when we concluded that some part of our beliefs or feelings require self-hatred. In these moments, we rejected ourselves at some level of consciousness.

It could be said that forms of self-hatred are to be expected, especially during adolescence (Lave-Gindhu & Schonert-Reichl, 2005) or after feelings of defeat or failure (Turp, 2003). However, there are people who have made a lifestyle out of hating themselves. The thought of loving themselves becomes a frightening experience. They rather accept a tolerance for self-hatred than begin seeing themselves in a positive light. For these people, being addicted to self-hatred becomes a way of life. Self-hatred runs deep within some people's existential meaning, and the thought of personal acceptance becomes an untenable belief. For these people, a self-hatred addiction can alter the basic meaning in their lives, and can cause serious consequences for physical or psychological violence and destruction.

In counseling, we try methods to help these clients, only to realize that none of our attempts work without acknowledgement, acceptance and appreciation of clients as people. Self-hatred can be an addiction that sabotages many counseling sessions with its dependency on clients seeing themselves as unacceptable. Experienced counselors know the frustration felt when we have finally helped clients restart their lives, only to watch them tear down their recovery through self-hatred.

Case Study

Sally came from an alcoholic family where the core belief was that the children were never good enough. Her father and mother would become intoxicated and beat her two sisters and her brother. Over the years, she despised them for what they had done. The echoes of her father's voice still resonated in her ears, "You are no damn good. Get the hell out of here!" were phrases that she remembered verbatim even till the present day. Her parent's rejection made life unbearable, and Sally never seemed to recover from putdowns from the past. Underneath, Sally hated herself. No matter how many people told her that she was a wonderful person, Sally simply rejected compliments. In fact, she went out of her way to prove how miserable a person she had turned out to be.

Even though Sally was remarkably beautiful and had many admirers, when she looked into the mirror, she saw a disgusting creature. She was also very intelligent and would get almost perfect grades, but made excuses of being a bookworm, and not to be taken seriously. Furthermore, she was tall and slender, but believed that she was too tall, and too skinny, and needed to gain weight. However, when she did gain weight, she thought she was fat and ugly and resorted to isolation.

When she finally arrived for counseling her counselor, Lisa, recognized the many contradictions in Sally's perception of herself. Some people are afraid of failure. In Sally's case, she was afraid of success, and would sabotage growth whenever she came near it. She was so self-destructive that Lisa could almost predict what she was going to do next. One example was the time that Sally kept talking about how accident prone she was, and how others never seemed to hurt themselves. Hearing this, Lisa wrote a message on a piece of paper and sealed it in an envelope, and told Sally to bring it back next week. One week later, Sally entered Lisa's office with her arm in a sling. Lisa told her to open the envelope written the previous week. It said, "In the next week you will hurt yourself." Sally looked at Lisa and said, "How did you know that?" Lisa answered that it had nothing to do with any psychic powers "I watched you set yourself up for some form of self-hatred behavior, and guessed it was only a matter of time before you hurt yourself, in some way."

Lisa went on to tell Sally that she believed she had an addiction; however, her addiction was based on self-hatred. Lisa believed that Sally had been practicing a pattern of self-hatred for so long that she depended on it. She depended on hating herself, but was in denial when told she hated herself. She had developed a tolerance for self-hatred, and she compulsively rejected anyone who tried to give her compliments. For the next several months, Sally and Lisa worked on ways to practice self-love. As simple as that seemed at the time, it became one of the major turning points in Sally's life.

It is hard to say when the emotional addiction of self-hatred began for

Sally. By most accounts, it probably dated back to the alcoholism of Sally'
parents. One of the possible fallout experiences from living in an alcoholi
family could be a self-hatred addiction. In Sally's case, her alcoholic paren
did not pass on an addiction to alcohol. If we think about it, alcohol was n
what most influenced her as a child. It was the constant barrage of rejectio
alienation and condemnation she received that started this addictive pattern
behavior. Sometimes, people with physical addictions can pass on more tha
patterns of alcohol or drug abuse. They can pass on emotional addictior
where their children become addicted to a specific emotion rather than
physical addiction.

The Experience of Self-Hatred

Hating yourself has to start somewhere. People are not born with forms
genetic hatred. Unlike anger or anxiety, self-hatred does not have biologic
roots. In order to begin hating yourself, some outside experience or outsid
person or persons must reject you. The basis of self-hatred may lie in rejectio
whether it is, rejection within a family, rejection of one's personality, or reje
tion of one's race (Figure 10). Being rejected has an emotional impact on pe
ple who are trying to belong, and constant rejection can leave people vulnei
able to low self-esteem, self-consciousness and guilt. People who experienc
self-hatred may retreat from others, and have difficulty forming bonds
friendship or intimacy (Bennet, 2000).

In the case study, Sally's parents constantly rejected her, and told her t
get away from them. The message implied in their rejection was that Sally wa
not a good person. As a young girl, Sally was caught. If she wanted to love he
parents, then she had to accept their rejection. If she accepted their rejectio
then she may reject herself. In this example, self-hatred, ironically, begins o
of Sally's attempt at loving her parents, yet their rejection influenced Sally t
reject herself.

People who are constantly being rejected, form a reaction in order to protect themselves. A common practice is to pull back and put up emotional shields for protection against constant rejection. Unfortunately, putting up emotional barriers between yourself and others has its consequences. The intention is to avoid rejection, but the outcome can be a sense of alienation from others (Newman & Newman, 2002). For example, in the case study, Sally did not see herself as others saw her. She was afraid of rejection from others, and made attempts to reject herself first. Even when given constant compliments about her intelligence and beauty, Sally was too alienated to accept these compliments. On the contrary, she saw compliments as threats that would draw her out from behind her veil of alienation.

In counseling, this phenomenon seems a paradox, especially to new counselors in the field. In our case study, why would Sally who is intelligent, beautiful and fundamentally a good person, not accept statements that could reinforce her self-esteem? Possibly, the answer lies in constant reliance on keeping up emotional walls for protection (Caplan, 1955). In many counseling situations, circumstances from the past have changed, but the experience of rejection and protecting yourself from it, resist change. People experiencing self-hatred may seek out emotional protection from potential rejection, only to find a larger problem in the experience of alienation.

Rejection and alienation are powerful forces in the experience of self-hatred. They have a tendency of drawing people toward conclusions about themselves that are not necessarily based on accuracy. Constant rejection and alienation isolates people where they sense others do not understand their true, unacceptable nature. For example, in the case study, people gave Sally constant compliments, yet she found ways to put a negative spin on them. She found methods to condemn herself regardless of the facts. Her sabotage of

positive input became counter productive where her condemnation of herself
reinforced more rejection and isolation, making it difficult to appreciate her
many qualities (Figure 10).

In counseling, we find people who seem to hate themselves by constantly
condemning or, at least, not accepting the positive growth pointed out by their
counselors. The scenario sounds something like this, "You are saying all of
these positive things but if you really knew me, you would not be thinking that
way." At the core of these clients is a sense that it does not matter what they
accomplish, they still remain fundamentally no good. The condemnation stage
in self-hatred becomes important because it shifts people experiencing self
hatred from *reacting* through rejection and alienation to *acting* through con
demnation (Reno, 2004). No longer is self-hatred a reaction to others. It now
becomes an intentional act of condemnation. In counseling, resistance to posi
tive growth becomes difficult when clients practice self-condemnation. In
many ways, we as counselors are faced with the existential problem of revers
ing a view of self that does not necessarily reflect the personalities of our cli
ents.

People practicing self-hatred may practice some form of self-inflicted
physical or psychological violence. Constant rejection by one's self or others
builds emotional walls ending in alienation and personal condemnation, and
both are criteria for self-inflicted punishment (Figure 10). Hurting yourself
seems to be the most dramatic experience in the phenomenon of self-hatred. In
the case study, Sally wanted to love herself, but sabotaged all attempts by her
counselor to help her. It was as if she wanted to punish herself for being, her
self. She practiced psychological violence by refusing to see herself in a posi
tive light.

In counseling, we sometimes see clients practicing self-hatred by destruction. It could be said that portions of anorexia nervosa, bulimia and other violent acts against one's body have roots in self-hatred (Gardner, 2001). Self
hatred seems grounds for many different types of addictions and disorders
Who is to say how much of any addiction or mental health disorder originated
with self-hatred? Furthermore, after successful treatment for an addiction or
disorder, who is to say whether the phenomenon of self-hatred has been

successfully treated? People can be drug free and disorder free and still hate themselves. We should consider that not all self-inflicted physical and psychological violence emanating from addiction or disorders were solely the responsibility of these addiction or disorders. Sometimes self-hatred is the breeding grounds for self-inflicted violence regardless of the addiction or the disorder.

The ultimate goal of anyone practicing self-hatred is to destroy something, regardless of whether the person is conscious of their self-destruction (Figure 10). If you look at the underlying structure of self-hatred this statement may make sense. We are considering a profile of people who reject themselves, have become alienated from others, and practice personal forms of condemnation, resulting in some form of self-inflicted physical or psychological violence. Within this structure, destruction may seem inevitable. In the case study, Sally's counselor could actually predict when she would physically hurt herself. Lisa was not some clairvoyant who could read the future. She was a therapist who saw a pattern of behavior where Sally constantly exhibited rejection, alienation, and condemnation of herself, leading to some form of violent act (Ladd, 2005). It was only a matter of time before Sally destroyed something. Lisa's secret prediction was not much of a risk. Sally had made gestures toward some form of self-destruction. Writing a note saying Sally would hurt herself in the near future was an educated guess. Sally was in a position to destroy something much more than create a positive experience.

Some of us have had bouts with self-destructive behavior, and possibly questioned our actions. It could have been a phase in life where being self-destructive had a higher probability of revealing itself, such as in adolescence. There are other possible cases where this may occur including, a period in life where personal loss forced us into self-destructive behavior, or it could have been demons from our past where self-destructive tendencies were a part of an overall tendency to hate ourselves. Self-hatred attracts self destruction, and self-destruction can be a phenomenon that acts as an endpoint in self-hatred.

Self-destructive behavior is rarely seen in a positive light. Often, when we hear of someone being self destructive, we begin to question their motives. Common sense would tell us that being self-destructive does not reinforce one's ability to ward off future rejections from others. In most cases, the opposite is closer to the truth. People who are not self-destructive and do not hate themselves are more likely to cope effectively with rejection from others. Self hatred destroys many things, the least of which is self esteem. Self esteem is that magic phenomenon that protects us from rejection, and guards us from self-destructive behavior. Without it, we become vulnerable to the rejection of others. Self-hatred may be the diametric opposite of self esteem. Within self hatred we find people who are vulnerable to rejection (Figure 10). These are people who you have to be careful in what you say, because any form of rejection can be a devastating experience. In the case study, Sally's counselor found clever ways of exposing Sally's self-hatred. Her use of a note about the future was an attempt to show Sally how self-destructive she had become. Lisa was sensitive to the fact that Sally was vulnerable to any forms of rejection. Lisa's counseling skills pointed out self-destructive behavior, in an empathic and accepting manner.

We all have had moments of being vulnerable to rejection by others. That does not mean we hate ourselves. However, it may mean we are going through a period in life where certain traumas have made us vulnerable to the rejection of others. Continuing in such a pattern may begin to raise the walls of alienation, condemnation and self-destruction. Self-hatred is a pattern of behavior where we can become our own worst enemy.

How a Self-Hatred Addiction Works

Self-hatred as an addiction can be passed on to people who have experienced rejection. In many respects, self-hatred seems more of an addiction than an emotion we experience in our everyday lives. For example, anger and resentment can have addictive characteristics, yet they also can be emotions that we experience on a daily basis. Self-hatred is less an everyday experience and more of a pattern where peoples' personalities are shaped by rejection, alienation and condemnation. In the field of mental health and addictions counseling, such a pattern can have consequences beyond physical addiction or mental health disorders, and it can be one of the key elements influencing these phenomena. Furthermore, it seems to be an addiction that has roots embedded in traumatic events (Geller, & DeBello, 2003). It seems unlikely that someone who does not hate themselves will show signs of self-hatred suddenly, or without some history of rejection or alienation from their past. Sometimes, self-hatred is the legacy left to children of addicted parents while at other times it can be attributed to physical or sexual abuse. Nevertheless, it shows itself in the counseling sessions of mental health and addiction's counselors, and may be regarded as a stumbling block when recovery from other addictions and disorders seem to fail.

Rejection and Tolerance—Some of us have experienced moments in our lives where we were rejected by another. For example, the process of going through a divorce or losing a job, are such moments where the overriding feeling is rejection. During these moments, our sensitivity to the world around us can be elevated, and our response to rejection may be a dramatic or a traumatic display of feelings (Catherall, 2005). When looking back on such events, they may stand out as moments in our lives that we vividly remember. Rejection and alienation may be burning memories of a relationship that had gone bad, or an employment situation that became unbearable. Through it all, we may still remember how we were treated, and the rejection and isolation that accompanied these experiences. This does not appear to be the case in a self-hatred addiction. People who hate themselves seem to develop a tolerance for such rejection. Rejection no longer is a memorable event. It becomes something to tolerate, and to make adjustments while living one's life. For example, in the case study, Sally, over the years, learned to tolerate the rejection of her alcoholic parents. It became a normal part of her everyday experience. Even though she felt that life was unbearable at times, her tolerance levels grew. She learned to survive rejection by building emotional walls for protection. Her tolerance levels became so refined that compliments from others were not acceptable. Ironically, she could tolerate rejection more than positive forms of acceptance.

Counselors who treat clients with self-hatred tendencies may see this first hand. Clients may have little difficulty describing how they tolerated rejection from others yet giving these clients positive regard may cause embarrassment. In the case study, Sally did not want to hear that she was beautiful or intelligent. She had learned to tolerate forms of rejection, and believed it was easier to make negative excuses for these compliments. One could question, "How important is it for a client to accept a compliment? In some circumstances very important, if it represents a long standing tolerance of rejection, and an equally long intolerance for acceptance. Over time, people addicted to self-hatred can find themselves developing such a tolerance where rejection is taken for granted, and acceptance becomes more problematic.

Alienation and Dependency—At first, people suffering from a self hatred addiction may welcome building emotional walls between themselve and others. In the case study, this seemed to be Sally's way of survival agains her alcoholic parents. The problem that eventually emerged was not that Sal put up walls as a defense against constant rejection; but rather, it was that sh kept them up and began to depend on them. The decision to put up emotion walls in response to abusive families, marriages or institutions can be observe in numerous counseling situations. Putting up walls of alienation may be th only survival skill believed possible at the time. The problem that can emerg is keeping up these walls, even after circumstances causing alienation hav passed (Rovane, 2004). In the case study, Sally had become a successful pe son who faired well in the world, yet she still hid behind emotional walls th alienated her from experiencing many of the joys in life. Even when co fronted by her counselor, she kept her walls intact. It would be hard to belie that Sally enjoyed her alienation from the world. More likely, she had deve oped a dependency on these walls. By hiding behind emotional walls, Sal could tolerate rejection. However, her dependency on feeling alienated limite the scope of her life.

For counselors, it becomes problematic when people experiencing sel hatred continue to depend on staying alienated. In some cases, their depen ency on hiding behind emotional barriers is stronger than their need for affe tion, appreciation and love. In the case study, Sally acted in paradoxical way She wanted to be loved but depended on alienating herself from others. Muc as in describing a physical addiction, an alcoholic would like to stop drinkin but depends on drinking to get through the day. It seems to be the dependenc to stay behind emotional walls that makes resistance to change a major prob lem in a self-hatred addiction.

Condemnation and Addictive Thinking—In counseling, when askir clients with a self-hatred addiction why they are so hard on themselves, the a swer has a tendency to follow the addictive thinking of people with a physic addiction. Many times, it will lack any real attempt at critical thinking. For e ample, in the case study, Sally perceived herself the exact opposite of ho others perceived her. No matter what others said to compliment her on intell gence, beauty or success, she found ways to condemn herself. Her consta self-condemnation was based on a way of thinking that did not allow her feel good about herself. She practiced addictive thinking that reinforced h personal condemnation. Addictions counselors see similar addictive thinkir when counseling their clients. It is a method of thinking that; does not follo logic, does not make a critical analysis of the facts, and does not accept the r liability or the validity of others (Donovan & Marlatt, 2005). In Sally's ca her thoughts had to pass through a filter of condemnation in order to be unde stood. Her addictive thinking would only allow her to associate wi thoughts that validated her self-rejection and alienation. She did not have the ability to look at life from a critical perspective. It was only after her counselor described how she was addicted to self-hatred that she began to think differently about her life.

The power of addictive thinking is in its ability make any complicated experience; black or white, good or bad. In Sally's case, it did not matter whether life experiences were complicated and in need of critical thinking. Her addictive thinking followed the simple formula where, no matter what she did, some form of condemnation would follow. Recovering alcoholics sometimes fall into a similar pattern of addictive thinking where they condemn their behavior to the point of inhibiting positive growth. Sometimes alcoholics find themselves at Alcoholic Anonymous meetings condemning their behavior while giving little thought to the success of their recovery.

Physical and Psychological Violence and Compulsive Behavior—
People addicted to self-hatred have an investment in some form of physical or psychological violence (Roy, 2002). Such thinking is reflected in statements such as this, "Condemned people should be punished." or, "Condemned people should experience some form of harm." Obviously, not all people who hate themselves will think this way, yet it may be that similar beliefs lead these people into some form of compulsive violent acts. For example, in the case study, Sally's counselor predicted that Sally would hurt herself in the near future. Lisa did not believe that Sally wanted to hurt herself. She believed that Sally's compulsive behavior would create a scenario for some form of physical or psychological violence. When she entered the office with her arm in a sling, it was no surprise to Lisa. She had watched Sally reject, alienate and condemn herself. Doing some form of violence to herself seemed a natural next step in lieu of her self-destructive behavior.

Compulsive acts of violence are familiar to counselors in addictions and mental health counseling. An addiction to "Crystal Meth" may lead to compulsive acts or violence. Or people with conduct disorder may perform compulsive violent acts. Yet, let us consider the compulsive nature of a self-hatred addiction as having similar characteristics. In the case study, Lisa could predict that Sally would hurt herself, not because of any clairvoyant gift, but because of the compulsively violent nature of a self-hatred addiction. Outward acts of violence grab our attention in their drama, but the compulsive act of self-destruction found in a self-hatred addiction effects our sense of trauma.

Destruction and Withdrawal—In the end, some form of self destruction seems mandatory for people with a self-hatred addiction. Self-hatred requires something or someone to be destroyed in order for it to be justified and meaningful. For example, in the case study, what sense would Sally's life make if she did not eventually sabotage or destroy something. All of her investment in; rejection, alienation, condemnation and self inflicted violence,

would hold little meaning if, in the end, it seemed a waste of time. Ironic as
may sound, Sally was at war with herself. On the outside, she was trying t
live a productive life while inside she was trying to destroy herself. Howeve
if you asked Sally whether the latter statement was correct, chances are sh
would say, no. Unfortunately for Sally, the strength of her self-hatred addic
tion forced her into self-destructive behavior. Parenthetically, her attempts
controlling her self-destructive behavior produced withdrawal symptoms. Fo
example, even if Sally wanted to become more positive and productive, he
destructive nature would fight such a change. She might even experienc
withdrawal symptoms when trying to take a positive outlook on her life. Th
phenomenon has been the topic of discussion for many counselors when
seems difficult to believe that clients would continue to destroy themselve
even when faced with this discussion from their counselors. The answer ma
be in the withdrawal symptoms they experience when trying to stop destroyin
themselves.

In counseling, self-destructive clients seem to have attacks of anxiet
when beginning to show growth. For example, there was a client sufferin
from a self-hatred addiction who constantly experienced what could be calle
the "Eleventh Hour Syndrome." Five times she almost recovered and fiv
times at the eleventh hour she sabotaged her growth. Why would she sabotag
all of her hard work?" To answer this question, it may be important to unde
stand the withdrawal symptoms experienced in people with a self-hatred ac
diction. Her anxiety, apathy, and other emotions would not allow her to accep
herself.

Vulnerable to Rejection and Denial—Unfortunately, self-destructiv
behavior does not seem to deter people with a self-hatred addiction from fa
ling victim to more rejection. The vulnerability in hating yourself can be cov
ered up by denying any of the experience exists (Bjork, 1996). To put it ar
other way, people do not seem open to admitting they hate themselves. How
ever, denial of self-hatred leaves open the possibility for more rejection, thu
starting the vicious cycle to repeat itself. It is in the denial of self-hatred wher
people find themselves more vulnerable, and where the possibility for mor
self-hatred can be reinforced.

In the case study, Sally was vulnerable her entire life to more rejectior
By denying a problem existed, she continued to cycle through her self-hatred
leaving her vulnerable for more of it. Self-hatred seems to be a phenomeno
that grows stronger each time people become vulnerable to another round c
rejection. Like "Velcro" one rejection sticks to another until people becom
vulnerable to an overwhelming mass of self-hatred. Denial of this phenome
non allows self-hatred to grow and flourish while those with it slowly destro
themselves. In many respects, self-hatred is one of the most vulnerable c

emotional addictions. Denying its existence allows it to clearly express its self-destructive nature.

Emotional Connections

Self-hatred seems to hold a core characteristic in many addictions and disorders. This makes it difficult to pinpoint one or two for discussion. In the course of counseling, self-hatred may reveal itself as a starting point for numerous physical addictions, and it may be what is left after addicts have attempted recovery. It may be at the heart of different disorders such as, anorexia nervosa or depression, and may still exist after successful treatment for these disorders. In this section, a connection between self-hatred and adult children of alcoholics will be discussed. Here is where descendants of alcoholics may be focusing on the impact of alcoholism, and not realize they may have an emotional addiction to self-hatred. Treating relatives of alcoholics may be improved by considering an emotional pattern of self-hatred as one possibility in surviving the abuse of their parents.

Another possible area to consider can be found in rape victims who have had forms of physical and psychological violence inflicted on them. Victims may find patterns of rejection, alienation and condemnation emerging on the violent acts of others.

Self-Hatred and Adult Children of Alcoholics—Groups such as Al-Anon and Alateen have a long history of helping the descendents of alcoholic parents. Within these groups support is given for those who have suffered physical and psychological damage in their association with drug induced, abusive behavior of their parents. Much time is spent in these groups in trying to understand the impacts of alcohol and abuse on people's personal lives. Sometimes group members have become alcoholics in their own right, and other times it is the emotional fallout from such families that draw these people together in a formal setting. However, another reason may be present; even though, it may be hidden behind the alcohol abuse of one's parents. It may be possible that adult children of alcoholics are struggling with some form of emotional addiction. We have already talked about one of these addictions in Chapter 1 of this book, in the connection between an anger addiction and inter-generational child abuse. Another possibility to consider is the connection between a self-hatred addiction and the fallout experienced by adult children of alcoholics (Lester & Zuckerman, 2000).

Counselors understand the traumatic impact of people who have survived the alcoholism of relatives, and time is spent in counseling trying to reverse the fallout from alcoholic behavior. Beyond such counseling practices lies another possibility. Mental health and addiction's counselors may want to consider that adult children of alcoholics may have developed a pattern of survival that leaves their self-esteem and self-worth in shambles, through rejection condemnation and self-destruction.

Example—Horace religiously attended Al-Anon meetings each week and benefited greatly from these meetings. He had made peace with his parents and slowly understood the characteristics of an addiction to alcohol. His growth was found in sharing his past with others who gave him emotional support that continued as long as he went to meetings each week. His time spent at Al-Anon was well worth the effort, yet Horace did not seem to go beyond simply coping with life. It appeared that he was only keeping his head above water, and could not truly enjoy life or himself.

This was his state of mind when he entered the office of Steve, an addictions counselor. He told him that fundamentally he still remained unhappy and seemed to carry a weight around his neck where feeling confident around others felt impossible. However, any attempts by Steve to point out the positive aspects of Horace's life were met with rejection. Horace was extremely hard on his evaluation of himself. He wanted to be happy, but when happiness was near, he found ways to sabotage it. This was obvious in his relationships with women. He had been in numerous relationships where women went out of their way to make him happy. He revealed in counseling that any one of them would have made him happy, if he only had let their efforts alone. Horace had a habit of being in successful relationships, but eventually finding ways to sabotage them. In fact, Steve noticed a pattern of self-destructive behavior that permeated most of Horace's life. Steve would ask Horace. "Why do you destroy the things you love most?" Horace's answer was revealing. He said, "I do not know."

After much counseling with Steve, Horace began to understand his self-destructive nature. As an adult child of alcoholic parents, Steve explained:

> You experienced constant rejection and began developing ways to cope with this rejection. Over time, accepting yourself became a problem. You were so used to condemning yourself that acceptance seemed unreachable. When others found you acceptable, you found ways of sabotaging their efforts. Over time, you practiced forms of physical and psychological violence against yourself. Though this was diametrically opposed to what you wanted out of life, your self-hatred addiction did not allow you to feel confident, or free to pursue your dreams.

After the self-hatred addiction was exposed, Steve and Horace worked on ways of changing this subtly addictive pattern. Over time, Horace realized that he did not have to hate himself, and that being an adult child of alcoholic parents had left him suffering from an addiction.

Summary—Not all adult children of alcoholics suffer from a self-hatred addiction. However, it seems to be a common theme with people who are trying to understand their alcoholic relatives (Dupont, 1997). In the example, Horace tries to be happy in life, yet sabotages all major attempts at happiness. If all that needed to be considered was Horace's free will, then he could logically change his thinking and behavior, and live a happy life. This was not all that was needed. First of all, Horace would have to stop his addictive thinking. He rejected himself based on an addictive pattern, not on the facts portraying his life. For example, women loved him and wanted to be with him, but Horace rejected their acceptance of him. He practiced rejection, alienation, condemnation and self-destruction as a response to his success. Horace was addicted to hating himself, and as an adult child of alcoholic parents, he could justify his actions by a history of rejection that began in his childhood.

Sometimes people go with what they know. Horace knew that he was unhappy and that happiness eluded him. What Horace did not know was that his parents rejected him, and condemned him to a life of self-destructive behavior. He never knew how vulnerable his feelings were to any forms of rejection, even personal rejection. As counselors, we may want to consider that some of our clients, who are adult children of alcoholics, may suffer from a self-hatred addiction, but are in denial of its existence. This may be a denial of their present human condition, leaving them vulnerable to future self-destructive behavior.

Self-Hatred and Victims of Rape

Self-Hatred and Victims of Rape—Victims of rape have many issues to contend with beyond the rape itself. Such an extreme act of violence can create problems for victims long after rape has occurred. Feelings of guilt and rage are two of the more common experiences for rape victims (Hilberman, 1976). Rage over the act of rape continues to be one of the major counseling themes in treatment for these violent acts (Groth & Birnbaum, 1979). Guilt is another counseling theme, especially, when the family, court or society raises doubts about a victim's behavior. Embarrassment can accompany public scrutiny of victims going through a public's need to better understand these incidences.

Another phenomenon to consider beyond the rage and the guilt is the impact such events can have on self-acceptance. First of all, rapists destroy more than some form of physical violation. In many respects, they practice a form of hatred against their victims. They reject their victims as being human or having feelings. They alienate themselves against having any compassion for the victims they rape. They condemn their victims to a traumatic event that may pose difficulty in recovery. Most apparent is the difficulty in recovery from physical and psychological violence. Finally, they destroy something within the victims they attack.

In some cases, destruction comes in the victim's inability to love and e
pecially, self love. Some clients will state that the rape incident made the
feel dirty or tarnished, and that intimacy with others feels impossible. Son
say that life has changed and being open to others may never come again. F
these people, the possibility of self-hatred has increased, and over time, ma
evolve into an emotional addiction.

Example—Rachel did not know how it happened. She did not feel well a
ter entering a party of one of her friends, and decided to lie down on a bed
an upstairs bedroom. He was on her before she could scream. His powerf
muscles held her down while he forcibly raped her numerous times. When
left, all she could focus on was his smell, and the pain between her legs. Sh
was hurt by someone she did not even know, and in the moments that fc
lowed, she realized that recognizing him would be impossible. This is wh
she shared with the police during their thorough investigation of the event.
the end, someone had raped her, but finding that someone continued to b
come more problematic. With time, people made rumors that maybe it nev
happened and Rachel may be going through some tough times, and could hav
been looking for attention. At first, these allegations infuriated her. She wou
lash out with rage, followed by periods of guilt, especially when she could n
supply proper identification of her victim. With time, her rape had drift
away into the unconscious minds of her friends. Rachel was asked to join i
much in the manner that she demonstrated before the rape incident. Howeve
Rachel had changed. She now was extremely hard on herself, and found wa
to condemn different aspects of her behavior. This was especially evident
her relationships with men. It was not that she hated them. It was more that sh
hated herself when in their presence. As the years past, Rachel pulled mo
within herself. As fate would have it, the person who raped her finally w
caught, and admitted to the incident. Instead of this putting an end to a chapt
in Rachel's life, it seemed to make matters worse. Now, her hatred for the ma
who raped her was matched by her own self-hatred.

Over time, she realized that something had to be done. Her self-hatre
continued to increase, and life was taking a negative turn where she becam
self-destructive both physically and psychologically. Within the course of tw
years, she had gained over two hundred pounds, and had quit her job. In de
peration, she made an appointment to see a mental health counselor. Judy wa
a counselor recommended to her by friends. In fact, Judy herself had been
victim of rape, and Rachel immediately felt comfortable with her. As tim
passed, Judy revealed that her rapist left her with more than extreme traum
He also set the stage for her to begin hating herself, and that her self-hatre
had formed into an addiction. For the next year, Judy helped Rachel face

addictive pattern based on self-hatred. She helped her break through this pattern and love herself again.

Summary—One of the tragedies in Rachel's rape was the addictive pattern of self-destruction that had emerged from the rape incident. It appeared that talking through the rape itself was not enough to help Rachel with her problem. She needed to understand how the rape incident developed into a self-hatred addiction that became almost impossible to break without her counselor's help. Talking about the rape incident with an experienced counselor was therapeutic and productive, but talking about how Rachel, in a sense, continued to feel raped needed more work. It required a better understanding of how people inadvertently can fall into an addictive pattern based on a traumatic event. This certainly was the case for Rachel. The rape incident changed her view of herself. On some unconscious level, Rachel began to; reject herself, put up emotional walls, indirectly condemn herself, and violate herself with self-destructive behavior. She had developed an emotional addiction based on self-hatred.

Being raped can change peoples' perspectives as to how they look at themselves. Dramatically, rape can change a person from accepting, acknowledging and appreciating their personalities, to rejecting, alienating and condemning the same personalities. The danger in rape seems to go beyond the violent act. It plants seeds of destruction that may grow within the minds of its victims. Anytime counselors experience constant rejection in their clients, it may be important to consider a self-hatred addiction.

Potential Counseling Solutions

- One phenomenon that seems to accompany a self-hatred addiction i when clients do not accept compliments. This seems to be a symbo for deeper problems that need exploration. Some form of existentia counseling may be required to help get to the roots of self-hatre (Miars, 2002).

- Self-hatred can be very self-destructive. Look for signs of self destructive behavior, both physically and psychologically. Clients ad dicted to self-hatred may have a history of sabotaged experiences Find out about these experiences and connect them for the client.

- It may be important to let clients know that no genetic link is presen in self-hatred. It is a learned pattern of behavior that probably ha evolved over time. Some form of cognitive behavioral therapy ma be necessary to convince clients that they are not by nature bad peo ple (Basco & Rush, 2005).

- Sometimes it is difficult getting people who practice self-hatred t accept this addictive pattern. Hardly anyone wants to admit that the hate themselves. Re-focus the counseling on an addictive pattern o behavior where the emotional addiction of self-hatred creates a de pendency on it. If you suspect that a client is practicing self-hatred look into their past and determine what event or what lifestyle ha created this pattern. Clients do not hate themselves without reasons Some form of rejection may have taken place that has allowed thi emotional addiction to grow. Some form of free association about the past may be necessary (Shaffer & Lazarus, 1952).

- When working with victims of rape, consider an addictive pattern o self-hatred to be a possibility. Rape is an act of hateful behavior tha can plant the seeds of hatred within the victims of rape. It can possi bly create a scenario for self-destruction within a client's everyda living. Explain how a self-hatred addiction works, and how it be comes important to not mimic the pattern within one's self.

- Counseling clients with self-hatred can be discovered by understand ing other emotions such as, guilt or anxiety. However, just focusin on these emotions may not go deep enough in shorting out an addic tion where self-destructive behavior is present. Sometimes guilt an anxiety are symptoms of self-hatred, and clients should have the op portunity to understand this phenomenon.

elf-Hatred Addiction Short List

- Few clients want to admit they hate themselves. Look for denial being a factor in counseling.

- Encourage clients to find ways of loving themselves, even if it is small gestures of positive regard.

- Let clients with self-hatred explore rejection from their past.

- Watch out for addictive thinking. Clients with self-hatred have a tendency to think in black or white terms.

- Point out compulsive acts of putting down one's behavior, emotions and thoughts.

- Be compassionate toward people who may hate themselves through the rejection of others. Use some form of positive regard to counteract this phenomenon.

- Watch for signs of self-destruction both physically and psychologically. Sometimes clients will show how they hate themselves through self-destructive behavior.

- Have victims of rape consider the possibility that the act of rape can continue within the victim of rape through self-hatred.

- Try to have clients with self-hatred control their self-defeating behavior through some form of positive regard.

- Recognize that adult children of alcoholics may have some form of self-hatred as the basis of their problems.

- Compulsive, self-destructive behavior should not be confused with someone planning to destroy portions of their lives.

Format for Other Emotional Connections

This is an opportunity to develop a connection between a self-hatred addiction and some other real life experience. This could mean making a connection between a self-hatred addiction and some form of physical addiction, or a connection with another process oriented addiction. Also, this could be a connection between a self-hatred addiction and a mental health disorder. Finally, this could be a connection between a self-hatred addiction and an everyday life experience where a self-hatred addiction makes an impact on this experience:

Briefly describe the connection between a self-hatred addiction and your chosen phenomenon:

Write an example of how a self-hatred addiction is connected to your chosen phenomenon:

Summarize your thinking on this connection:

Glossary

Aberrant Behavior: Irregular behavior that deviates from what is considered normal. It can be found as a diagnosis for such mental disorders as, oppositional defiant disorder or conduct disorder.

Aberrant Response: an abnormal or atypical behavior, commonly targeted during a behavioral intervention

Active Listening: a psychotherapeutic technique in which the therapist listens to a client closely and attentively, asking questions as needed, in an attempt to fully understand the content of the message and the depth of the client's emotion. The therapist typically restates what has been said to assure the client that he or she has been understood. Active listening is particularly associated with Client-Centered Therapy.

Acute Stress Disorder (ASD): a disorder representing the immediate psychological aftermath of exposure to a traumatic stressor. In addition to characteristics of posttraumatic stress, ASD may also include elements of dissociation and disorientation. ASD does not necessarily develop into posttraumatic stress disorder.

Adult Children of Alcoholics: Refers to adults who had one or more parents or other close family members who abused alcohol. Alcoholism creates an inconsistent or abusive home environment, causing children to learn ways of relating to the world that may hurt them later on.

Adolescence: the period of human development that starts with puberty (10-12 years of age) and ends with physiological maturity (approximately 19 years of age), although the exact age span varies across individuals. During this period major changes occur at varying rates in sexual characteristics, body image, sexual interest, social roles, intellectual development, and self-concept.

Agoraphobia: anxiety about being in places or situations for fear of having uncontrolled panic systems or a panic attack. Apprehension is typically focused on fear of being unable to avoid a situation from which escape may b difficult or to control the panic symptoms that may result from exposure to th situation.

Al-Anon: Al-Anon's purpose is to help friends and families of alcoholics re- cover from the effects of living with the problem drinking of a relative or friend.

Alateen: Alateen is a part of Al-Anon, which helps families of alcoholics re- cover from the effects of living with problem drinking of a relative or a friend Alateen is a recovery program for young people.

Alcoholism (Dependence): a cluster of cognitive, behavioral, and physiolog cal symptoms indicating continued use of alcohol despite significant alcoh(related problems. There is a pattern of repeated alcohol ingestion resulting i tolerance, and an uncontrollable drive to continue use. Alcohol dependence i known popularly as alcoholism.

Alienation: 1. A deep-seated sense of dissatisfaction with one's personal ex periences that can be a source of lack of trust in one's social or physical env ronment or in oneself. 2. The experience of separation between thoughts an feelings, sometimes seen in obsessive-compulsive disorder and schizophrenia

Anger Management: These are techniques used in counseling or therapy control inappropriate reactions to anger-provoking stimuli, and to express fee ings of anger in appropriate ways that are respectful of others. Such technique include using relaxation methods to reduce physiological responses to ange replacing exaggerated or overly dramatic thoughts with more rational one communicating more calmly and thoughtfully about one's anger, and remov ing oneself from situations or circumstances that provoke anger or avoidin them altogether.

Anti-Anxiety Drugs (anxiolytics): a class of drugs used in the control (anxiety, mild behavioral agitation, and insomnia. Formerly called minor tra quilizers, they can also be used as adjunctive agents in the treatment of depre sion and panic disorder.

Anti-Depressant Drugs: a class of psychotropic drugs administered in th treatment of depression. Although exact mechanisms of action remain unclea antidepressants apparently work by altering levels of various neurotransmitte available at receptor sites in the brain. Al least four classes of antidepressan are in current clinical use.

Antisocial Personality Disorder: a personality disorder characterized b chronic antisocial behavior that is not due to severe mental retardation, schizc phrenia, or manic episodes. This behavior pattern, which is more common i males than females, starts before age 15 with such infractions as lying, stealing, fighting, truancy, vandalism, theft, drunkenness, or substance abuse. It then continues after age 18 with at least four of the following manifestations: (a) inability to work consistently (b) inability to function as a responsible parent (c) repeated violations of the law (d) inability to maintain an enduring sexual relationship (e) frequent fights and beatings inside and outside the home (f) failure to repay debts and provide child support (g) travel from place to place without planning (h) repeated lying and conning, and (i) extreme recklessness in driving and in other activities.

Attention Deficit Disorder: A former and still commonly used name for attention-deficit/hyperactivity disorder.

Behavior Therapy: a form of psychotherapy that applies the principles of learning, operant conditioning, and pavlovian conditioning to eliminate symptoms and modify ineffective or maladaptive patterns of behavior.

Borderline Personality Disorder: a personality disorder characterized by a long-standing pattern of instability in mood, interpersonal relationships, and self image that is severe enough to cause extreme distress or interfere with social and occupational functioning.

Bulimia: insatiable hunger for food. It may have physiological causes, such as a brain lesion or endocrine disturbance, or be primarily a psychological disorder.

Bullying: Bullying is the act of intentionally causing harm to others, through verbal harassment, physical assault, or other more subtle methods of coercion such as manipulation.

Chronic Depression: depression conditions or symptoms that persist or progress over a long period of time and are resistant to cure.

Cognitive Behavior Therapy (CBT): a form of psychotherapy that integrates theories of cognition and learning with treatment techniques derived from cognitive therapy and behavior therapy. CBT assumes that cognitive, emotional, and behavioral variables are functionally interrelated. Treatment is aimed at identifying and modifying problematic behaviors through cognitive restructuring and behavioral techniques to achieve change.

Cocaine: a drug, obtained from leaves of the coca shrub that stimulates the central nervous system, with effects of reducing fatigue and increasing well-being. These are followed by a period of depression as the initial effects diminish. The drug acts by blocking the reuptake of the neurotransmitter dopamine, serotonin, and norepinephrine.

Common Ground: This is a term that is increasingly being used in the area of conflict resolution. It refers to an area of agreement, something mutually agreed upon, especially as a basis for negotiation.

Conflict Resolution: This term usually refers to the process of resolving dispute or a conflict, by providing both sides an adequate addressing of their needs and addressing an adequate outcome. The reduction of discord and friction between individuals or groups is usually through the use of active strategies, such as, conciliation, negotiation, and bargaining.

Cynicism: An attitude of scornful or jaded negativity, especially a general distrust of the integrity or professed motives of others.

Critical Thinking: a form of directed, problem-focused thinking in which the individual tests ideas or possible solutions for errors or drawbacks. It is essential to such activities as examining the validity of a hypotheses or interpreting the meaning of research results.

Defense Mechanisms: Found in classical psychoanalytic theory, an unconscious reaction pattern employed by the ego to protect itself from the anxiety that arises from psychic conflict. Such mechanisms range from mature to immature; depending on how much they distort reality, whereas sublimation is one of the most mature forms of defense because it allows indirect satisfaction of a true wish. In more recent psychological theories, defense mechanisms are seen as normal means of coping with everyday problems, but excessive use of any one or the use of immature defenses may cause problems.

Depression: 1. Dysphoria that can vary in severity from a fluctuation in normal mood to an extreme feeling of sadness, pessimism, and despondency. 2. in psychiatry, any of the depressive disorders.

Domestic Violence: Domestic violence occurs when a family member, partner or ex-partner attempts to physically or psychologically dominate another.

Detoxification: Detoxification can also refer to the period of withdrawal during which a person's body takes to return to homeostasis after long-term use of addictive substances. - a therapeutic procedure that reduces or eliminates toxic substances in the body

Dry Drunk: people who have given up drugs and alcohol but have not made any internal emotional change. They stay the same as when using but the substance is gone.

DSM-IV-TR: the text revision of the fourth edition of the *Diagnostic and Statistical Manual of Mental Health Disorders* prepared by the Task Force on *DSM-IV* of the American Psychiatric Association and published in 2000.

EAP Counseling: counseling for individuals in the Employee Assistance Program

Ecstasy: A psychedelic drug that puts people in a trance-like state in which they transcend normal consciousness. It is a state of intense pleasure and elation, including some mystical states, orgasms, aesthetic experiences, and drug-induced states. Such extreme euphoria also occasionally occurs in the context of a Hypomanic Episode or a Manic Episode.

Flashbacks: The reliving of a traumatic event after the initial adjustment to the trauma appears to have been made. Flashbacks are part of post traumatic stress disorder. Forgotten memories are reawakened by words, sounds, smells, or scenes that are reminiscent of the original trauma (e.g., when a backfiring car elicits the kind of anxiety that a combat veteran experienced when he or she was the target of enemy fire).

Free Association: a basic process in psychoanalysis and other forms of psychodynamic psychotherapy, in which the patient is encouraged to verbalize freely whatever thoughts come to mind, no matter how embarrassing, illogical, or irrelevant, without censorship or selection by the therapist. The object is to allow unconscious material, such as traumatic experiences or threatening impulses, and otherwise inhibited thoughts and emotions to come to the surface where they can be interpreted. Free association is also posited to help the patient discharge some of the feelings that have given this material excessive control over him or her.

General Anxiety Disorder: excessive anxiety and worry about a range of events and activities (e.g., world events, finances, health, appearance, activities of family members and friends, work, or school) accompanied by such symptoms as restlessness, fatigue, impaired concentration, irritability, muscle tension, and disturbed sleep. The anxiety occurs on more days than not and is experiences as difficult to control.

Heroin: a highly addictive opioid that is a synthetic analog of morphine and three times more potent. Its rapid onset of actions leads to an intense initial high, followed by a period of euphoria and a sense of well-being.

Homeostasis: 1.The regulation by an organism or all aspects of its internal environment, including body temperature, salt-water balance, acid-base balance, and blood sugar level. This involves monitoring changes in the external and internal environments by means of receptors and adjusting bodily process accordingly. 2. Maintenance of a stable balance, evenness, or symmetry.

Hyper-Vigilant Behavior (hypervigilance): a state of heightened alertness, usually with continual scanning of the environment for signs of danger.

Intractable Pattern of Behavior: A pattern of behavior that is difficult to change. A common term used in conflict resolution for difficult disputes.

Machismo: is a prominently exhibited or excessive masculinity. As attitude, machismo ranges from a personal sense of virility to a more extren male chauvinism. In many cultures, machismo is acceptable and ev expected.

Mono-Theistic: This is a doctrine and beliefs that there is only one god. Primarily came into existence with the modern religions.

Narcissism: excessive self-love or egocentrism. The ability to constantly focus on one's self.

Obsessive Compulsive Disorder (OCD): an anxiety disorder characteriz by recurrent obsessions, compulsions, or both that are time consuming (mo than one hour per day), cause significant distress, or interfere with the indivi ual's functioning. The obsessions and compulsions are recognized as excessi or unreasonable.

Oppositional Defiant Disorder: a behavior disorder of childhood characte ized by recurrent disobedient, negativistic, or hostile behavior toward authori figures that is more pronounced than usually seen in children of similar ag and lasts for at least 6 months. It is manifest as temper tantrums, active de ance of rules, dawdling, argumentativeness, stubbornness, or being easily a noyed.

Oppression: is the act of using power to empower and/or privilege a group the expense of disempowering, marginalizing, silencing, and subordinati another group. Oppression does not need established organizational support; can be rendered on a much smaller individual scale. It is closely associat with nationalism and derived social systems, where identity is built antagonism to the other. The term itself derives from the idea of bei "weighted down."

Panic Disorder: an anxiety disorder characterized by recurrent, unexpect panic attacks that are associated with (a) persistent concern about having a other attack, (b) worry about the possible consequences of the attacks, (c) si nificant change in behavior related to the attacks (eg. Avoiding situations, e gaging in safety behavior, not going out alone), or (d) a combination of any all of these.

Physical Addictions: the state of an individual who has repeatedly taken drug and will experience unpleasant physiological symptoms if he or she sto taking the drug. In DSM-IV-TR, substance dependence with physical depen ence is diagnosed if there is evidence of withdrawal of tolerance.

Possessive Love: A form of intimacy where one person objectifies another and treats them as a possession.

Post Traumatic Stress Disorder: a disorder that results when an individual lives through or witnesses an event in which he or she believes that there is threat to life or physical integrity and safety and experiences fear, terror, or helplessness. The symptoms are characterized by (a) re-experiencing the trauma in painful recollections, flashbacks, or recurrent dreams or nightmares; (b) diminished responsiveness (emotional anesthesia or numbing), with disinterest in significant activities and with feelings of detachment and estrangement from others; and (c) chronic physiological arousal, leading to such symptoms as exaggerated startle response, disturbed sleep, difficulty in concentrating or remembering, guilt about surviving when others did not, and avoidance of activities that call the traumatic event to mind.

Prejudice: a negative attitude toward another person or group formed in advance of any experience with that person or group. Prejudices include as affective component (emotions that range from mild nervousness to hatred), a cognitive component (assumptions and beliefs about groups, including stereotypes), and a behavioral component (negative behaviors, including discrimination and violence). They tend to be resistant to change because they distort the prejudiced individual's perception of information pertaining to the group.

Process Oriented Addictions: Forms of addictions where a physical substance is not involved such as, a sexual addiction or a gambling addiction.

Professional Jealousy: A form of jealousy where others are afraid of the success of another and want to claim their work for their own.

Psychedelic Drugs: a name for hallucinogens proposed in 1956 by Humphry Osmond

Purging: A term closely associated with the disorder, bulimia. It is the act of purging food after a meal. Also, considered a method used with other eating disorders. It is the activity of expelling food that has just been ingested, usually by vomiting or the use of laxatives. Purging often occurs in conjunction with an eating binge in anorexia nervosa or bulimia nervosa; its purpose is to eliminate or reduce real or imagined weight gain.

Racism: a form of prejudice that assumes that the members of racial categories have distinctive characteristics and that these differences result in some racial groups being inferior to others. Racism generally includes negative emotional reactions to members of the group, acceptance of negative stereotypes, and racial discrimination against individuals; in some cases it leads to violence. It is the belief that inherent differences among the various human races determine cultural or individual achievement, usually involving the idea that one's own race is superior and has the right to rule others.

Rave: A rave or rave party is a term in use since the 1980's, to describe danc parties, often all night events.

Reconciliation: The reestablishment of cordial relations. It is professionally used in conflict resolution as a way of stabilizing the differences between peo- ple.

Sexual Addiction: Sexual addiction is best described as a progressive int macy disorder characterized by compulsive sexual thoughts and acts. A prob lematic sexual behavior, such as a paraphilla or hyper sexuality, regarded as form of addiction similar to drug addiction. The defining features of a sexua addiction include sexual behavior that has become out of control, has severel negative consequences, and that the addict is unable to stop, despite a wish t do so. Other features include persistence in high risk, self-destructive behav ior; spending large amounts of time in sexual activity or fantasy; neglect of so cial, occupational, or other activities; and mood changes associated with sex ual activity.

Social Phobia: It is an anxiety disorder characterized by overwhelming anx ety and excessive self-consciousness in everyday social situations. It is a anxiety disorder that is characterized by extreme and persistent social anxiet or performance anxiety that causes significant distress or prevents participa tion in everyday activities. The feared situation is most often avoided alto gether or else it is endured with marked discomfort.

Social Pressure: the exertion of influence on a person or group by anothe person or group. Like group pressure, social pressure includes rational argu ment and persuasion (informational influence), calls for conformity (normativ influence), and direct forms of influence, such as demands, threats, or persona attacks on the one hand and promises or reward or social approval on the othe (interpersonal influence).

Solution Focused Brief Therapy: Short-term therapy that focuses on prob lems in the here and now, with specific goals that the client views as importar to achieve in a limited time.

Stress Management: the use of specific techniques, strategies, or programs such as relaxation training, anticipation of stress reactions, and breathing tech niques- for dealing with stress-inducing situations and the state of bein stressed.

Substance Induced Anxiety Disorder: clinically significant anxiety (e.g generalized anxiety, panic attacks, phobic symptoms, or obsessive-compulsiv symptoms) caused by the direct physiological effects of exposure to a drug toxin, or other substance. The anxiety symptoms may be associated wit substance intoxication (e.g., alcohol, amphetamines, caffeine) substance withdrawal (e.g., alcohol, cocaine, sedatives) medication use (e.g., anesthetics, anticholinergics, thyroid medication) or exposure to heavy metals and toxins (e.g., gasoline, paint, carbon dioxide).

Suicide Ideation: suicidal though or a preoccupation with suicide, often as a symptom of a major depressive episode. Most instance of suicidal ideation do not progress to attempted suicide.

Traumatic Cues: Those incidences during everyday living that can set off some form of mental health disorder.

Values Clarification: 1.Any process intended to promote an individual's awareness and understanding of his or her moral principle and ethical priorities and their relationships to behavior. 2. In psychotherapy, a series of exercise used to help an individual identify his or her personal values and evaluate their impact on or place in daily life.

Victimization: an individual who has experienced as accident or natural disaster and has suffered consequences from this disaster.

References

Abalos, D. T. 2002. *The Latin male: Radical redefinition.* Boulder, CO: Lynne Rienner.

Allcorn, S. 1994. *Anger in the workplace: Understanding the causes of aggression and violence.* Westport, CT: Quorum Books.

Andreasen, N. C., 2003. *.Brave new brain: Conquering mental illness in the era of the genome.* New York: Oxford University Press.

Arias, I. & T. Laughren. 200. Teen suicide up sharply for first time in years. *Scout News.* September, 2007.

Arieti, S., D. X. Freedman, & J. E. Dyrud, 1975. *Treatment.* New York: Basic Books.

Ashenberg, S. A. 2004. *Clinical work with substance-abusing clients.* New York Guilford Press.

Ashkanas, M., C. E. Hartell & W. J. Zerbe, 2000. *Emotions in the workplace: Research, theory and practice.* Westport, CT: Quorum Books.

Austrian, S. G. 2000. *Mental health disorders, medications and clinical social work.* New York: Columbia University Press.

Baer, M. A. 2002. Medication, testing and psychotherapy – be critical. *Annals of the American Psychological Association.* Vol. 5 (4) 5.

Balraman, G., D. Bux, J. Hahn, H. Wallace & J. Volpicelli. 1999. The role of controllable trauma in the development of PTSD and alcohol addiction. *Alcohol Research and Health.* Vol. 23 (4) 256

Barber, J. P. & P. Crits-Christoph. 1995. *Dynamic therapies for psychiatric disorders: Axis I.* New York: Basic Books Pub.

Barnes, K. L. & S. M. Moon. 2006. Factor structure of the psychotherapy supervisor development scale. *Measurement and Evaluation in Counseling and Development.* Vol. 39 (3) 130+.

Basco, M. R., & A. J. Rush. 2005. *Cognitive behavioral therapy for pi-polar disorder.* New York: Guilford Press.

Bashford, A. & A. Strange. 2003. *Places and practices of exclusion.* New York: Routledge.

Beabout, G. A. 1996. *Freedom and its misuses: Kierkegaard on anxiety and despair* Milwaukee: Marquette University Press.

Beck, A. T., G. Emery & R. L. Greenburg. 1985. *Anxiety disorder and pho bias: A cognitive perspective.* New York: Basic Books.

Bell, T. L. 2002. Pretreatment: Getting ready for recovery. *Reclaiming Chil dren and Youth.* Vol. 11 (3) 168+.

Bennet, J. B. 2000. *Time and intimacy: A new science of personal relation ships.* Mahwah, NJ: Lawrence Erlbaum Associates.

Bergesen, A. J. & H. Yi. 2005. New directions for terrorism research. *Inter National Journal of Comparative Sociology.* Vol. 46 (1-2) 133+

Berson, I. R. & M. J. Berson. 2008. Weathering natural disasters with safety net. *Social Education.* Vol. 72 (1) 27+.

Bevan, J. L., & Samter, W. 2004. Toward a broader conceptualization o jealousy in close relationships: Two exploratory studies. *Communica tion Studies.* Vol. 55 (1) 14+.

Beyan, J. L. 2004. General partner and relational uncertainty as cones quences of another person's jealousy expression. *Western Journal o Communication.* Vol. 68 (2) 195+.

Bielski, L. 2002. The great risk debate: Basal committee proposals and a tough business climate push operational risk to the fore: The question remains, how to manage it best. *ABA Banking Journal.* Vol. 94 (2 58+.

Bjork, P.B. 1996. *The novel of Toni Morrison: The search for self and place within the community.* New York: Peter Lang.

Blackman, J. S. 2004. *101 defenses: How the mind shields itself.* New York Routledge.

Blanchfield K., T. Blanchfield, & P. D. Ladd. 2007. *Conflict resolution for law enforcement: Street smart negotiating.* Flushing, NY: Looseleaf Law Publications.

Blocher, D. H. 2000. *Counseling: A developmental approach.* New York Wiley.

Blum, P. 2001. *A teacher's guide to anger management.* London: Routledge Falmer.

Blumstein, A. 1995. Youth violence and the illicit drug industry. *Journal of Criminal Law and Criminology.* Vol. 86 (1) 10-36

Bourque, P. & D. J. Cyr. 1982. Evaluation of an assertiveness training pro gram in a maximum security correctional setting. *Journal of Canadian Criminology* Vol. 24 (1) 51.

Brown, R. A., C. W. Kahler, S. E. Ramsey, J. P. Read, & G. L. Stuart. 2004 Discriminating between substance-induced and independent depressive episode in alcohol dependent patients. *Journal of Studies on Alcohol.* Vol.6 (5) 672+.

Brown, S. I. & M. I.Walter. 2005. *The art of problem posing.* Mahwah, NJ: Lawrence Erlbaum.

Burgess-Jackson, K. 2003. Deontological egoism. *Social Theory and Practice.* Vol. 29, (3) 357+

Bush, R. 2003. The civil rights movement and the continual struggle for redemption America. *Social Justice.* Vol. 30 (1) 42+.

Cahill, A. J. 2001. *Rethinking rape.* Ithaca, NY: Cornell University Press.

Caplan, G. 1955. *Emotional problems of early childhood.* New York: Basic Books.

Catherall, D. R. 2005. *Family Stressors: Interventions for stress and trauma.* New York: Brunner Routledge

Chafetz, M. E. & H. W. Demone. 1962. *Alcoholism and society.* New York: Oxford University Press.

Chalk, P. 1998. The response of terrorism as a threat to liberal democracy. *The Australian Journal of Politics and History.* Vol. 44 (3) 373.

Champion, D. 2002. *Narcissism and entitlement: Sexual aggression and the college male.* New York: LFB Scholarly Publishing.

Chin, A. 2003. Increasing the accountability of state actors in prison systems a necessary enterprise in guaranteeing the eight amendment rights of prison inmates. *Journal of Criminal Law and Criminology.* Vol. 93 (4) 913+.

Christian Century Foundation. 2001. *Overcoming fear.* Vol. 118, (29) 5.

Churchill, A. M. 2004. *The Expressions of hope among Native American Children* .Ottawa, Ont.: Carlton University Press.

Christian, G. 2004. Hiding from humanity: Disgust, shame, and the law. *The Christian Century.* Vol. 121 (10) 41+.

Claiborne, L. 2005. *Investigate the levels of dating among American teenagers.* New York: Liz Claiborne Inc.

Clark, A. J. 2007. *Empathy in counseling and psychotherapy.* Mahwah, NJ: Lawrence Erlbaum, Associates.

Clark, A. 1999. *Defense mechanisms and the counseling process.* San Francisco: Sage Pub.

Clendinning, A. 2006. Keeping up with the Joneses: Envy in American consumer society. *Urban History Review.* Vol. 34 (2) 58+.

Conrad, S. D. & R. S. Morrow. 2000. Borderline personality organization, dissociation, and willingness to use force in intimate relationships. *Psychology of Men and Masculinity* Vol. 1.

Conyne, R. K. 2004. *Preventive counseling: Helping people to become empowered in systems and settings.* New York: Brunner-Routledge.

Cook, A. J. 2004. Columbine author speaks at conference. *Reclaiming Children and Youth.* Vol. 13 (3) 181+

Cook-Cottone, C., & L. Phelps. 2004. Body dissatisfaction in college women: Identification of risk and protective factors to guide college counseling practices. *Journal of College Counseling.* Vol. 6 (1) 80+.

Corby, B. 2006. *Child abuse: Towards a knowledge base.* Maidenhead England: Open University Press.

Cordesman, A. H. 2003. *The Iraq war, strategy, tactics, and military lessons.* Westport, CT: Praeger.

Crawford, T. N., P. C. Cohen, J. G. Johnson, J. R. Sneed & J. S. Brook. 2004. The course and psychological correlates of personality disorder symptoms in adolescence: Erikson's developmental theory revisited. *Journal of Youth and Adolescence.* Vol. 33 (5) 273+.

Davis, D. R. & C. G. Jansen. 1998. Making meaning of alcoholics anonymous for social workers: Myths, metaphors and realities. *Social Work.* Vol. 43 (2) 169+.

Davidson, J. E. & R. J. Sternberg. 2003. *The psychology of problem solving.* Cambridge, England: Cambridge University Press.

Davidson, J. 2004. Optimism in an era of uncertainty. *Public Management* Vol. 86 (10) 22+.

Deluca, T. 1995. *The two faces of apathy.* Philadelphia, PA: Temple University Press.

Dilulio, J. 2006. Age of apathy. *The Soap Box.* Vol. 2 (2) 9+.

Donovan, D. M. & G. A. Marlatt. 2005. *Assessment of addictive behavior.* New York: Guilford Press.

Dryden, W. & M. Neenan. 2004. *Cognitive therapy: 100 key points.* New York: Brunner Routledge.

Dupont, R. L. 1997. *The selfish brain: Learning from addiction.* Washington, DC: American Psychiatric Association.

Durham, M. S. 2000. *The therapist's encounters with revenge and forgiveness.* London: Jessica Kingsely.

Edwards, J. 2000. Passion, activity and "the care of self". *The Hastings Center Report.* Vol. 30 (2) 31.

Eliot, A. O. 2004. A concept of eating-disordered adolescent girls. *Annals of the American Psychological Association.* Vol. 7 (1)14+.

Elliot, M., 1994. Who's homeless and why. *The Christian Century.* Vol. 11 (25) Sept.

Engel, B. 2002. *The emotionally abused relationship: How to stop being abused and how to stop abusing.* Hoboken, NJ: Wiley Pub.

Einarsen, S., H. Hoel, D. Zapf & C. L. Cooper, Eds. 2003. *Bullying and emotional abuse in the workplace: International perspectives in research and practice.* London: Taylor & Francis.

Epting, F., & S. R. Webster. 2003. Counselor's perceptions of female and male clients. *Journal of Counseling and Development.* Vol. 81 (2) 131+.

Esterly, R. & W. T. Neely. 1997. *Chemical dependency and compulsive behavior.* Mahwah, NJ: Lawrence Erlbaum Associates.

Fall, K. A., J. M. Holder & A. Marquis. 2003. *Theoretical models of counseling and psychotherapy.* New York: Brunner-Routledge.

Faupel, C. E. 1991. *Shooting dope: Career patterns of hard-core heroin users.* Gainesville, FL: University of Florida Press.

Fien, M. L. 1993. *A common sense guide to coping with anger.* WestPort CT.: Praeger Publishers.

Feindler, W. L. Ed. 2006. *Anger related disorders: A practitioner's guide to comparative treatments.* New York: Springer Publications.

Fichman, L., R., D. C. Koestner, M. Zuroff. 1996. Dependency , self-criticism and perceptions of inferiority at summer camp. *Journal of Youth and Adolescence.* Vol. 25 (1) 113+.

First, M. 2000. *Diagnostic and statistical manual of mental disorders IV ed.* Washington D.C.: American Psychiatric Association.

Fitzgerald, H. E., B. M. Lester & B. S. Zuckerman. 2000. *Children of addiction.* New York: Garland.

Frankl, V. 1997 opt ed. *Mans search for meaning.* New York:Pocket Books.

Freedam, S. 1998. Forgiveness and conciliation: The importance of understanding how they differ. *Counseling and Values.* Vol. 42 200+

Gardner, F. 2001. *Self-Harm: A psychotherapeutic approach.* Hove, Eng - land: Brunner-Routledge.

Garland, A. & R. G. Moore. 2003. *Cognitive therapy for chronic a persistent depression.* Chichester, England: Wiley Pub.

Gaylin, W. 2003. *Feelings: Our Vital Signs.* New York: Harper Row.

.Geller, B., & M. P. DeBello, 2003. *Bipolar disorder in childhood and early adolescence.* New York: Guilford Press.

Gerhardt, L. B. 2000. Uniqueness of self. *Journal of Humanities and Peace.* Vol. 16, 71.

Gerson, L. P. 2004. Plato on identity, sameness and difference. *The review metaphysics.* Vol. 58 (2) pp. 305+.

Glazer, N. 2000. The culture of achievement. *Public Interest.* Summer, 49.

Greenberg, J. 2003. *Trauma at home 9/11.* Lincoln NE: University of Ne - braska Press.

Griffths, P. E. 2002. What is innateness? *The Monist.* Vol. 85 (1) 70+.

Griffith-Shelley, E. 1997. *Sex, addiction and love: Addiction, treatment and recovery.* Westport, CT: Praeger.

Grinberg, L. & C. Tollope. 1992. *Guilt and depression.* London: Karnac Books.

Groth, A. N. & H. J. Birnbaum. 1979. *Men who rape: The psychology of the offender.* New York: Plenum Press.

Guerro, L. K., P. A. Anderson & W. A. Afifi. 2001. *Close encounters: Communicating in close relationships.* Mountain View CA: Mayfield Publishing.

Haddad, S. 2004. A comparative study of Lebanese and Palestinian perceptions of suicide bombings: The role of militant Islam and socioeco - nomic status. *International Journal of Cooperative Sociology.* Vol. 45 (5) 337+.

Halpern, D. F., 2003. *Thought & knowledge: An introduction to critical thinking.* Mahwah, NJ: Lawrence Erlbaum Associates.

Harpriva, B. A. & A. D. Schmetzer. 2007. Pharmacotherapy of combat re - lated post-traumatic stress disorder. *Annals of the American Psychotherapy Association.* Vol. 10 (4) 28+.

Hazler, R. J., J. V. Carney, S. Green, R. Powell & L. S. Jolly. 1997. Areas of expert agreement on identification of school bullies and victims, *School Psychology International*, 18, 3—12.

Henderson, E. C. 2000. *Understanding addiction.* Jackson, MS.: University Press of Mississippi.

Hensely, L. G. 2001. College student binge drinking: Implications for a constructivist approach to college counseling. *Journal of College Counseling.* Vol. 4 (2) 100+.

Herman, J. L. 1997. *Trauma and recovery.* New York: Basic Books.

Hier, S. P. 2002. Raves, risks and the ecstasy panic: A case study in the subversive nature of moral regulation. *Canadian Journal of Sociology.* Vol. 27 (1) 2002, 33+.

Hilberman, E. 1976. *The rape victim: A project of the committee on women of the American Psychiatric Association.* New York: Basic Books.

Hodgson R. R. & R. J. Kizior. 1998. *Saunders nursing drug handbook.* Philadelphia: Harcourt Brace & Co.

Holloway, H. 1969. *The politics of the southern Negro: From exclusion to big city organization.* New York: Random House.

Honess, T. & K. Yardley. 1987. *Self and identity: Perspectives across the lifespan.* London: Routledge & Kagan Paul.

Honig, W. K. & J. G. Fetterman. 1992. *Cognitive aspects of stimulus control.* Hillsdale, NJ: Lawrence Erlbaum Associates.

Hood, E. 2005. Addiction/addiction connection. *Environmental Health Perspective.* Vol. 113 (12) 812+.

Hook, S. 1959. *Psychoanalysis and the scientific method.* New York: New York University Press.

Hudgin, K. M. 2002.*The experiential treatment for ptsd.* New York:Springer Pub.

Idhe, D. 1976. *Listening and voice a phenomenology of sound.* Athens OH: Ohio University Press.

Jeffrey, H. D. & C. White C. 2005. Teaching multi-cultural counseling: Collaborative endeavors to transcend resistance and increase awareness. *Journal of Humanistic Counseling, Education and Development.* Vol. 44 (2) 225+.

Jenkins, R. 2004. *Social Identity.* New York: Routledge.

Jensen, J. M. 2005. Reflections on natural disasters and traumatic events. *Social Work Research.* Vol. 29 (4) 195+.

King, P.A. & R. A. Shearer. 2001. The powerless-employment scale: Measurement of substance abuse. *Journal of Addictions and Offender Counseling.* Vol. 21 (2) 68.

Johnson, E. H. 1990. *The deadly emotions: The role of anger, hostility, and aggression in health and emotional well-being.* New York: Praeger Pub.

Johnson, H. D., E. Brady, R. Monair, D. Congdon, & J. Niznik. 1995. Identity as a moderator of gender differences in the emotional closeness of emerging adults. *Adolescence.* Vol. 42 (165) 1+.

Johnson, W. 1946. *People in quandaries.* San Francisco.

Kirk, A., 2006. Judgment days: Lyndon Baines Johnson, Martin Luther King Junior and the laws that challenged America. *Journal of Southern History.* Vol. 22 (4) 900+.

Kirkpatrick, E. M., Ed. 1989. Legitimacy and authority. *World Affairs.* Vol. 152 (2) 75.

Konstan, V., W. Holmes & B. Levine. 2003. Empathy, selfism, and coping as elements of the psychology of forgiveness. *Counseling and Values.* Vol. 47 (3) 172+.

Konstan, V., Chernoff, M. & Deveney, S. 200.1 Toward forgiveness: The role of shame, guilt, anger, and empathy. *Counseling and Values.* Vol. 46 (1) 26.

Kristiansson, K. 2002. *Justifying emotions: Pride and jealousy.* London: Routledge p. iii.

Kubany, E. S. & F. P. Manke. Cognitive therapy for trauma-related guilt: Conceptual bases and treatment outlines. *Cognitive and Behavioral Practice.* Vol. 2 23—61.

Kubany E. S. & S. B. Watson. 2003. Guilt: Elaboration of a multidimensional model. *The Psychology Record.* Vol. 53 (1) 51+.

Ladd, P. D. 2005. *Mediation, conciliation and emotions: A practitioner's guide for resolving emotions in dispute resolution.* Lanham, MD: University Press of America.

Ladd, P. D. 2007. Relationships and patterns of conflict resolution: A reference book for couples counseling. Lanham, MD: University Press of America.

Ladd, P. D. 1974. *A phenomenological approach to the experience of fear.* San Diego, CA: U.S. International University Press.

Ladd, P.D. 1976. *Resentment of authority; A phenomenological approach.* San Diego CA: U.S. International University Press.

Lafee, S. 2000. Profiling bad apples. *School Administrator.* Vol. 57 (2) 6.

Laidlaw, K., L.W. Thompson, L. Dick-Siskin & D. Gallagher-Thompson, D. 2003. *Cognitive behavioral therapy with older people.* Wiley: Hoboken, NJ.

Lamb, M. E. & B. Sutton-Smith. 1982. *Sibling relationships: Their nature and significance across the lifespan.* Hillsdale, NJ: Lawrence Erlbaum Associates.

Lambie, G.W. 2006.Burnout prevention: A humanistic perspective and structured group supervision activity. *Journal of Humanistic Counseling and Education and Development.* Vol. 45 (1) 32+.

Langone, J. 1995. *Tough choices: A book about substance abuse.* Boston Little, Brown and Co.

LaTorre, M.A. 2001. Therapeutic approaches to anxiety- holistic view. *Per spectives in Psychiatric Care.* Vol. 37 (1) 28.

Lave-Gindhu, A. & K. A. Schonert-Reichl. 2005. Non-suicidal self-harm among community adolescents: Understanding the "whats" and th "whys" of self-harm. *Journal of Youth and Adolescence.* Vol. 34 (5) 447+.

Leaman, T. L. 1992 *Health and anger related disorders.* New York: Plenum Press.

Leaman, T. L. 1992. *Healing the anxiety diseases.* New York: Plenum Press

Lee, V. L., 1988. *Beyond behaviorism.* Hillsdale, NJ: Lawrence Erlbaum As sociates

Lemanski, M. A. 2000. Addiction alternatives for recovery. *The Humanis* Vol. 60 (1) 14.

Lemoire, S. J. & C. P. Chen. 2005. Applying person-centered counseling to sexual minority adolescents. *Journal of Counseling and Development* Vol. 83 (2) 146+.

Lester, B. M. & B. S Zuckerman. 2000. *Children of addiction.* New York Garland.

Lewis, T. & C. J. Osborne. 2004. Solution focused counseling and motivetional interviewing.. *Journal of Counseling and Development.* Vol. (1), 38+.

Lloyd, R. 1995. *Closer and closer apart: Jealousy in literature.* Ithaca, NY Cornell University Press.

Longabaugh, R. & J. Morganstern. 1999. Cognitive-Behavioral coping skill therapy for alcohol dependence. *Alcohol, Research and Health.* Vol.2 (2) 78.

Lucas, A. R., 2004. *Demystifying anorexia nervosa: An optimistic guide to understanding and healing.* New York: Oxford University Press

Lundeberg, A. 1998. *The environmental and mental health: A guide for cli nicians.* Mahwah NJ: Lawrence Erlbaum.

Lusner, K. L. 2003 *Down and out, on the road: The homeless in America* New York: Oxford University Press.

Mano, H. 1991. The structure of intensity of emotional experiences: Methods and context convergence. *Multi-Variant Behavioral Research.* Vol 26 (3) 389.

March, J. S. & T. H. Ollendick, Ed. 2004. *Phobia and anxiety disorders in children and adolescents: A clinician's guide to effective psychosocia and pharmacological interventions.* New York: Oxford University Press.

Marlatt, G. A. & J. R. Gordon. 1985. *Relapse prevention: Maintenance strategies in the treatment of addictive behaviors.* New York: Guilford Press.

Marlatt,G. A. & D. M. Donavan. 2005. *Addictive behaviors.* New York: Guilford Press.

Massr, J. & A. H. Tuma. 1985. *Anxiety and anxiety disorders.* Hillsdale, NY: Lawrence Erlbaum Associates.

Martens, H. J. 2005. Therapy on the borderline: Effectiveness of behavioral therapy on patients with borderline personality disorder. *Annals of the American Psychotherapy Association.* Vol. 8 (4) 5+.

Matt, S. J. 2002. Envy and the emergence of the modern consumer ethic. *Journal of Social History.* Vol. 36 (2) 283+.

McLean, P. D. & S. R. Woody. 2001. *Anxiety disorder in adults: An evidence-based approach to psychological treatment.* New York: Oxford University Press.

Miars, R. D. 2002. Existential authenticity: A foundational value for counseling. *Counseling and Values.* Vol. 46 (3) 218+.

Moeller, F. G. & D. M. Dougherty. 2004. Antisocial personality disorder, alcohol and aggression. *Alcohol Research & Health.* Vol. 25 (1) 5.

Morrison, T., M., Erooga & R. C. Beckett. 1994. *Sexual offending against children: Assessment and treatment of male abusers.* New York: Routledge.

Neenan, M. & W. Dryden. 2002. *Life coaching: A cognitive behavioral approach.* East Essex, England: Brunner-Routledge.

Nelson, J. B. 2007. Alcohol addiction and Christian ethics. *The Christian Century.* Vol. 124 (3) 37+.

Nelson, R. J., Ed. 2006. *Biology of aggression.* New York: Oxford University

Neuman, J. 1999. Cognitive behavioral coping skills for alcohol dependence. *Alcohol Research and Health.* Vol. 23 (2) 78.

Neuman, D. 1992. How mediation can effectively address the male-female power imbalances in divorce. *Mediation Quarterly.* 9 (3) 227—239.

Newman, B. M. & P. R. Newman. 2002. Group identity and alienation: Giving the we its due. *Journal of Youth and Adolescence.* Vol. 30 (5) 515.

Nicholson, N. 2001. The new word gossip. *Psychology Today.* 34, 40—46.

NIDA, 2005. Cost of drug abuse in the United States. *National Institute for Drug Abuse.* Washington, DC: NIDA.

NIMH, 2004. *Research on withdrawal symptoms.* Lexington, KY: NIMH Addiction Research Center.

Nirenberg, J. 1998. Myths we teach, realities we ignore: Leadership education in business schools. *Journal of Leadership Studies.* Vol. 5 (1) 82.

Norman, D. M. & T. Ganser. 2004. A humanistic approach to new teacher mentoring: A counseling perspective. *Journal of Humanistic Counseling, Education and Development.* Vol. 43 (2) 129+.

O'Meara, K. P. 2001. A prescription for violence. *Insight on the News.* Vol. 17 (14) 14.

Owens, K. 1995. *Raising your child's inner self-esteem: The authoritative guide from infancy through the teen years.* New York: Plenum Press.

Parker, A. C.1989. *Seneca myths and folk tales.* Lincoln, NE: University of Nebraska Press.

Parker, G., D. Straton, K. Wilhelm, P. Mitchell, P., M. Austin, K. Eyers, H. Dusan, G. Malhi, & S. Grdovic. 2002. *Dealing with depression: Common sense guide to mood disorders.* Crows Nest NSW: Allen & Unwin Pub.

Parshall, D. P. 2003. Research and reflection: Animal-assisted therapy in mental settings. *Counseling and Values.* Vol. 48 (1) 47+

Peterson, R. D. 2002. *Understanding ethnic violence: Fear, hatred and resentment in twentieth century Europe.* Cambridge MA: Cambridge University Press.

Plunka, G. A. 2000. Freud and the psychology of neurosis: John Bosom's and neglect. *Papers on Language and Literature.* Vol. 36 (1) 93.

Powers, D. V., R. J. Cramer & J. M. Grubka. 2007. Spirituality, life stress and affective well-being. *Journal of Psychology and Theology.* Vol. 35 (3) 235.

Psychiatric Association. 1994. *Diagnostic and statistical manual of mental disorders.* Washington, DC: American Psychiatric Association.

Pyatt, S. E. 1986. Martin Luther King Junior: An annotated bibliography. New York: Greenwood Press.

Raeburn, J. 1984. *Fame became him: Hemingway as public writer.* Bloomington, IN: Indiana University Press.

Ralkowski, M., 2007. Introduction to phenomenological research. *The Review of metaphysics.* Vol. 60 (3) 658+.

Randall, P. 2001. *Bullying in adulthood: Assessing the bullies and their victims.* London: Brunner-Routledge.

Ray, J. 1990. *Alcohol and alcohol abuse.* New York: Delta Press.

Reiser, C. 1999. *Reflections on anger: Women and men in a changing society.* Westport, CT: Praeger Publishers.

Reno, R. R. 2004. Fear of redemption. *Journal of Religion and Public Life.* (144) 29+.

Retzinger, S. & Scheff, T. 2001. Strategies for community conferences: Emotions and social bonds. In *Restorative Justice: International Perspectives.*Edited by B. Galaway and J. Hudson, 315—336. Monsey, NY: Criminal Justice Press.

Rippin, A. 2004. Commanding right and forbidding wrong in Islamic thought. *Journal of the American Oriental Society.* Vol. 124 (1) 119+.

Robertson, S. I. 2001. *Problem solving.* Philadelphia: Psychology Press.

Ronczkowski, M. R. 2004. *Terrorism and organized hate crimes: Intelligence gathering, analysis and investigations.* Boca Raton, FL: CRC Press.

Ronen, T. & T. Ayet. 2001. *In and out of anorexia: The story of the client, the therapist ,and the process recovery.* London: Jessica Kingsley.

Rose, J. S., L. Chassin, C C. Presson, & S. J. Sherman, 2000. *Multivariate approach in substance abuse research.* Mahwah, NJ: Lawrence Erlbaum and Associates.

Roseman, I. J., C. Weist & T. S. Schwartz. 1994. Phenomenology, behaviors and goals differentiate discrete emotions. *Journal of Personality and Social Psychology. Vol.* 67, 206—221.

Ross, A. & P. Rose. 1994. *Moral panic: The media and the British rave culture.* London: Routledge.

Rotgers, F. & M. Maniacci. 2006. *Antisocial personality disorder: A practitioner's guide to comparative treatments.* New York: Springer.

Roy, J. M. 2002. *Love to hate: America's obsession with hatred and violence.* New York: Columbia University Press.

Rushbult, C. E. & P.A. Van Lange. 2003. Interaction and relationships. *Annual Review of Psychology.* 351+.

Rycroft, C., *Anxiety and neurosis.* 1988 London: Maresfield Pub.

Sabin, R. 1999. *Punk rock, so what?: The cultural legacy of punk.* London: Routledge.

Schaeffer, R. C. 1988. *Resentment against achievement: Understanding the assault on ability.* New York: Prometheus Books.

Scheff, T. J. 1997. *Bloody revenge: Emotions, nationalism, and war.* Boulder, CO: West View Press.

Scheler, M. 1961. *Resentiment.* New York: Schoken Books.

Schlipp, D.A. 1997. *The philosophy of Jean Paul Sartre.* LaSalle, IL: Open Court.

Schwartz, M. S. & F. Andrasik. 2003. *Biofeedback; A practitioner's guide.* New York:Guilford Press.

Schwarzer, R., Ed. 1986. *Self-related cognitions in anxiety and motivation.* Mahwah, NJ: Lawrence Erlbaum Associates.

Scrull, T. K. & R. S. Wyer. 1993, *Perspectives on anger and emotion.* Hillsdale NJ: Lawrence Erlbaum Associates.

Seligman, C., J. M. Olson & M. P. Zanna. 1996. *The Psychology of values.* Mahawah, NJ: Lawrence Erlbaum and Associates.

Siegman, A. W. & T. W. Smith. 1994. *Anger, hostility and the heart.* Hillsdale, NJ: Lawrence Erlbaum Associates.

Shaffer, G. W. & R. S. Lazarus. 1952. *Fundamental concepts in clinical psychology.* New York: McGraw-Hill.

Shipway, L., 2004. *Domestic violence: A handbook for health professional.* New York: Routledge.

Shores, K. & D. Scott. D. 2007. The relationship of individual time perspective and recreation experience preferences. *Journal of Leisure Research.* Vol. 39 (1) 28+.

Siossat, R. 2005. *Overview of Alcohol and alcohol related disorders.* Cooperstown, NY: Barton Luter Graphics.

Sommer, J. F. & M. B. Williams. 1994. *Handbook of post-traumatic therapy.* Westport, CT:Greenwood Press.

Stack, E. 1971. Nieztsche's earliest essays. *Psychology Today.* 37, 153—170.

Sunderland, L. C. 2004. Speech, language and audiology service in public schools. *Intervention in School and Clinic.* Vol. 39 (4) 209+.

Taylor, S., Ed. 1999. *Anxiety sensitivity: Theory, research and treatment of fear of anxiety.* Mahwah, NJ: Lawrence Erlbaum.

Tewrski, A. J. 1990. *Addictive thinking: Why we lie to ourselves? Why do others believe us.* Center City MN: Hazeldon Foundation.

Thompson, R. A.. 2003. *Counseling techniques: Improving relationships with others, ourselves, our families, and our environment.* New York: Brunner Routledge.

Tiffany, G. 2002. Shakespeare and Santiago de composeta. *Renascence Essays on Values.* Vol. 54 (2) 82+.

Timmer, D. E. 1989. Biblical exegesis and the Jewish-Christian controversy in early twelfth century. *Church History.* Vol. 58 (3) 309

Tinder, G. 1997. Augustine's world and ours. *Journal of Religion and Public Life.* Issue, 78, 35+

Todd, J. T. & E. K. Morris. 1995. *Modern Perspective on the behaviorism of B.F. Skinner and modern behaviorism.* Westport, CT.: Greenwood Press.

Troester, R. 1996. *Jimmy Carter as peacemaker: A post-presidential biography.* Westport, CT.: Praeger Publishers.

Turell, S., 2003. The abuse of men: Trauma begets trauma. *Sex Roles: Journal of Research.* 93.

Turp, M. 2003. *Self-harm: Narratives from psychotherapy.* London: Jessica Kingsley.

Wahl, O. F. 1995. *Media madness: Public images of mental illness.* New Brunswick NJ: Rutgers University Press.

Wainrib, B. R. 2006. *Healing crisis and trauma with body, mind and spirit.* New York: Springer.

Wall, A. & C. Werkle. 2002. *The violence and addiction equation. Theoretical and clinical issues in substance abuse and relationship violence.* New York: Brunner/ Routledge.

Watkins, C. E. & V. L. Campbell. 2000. *Testing and assessment in counseling practice.* Mahwah, NJ: Lawrence Erlbaum Associates.

Weiss, R. P. 2001. Deconstructing trainer's self-image: How to get the respect you deserve. *T&D.* Vol. 55 (12) 34+.

Wendt, A. C. & W. M. Slonaker. 2002. Sexual harassment and retaliation: A double-edged sword. *SAM Advanced Management.* Vol. 67 (4) 49+.

Whittaker, D. J. 2004. *Terrorists and terrorism in the contemporary world.* New York: Routledge.

Williams, M. 1998. *Mediation: Why people fight and how to help them stop* .New York: Greenwood Press

Williams, B. 1993. *Shame and necessity.* Los Angeles: University of California Press.

Williams, K. D., J. P. Forgás & W. von Hippel, Eds. 2005. *The social ostracism, outcast: Social exclusion, rejection, and bullying.* Psychology Press: New York, NY.

Wilson, J. Q. 1998. Human remedies for social disorders. *Public Interest.* (131) 25+

Wong, P. & S. F. Prem. 1998. *The human quest for meaning: A handbook of psychological research and clinical applications.* Mahwah, NJ. Lawrence Erlbaum Associates

Wyer, R. S. & T. K. Srull. 1993. *Physical aspects of counseling.* Hillsdale, NJ: Lawrence Erlbaum and Associates.

Yoshimura, S. M. 2004. Emotional and behavioral responses to romantic jealous expressions. *Communication Reports.* Vol. 17 (2)   85+.

Young, A. 1995. *The harmony of illusions: Inventing post-traumatic stress disorder.* Princeton, NJ: Princeton University Press.

Zager, D., Ed. 2005. *Autism spectrum disorders: Identification, education and treatment.* Mahwah, NJ: Lawrence Erlbaum.

Index

About the Author

Peter D. Ladd, B.A., M.A., Ph.D., has been a tenured faculty member at St. Lawrence University in the Graduate School of Education for over twenty-five years. He coordinates the Certificate of Advanced Studies Program in Counseling, and has worked for thirty years in St. Lawrence University's satellite graduate school program on the Akwesasne Mohawk Reservation. Dr. Ladd has three books published in the area of social reform for Native people; *Sharing Solutions: First Nations Social Reform,* also, *First Nations Child and Family Services Joint National Policy Review,* and *Comprehensive Research Findings in Education and Training: Aboriginal Strategic Initiatives.* He has two books published in the area of conflict resolution; *Relationships and Patterns of Conflict Resolution: A Reference Book for Couples Counseling* and *Mediation, Conciliation and Emotions: A Practitioner's Guide for Understanding Emotions in Dispute Resolution.* He has one book published along with Kyle Blanchfield and Thomas Blanchfield called, *Conflict Resolution for Law Enforcement: Street Smart Negotiating.* He has written numerous articles in the areas of addictions counseling, Aboriginal studies, family counseling, and conflict resolution, and has authored chapters in books by Carl Rogers, *Freedom to Learn for the Eighties,* Robert Morris, *Students at Risk: Pitfalls and Promising Plans,* and has done extensive research in the phenomenology of emotions. He has contributed to institutional reform, by founding the Augsbury Institute for Youth and Families, the St. Lawrence Valley Teacher/Learning Center, the St. Regis Mohawk Counseling Center and co-founder with Kyle Blanchfield J.D., of the Northern New York Centers for Conflict Resolution. Dr. Ladd acts as the licensed clinical supervisor for the Tekanikonrahwa:kon Holistic Health and Wellness Program on the Akwesasne Mohawk Reservation, where he has practiced counseling and conflict resolution for twenty-five years.

Books from University Press of America

Mediation Conciliation and Emotions: A Practitioner's Guide for Understanding Emotions in Dispute Resolution, by Peter D. Ladd, received critical acclaim in a book review from Harvard Law School's *Negotiation Journal.* It was considered one of the top three books in the areas of negotiation and emotions. It offers guidance for understanding the emotional side of disputes.

Relationships and Patterns of Conflict Resolution: A Reference Book for Couples Counseling by Peter D. Ladd, is a best selling addition to the field of psychology. It emphasizes that relationships are not static entities. Couples can restructure their relationships and resolve conflict. It is a critical resource for those in training or in practice, who assist couples that want to restructure their relationships and resolve their conflicts.